the VEGAN BABY

Cookbook and Guide

the VEGAN BABY

Cookbook and Guide

100+ Delicious **Recipes** and Parenting Tips
for Raising **Vegan Babies** and **Toddlers**

ASHLEY NSONWU

 mango
PUBLISHING GROUP

CORAL GABLES

For permission requests, please contact the publisher at:
Mango Publishing Group
2850 S Douglas Road, 2nd Floor
Coral Gables, FL 33134 USA
info@mango.bz

For special orders, quantity sales, course adoptions and corporate sales, please email the publisher at sales@mango.bz. For trade and wholesale sales, please contact Ingram Publisher Services at customer.service@ingramcontent.com or +1.800.509.4887.

The Vegan Baby Cookbook and Guide: 100+ Delicious Recipes and Parenting Tips for Raising Vegan Babies and Toddlers

Library of Congress Cataloging-in-Publication number: 2023941641
ISBN: (p) 978-1-68481-245-5, (e) 978-1-68481-246-2
BISAC category code: CKB107000, COOKING / Baby Food

Printed in the United States of America

To my loving husband, Karl, and two children, Beyond and Wonder, who made me the mother I am and helped me build the community I have today.

To my community, who supported my work and motivated me to put this book out into the world for generations to come.

To the current and future generations of parents and kids ready to become the superheroes who change the world.

This book is for you.

Table of Contents

FOREWORD

By Genesis Butler

Genesis Butler is a teen environmental and animal rights activist and one of the youngest people ever to give a TEDx talk. She went vegan at age six and has earned numerous awards and recognitions for her activism, in addition to being featured on an episode of Marvel's Hero Project by Disney+. Genesis founded the Youth Climate Save movement, the first youth-led environmental organization focusing on animal agriculture's impact on climate change, and aims to give all young voices a platform.

It's never too early to be a vegan superhero! I stopped eating animals at age three after I asked my mom about the nuggets she was feeding me. She told me nuggets were an actual bird, so I didn't want to eat animals ever again. At age six, I found out the milk I was drinking came from mother cows. My mom was nursing my baby sister when I asked her where my milk came from, and when she told me it came from momma cows, I told her, "Well, that's like someone stealing milk from my baby sister and giving it to someone else." I went vegan that same day. Then, I got my parents to go vegan too. Now, my vegan superhero family also includes my four siblings. Two of them have been vegan since birth!

This decision began an entirely new lifestyle for my family and me, but it wasn't without its difficulties. Being a vegan superhero can present a unique set of challenges. You may face several questions from friends and family. Questions like, "Where do you get your protein from?" or "Isn't it hard to find vegan options at restaurants?" are common. Then there may be situations like family gatherings and parties where non-vegan food is the norm.

Our transition to a vegan lifestyle took place over a decade ago when the only cheese available tasted like coconut, so we had to overcome our challenges during a time when vegan alternatives were limited. Back then, my parents didn't have a comprehensive guide to help them navigate raising a vegan family in a non-vegan world. My mother and I would have loved to have a book like this to help us understand the variety of foods we could eat! This is why **The Vegan Baby Cookbook and Guide** will help many raise their little vegan superheroes easier! This book isn't just a cookbook; it's also a guide that provides you with strategies to navigate social situations and answer common questions about veganism confidently. Ashley's book will give families all the tips they need to overcome these challenges like a true superhero would! People may ask you questions and invite you to non-vegan parties; your children might question you just like I questioned my parents. After reading this cookbook and guide, you will be ready for any question or party.

Cutting meat and dairy from your family's diet positively impacts the animals and the planet. Choosing a plant-based dish over a dish made with meat and dairy will lower your carbon footprint more than any other action. Studies have shown[1] that avoiding meat and dairy is the single most effective way to reduce your environmental impact, as these food categories are responsible for nearly 60 percent of agriculture's greenhouse gas emissions despite providing only about a third of our protein and a fifth of our calories.

One of my favorite sayings, a wisdom passed down by Native Americans, reminds us, "We don't inherit the earth from our ancestors; we borrow it from our children." It invites us to question the kind of planet we want to leave for our children. Do we want to leave our children on a dying planet, or do we want to leave them on a thriving planet where all life can live in peace? You make this decision three times a day at mealtime.

I understand that transitioning to a vegan lifestyle may feel overwhelming, but remember, every journey starts with a single step. Don't worry if you feel you have to go vegan overnight and think it's impossible. Even the smallest steps can make a difference. I like to say, "Baby steps are better than no steps." Know you will make an impact every time you choose a plant-based meal!

I would like to thank each of you for taking the time to learn more about veganism. For those who are already vegan, thank you for contributing to a more compassionate world where sentient beings are recognized as individuals rather than objects. If you're standing at the edge, contemplating whether to take the plunge into veganism, just know that by even picking up this book and reading it, you are making a difference because you are taking the time to understand why

---

1   Poore, J., and T. Nemecek. 2018. "Reducing Food's Environmental Impacts through Producers and Consumers." **Science** 360 (6392): 987–992.

raising a vegan family is important. Being a vegan superhero is truly the best thing in the world, and I hope you join us and see for yourself how awesome it is to be a vegan superhero! I hope you explore this cookbook and guide with an open mind. Use it as a tool to navigate your vegan journey, answer tough questions, and make informed choices that align with your values.

Together, we have the power to make a difference—one plant-based meal at a time!

Part I

VEGAN SUPER KID GUIDE

01

RAISING A VEGAN SUPERHERO

Welcome to the Fam

Well, hey! I'm Ashley Nsonwu, a vegan mama and environmental advocate who earned a certificate from Cornell University via eCornell in plant-based nutrition (deepest thanks to the Food for Health Foundation for the scholarship) while I was pregnant with my first child, Beyond, and then another one in food and sustainability a year later. This book has truly been a labor of love—I wrote this cookbook and guide while pregnant with my second child, Wonder, to support vegan and vegan-curious parents and caregivers searching for clarity on how to raise their baby, toddler, and/or child on a healthy vegan lifestyle that fosters growth, confidence, and pure joy. If this book landed in your hands (thank you!) and you're ready to joyfully soak up this knowledge and learn some bomb baby recipes, then you're my people and welcome to the fam.

Upon becoming a mother, I went from being the only vegan I knew to having a vegan mini-me. I didn't grow up vegan, so I'm excited to watch my sons grow up in a completely different way from everything I knew as a little girl. My parents raised me the best way they could with the information they had at the time and I'm raising my children with the knowledge I have now too. You might be like me: you grew up eating corn dogs, rocking leather shoes, and visiting zoos and aquariums without thinking twice about it. But now that you're older, you've come to learn about the harmful impacts of everyday activities society taught us to normalize; and now you want to break that cycle in your family.

Raising my kids vegan means empowering them to care about animals, the planet, and their bodies. We teach kids that animals are their friends. Animals are in kids' books, cartoons, games, everywhere. So why feed our kids their friends? Of course, as a parent, I can only do my part to instill these values into my kids and hope they stick with them. Either way, I'm enjoying the ride.

So, here's the thing. While I've studied plant-based nutrition extensively, earned certificates on this subject from Cornell University, and had my vegan toddler taste test (and approve!) every recipe in this book—**I'm not a chef. I'm not a pediatrician. I'm not a dietician.** What I am is a mom trying my best to help shape a more healthy, sustainable, and animal-friendly world that my kids (and yours if you have any) can grow up in. We'll get into how vegan parenting impacts children's health, the environment, and animals in a minute—but first, a little about one of my favorite vegans on the planet—my son Beyond, who made this book possible.

Beyond, My Vegan Superhero

Meet Beyond, The Vegan Super Kid and the main character of this book! At the time of writing, he's a bubbly two-year-old foodie with the appetite of an Olympic swimmer. Breakfast, morning snack, lunch, afternoon snack, dinner—it doesn't matter; he's always ready to chow down and his favorite word is "more." His enthusiasm for food is the only reason I started to enjoy cooking. Before he came along, the kitchen was ironically my least favorite place to be. Now I see it as the cornerstone of our home—a place for love, bonding, and whipping up healthy meals that fuel my family's bodies, minds, and souls.

I'll never forget the words of my friend's husband when he met Beyond for the first time. "That's not a vegan baby," he insisted, shooting an incredulous look at my husband. "Come on; I know you're slippin' him some meat without Ashley knowing." Like him, many others have expressed the same sentiment, stemming from the assumption that all vegan kids must be underweight. "I've never seen a chunky vegan baby before," another recurring comment I get, reflects the shock people experience when their expectations of vegan kids don't meet the reality.

Not all heroes eat meat. Some heroes are three feet tall, thrive on plants, and aren't old enough to understand what a hero even is. When most people picture superheroes, they don't picture a vegan toddler—but that's how I want Beyond to eventually see himself and how I hope your kids will see themselves after implementing the tips and recipes in this book.

Fun Fact: Marvel Studios' *Moon Knight*, on Disney+, is the first show to have a vegan superhero and villain as main characters!

So, let's get into what's so super about raising a kid vegan.

Why Raise a Kid Vegan?

I started my vegan lifestyle in 2016 to take a stance against animal exploitation, and since then I have adopted a wide range of other reasons to further support that choice—from health to environmental to social justice issues.

Here are three of the most popular reasons to raise your child vegan: for the animals, planet, and health.

1. For the Animals

One of the most effective ways to help reduce animal suffering is to choose vegan options over animal-based products. While many adults have a hard time unlearning the food and lifestyle habits they acquired growing up, kids can adopt a way of eating and living consistent with their ethical beliefs, all while they are young enough to develop it into a lifelong habit.

A recent study[2] showed kids ages seven and under don't understand that meat and dairy come from animals, yet they classify animals as "**not okay** to eat." According to the paper, "One reason that children may exhibit confusion about animal-based food is because many parents in the United States are reluctant to talk with their children about the origins of meat."

The same holds true for dairy. Not many parents feel comfortable explaining to their kids that cows don't simply produce milk because "they are cows and that's what cows do." Cows produce milk because they are mothers who endure nine months of pregnancy, grueling labor, and birth, which then triggers their bodies to lactate to feed their babies, just like human moms. Only, they never get to experience motherhood because their calves are taken away and they become milk-producing machines for humans, leaving them unable to fulfill their most basic desires, such as nursing their young, even for a day. Kids aren't taught this reality though. Instead, they learn

that Old McDonald had a farm, and on that farm lived happy cows.

To make matters more difficult, the meat and dairy industry's efforts to conceal, to an extent, the realities of food production also contribute to children misunderstanding how food gets to their plates. From meat products bearing scant resemblance to the animals they started out as, to these products being marketed under non-animal names like beef, pork, ham, bologna, sausage, and meatballs, to name a few, it's easy to see how a lack of transparency can leave kids unsuspectingly eating a diet inconsistent with their feelings toward animals.

Kids love animals. Adults do too, but after years of consuming animal products, people eventually succumb to a form of cognitive dissonance known as the "meat paradox." Cognitive dissonance is a psychological term used to describe the mental conflict that occurs when one's behaviors don't line up with their beliefs. A recent review paper[3] explained that, at the center of the meat paradox, is this conflict: many adults wish to avoid harming animals, yet most will happily eat them. According to the paper, this phenomenon has grave negative consequences for animal welfare and the environment.

2   Hahn, Erin R., Meghan Gillogly, and Bailey E. Bradford. 2021. "Children Are Unsuspecting Meat Eaters: An Opportunity to Address Climate Change." **Journal of Environmental Psychology** 78 (December): 101705. https://doi.org/10.1016/j.jenvp.2021.101705.
3   Gradidge, Sarah, Magdalena Zawisza, Annelie J. Harvey, and Daragh T. McDermott. 2021. "A Structured Literature Review of the Meat Paradox." **Social Psychological Bulletin** 16 (3). https://doi.org/10.32872/spb.5953.

By raising kids to be vegan, we give them the opportunity to align their behaviors with their beliefs, before they reach an age where cognitive dissonance takes over. We give them the opportunity to demonstrate their natural recognition that animals should have the freedom to stretch their wings, raise their young, roam the land, and feel the warmth of the sun on their backs; we allow kids to essentially recognize an animal's right to be an animal and not a product.

Important Stats Every Family Should Know

★ Every day, over 200 **million** land animals are killed for food across the globe. According to the Food and Agriculture Organization of the United Nations (FAO),[4] over 85 **billion** land animals were killed by humans for food in 2020. These unimaginably huge numbers don't even include the **trillions** of aquatic animals killed for food each year.

★ In the US today, 99 percent of land animals used for food[5] live on massive industrial factory farms. Most won't even feel the warmth of the sun or breathe fresh air until the day they're led to slaughterhouses.

★ Many animals also die before they arrive[6] at the slaughterhouse, either in transport on the way to be killed or during the process of being raised under conditions of extreme abuse and confinement.

★ Animals raised for slaughter are not the only ones who are mistreated. The dairy industry is rife with abuse. Mother cows endure an endless cycle of coerced nine-month pregnancies and births just to have their babies taken away from them so they can continue lactating and producing milk for human consumption—a process that involves either being forced to procreate with a bull or being artificially inseminated in a brutal act of bodily violation.

★ Mother animals are routinely used and discarded. For example, once mother cows are no longer useful for milk production or mother hens begin to decline in egg production, they are sent for slaughter.

★ Meanwhile, if they give birth to males, this offspring is then sent to die. As just mere babies, male calves and male chicks are transported to slaughterhouses.

2. For the Planet

Avoiding animal products is the single biggest way[7] for your family to fight climate change and reduce its

4 FAO. 2022. "Crops and Livestock Products." www.fao.org. 2022. https://www.fao.org/faostat/en/#data/QCL.
5 Sentience Institute. 2019. "US Factory Farming Estimates." Sentience Institute. 2019. https://www.sentienceinstitute.org/us-factory-farming-estimates.
6 Sentient Media. 2022. "Slaughterhouses: The Harsh Reality of How Meat Is Made." Sentientmedia.org. July 1, 2022. https://sentientmedia.org/slaughterhouses/.
7 Poore, Joseph, and Thomas Nemecek. 2018. "Reducing Food's Environmental Impacts through Producers and Consumers." **Science** 360 (6392): 987–92. https://doi.org/10.1126/science.aaq0216.

environmental footprint. Our kids are growing up during a climate emergency and as parents, we have the unique challenge of guiding them through it. Climate change is likely the most challenging threat humanity has ever faced, and younger generations are well aware.

Okay, climate change, blah blah—what does that even mean? We hear it all the time, but **why** is it such a big deal?

Climate change refers to the process of our planet heating up and the resulting consequences. Wait, but warmer weather sounds like a year-round tropical vacation, right? I wish! This means that weather events will become more **severe** and **unpredictable**. We see it now, and it will only get worse for our kids.

Climate change is caused by the release of greenhouse gases into the atmosphere—and can you guess what one major cause is? Animal agriculture. This industry is responsible for at least 16.5 percent of global greenhouse gas emissions[8] and that's a conservative estimate.

Yes. In fact, the role food plays in climate change was acknowledged in the 2022 IPCC Special Report on Climate Change and Land,[9] which recognized the adoption of plant-based foods as a shift individuals can make to lower environmental impact in the effort to prevent catastrophic climate impacts. The IPCC is the United Nations' body in charge of assessing the science related to climate change. Suffice it to say, they know a thing or two about this stuff.

While the heavy lifting in addressing climate change will need to come via changes at the government and corporate level, we as parents can help influence mass behavioral change by raising kids to embrace eco-conscious, vegan lifestyles. This societal shift will be pivotal to securing a sustainable future for our kids and will likely be the most significant economic transition witnessed since the industrial revolution.

I once explained to a friend why being eco-conscious matters and she responded with, "I'm a mom; I don't have time to worry about the planet. My only priority right now is taking care of my kid." Now that I'm a mom, I finally understand where she was coming from. Parents have a million things to keep track of when raising a tiny human. Why can't someone else tackle climate change? Here's the thing, though: it's actually **because of our kids** that we should care about environmental issues and help our little ones adopt sustainable lifestyle habits. This starts with what's on their plate.

---

8 Twine, Richard. 2021. "Emissions from Animal Agriculture—16.5% Is the New Minimum Figure." **Sustainability** 13 (11): 6276. https://doi.org/10.3390/su13116276.

9 IPCC. 2019. "Chapter 5—Special Report on Climate Change and Land." Ipcc.ch. Special Report on Climate Change and Land. 2019. https://www.ipcc.ch/srccl/chapter/chapter-5/.

By raising kids vegan, we are not only showing them we care about protecting their generation and the other generations to come; we are also teaching them how to lead the way. They get to be the Captain Planets of their generation, inspiring their peers to be at the forefront of a green revolution during an unprecedented time in history when positive change is greatly needed.

Important Stats Every Family Should Know

★ Currently, farmed animals occupy nearly 30 percent[10] of the ice-free land on earth.

★ Meat and dairy provide[11] just 18 percent of calories consumed but use 83 percent of global farmland and are responsible for 60 percent of agriculture's greenhouse gas emissions.

★ It takes **144** gallons of water to produce just **1** gallon of milk[12] in the US and more than 93 percent of that water is used to grow feed for dairy cows.

★ Almost 70 percent of the world's wildlife populations have declined[13] since 1970, and animal farming is cited as a key reason.

★ Scientists say[14] a global shift to plant-based diets would reduce global land use for agriculture by 75 percent.

3. For Health

A carefully planned healthy vegan diet can set a child up for lifelong health success. What your child eats during the first few years of life can build a strong foundation, providing early prevention for the kind of illnesses that aren't symptomatic until **decades** later. Research shows[15] that many chronic diseases suffered in adulthood have their beginnings in childhood and kids who grow up on a Standard American Diet are at greater risk of developing these diseases. Focusing on whole foods and plant-based nutrition can be a preventative tool that allows kids to take control of their long-term health outcomes.

Nutrition can affect a variety of health conditions experienced during childhood as well, including allergies, constipation, acne, recurrent upper respiratory tract and ear

10 Alders, Robyn G, Angus Campbell, Rosa Costa, Guèye E Fallou, Ahasanul Hoque, Md, Raúl Perezgrovas-Garza, Antonio Rota, and Kate Wingett. 2021. "Livestock across the World: Diverse Animal Species with Complex Roles in Human Societies and Ecosystem Services." **Animal Frontiers** 11 (5): 20–29. https://doi.org/10.1093/af/vfab047.
11 Poore, J., and T. Nemecek. 2018. "Reducing Food's Environmental Impacts through Producers and Consumers." **Science** 360 (6392): 987–992.
12 WWF. 2019. "Milk's Impact on the Environment." World Wildlife Fund. 2019. https://www.worldwildlife.org/magazine/issues/winter-2019/articles/milk-s-impact-on-the-environment.
13 International, W. W. F. 2020. "Living Planet Report 2020 | Official Site | WWF." Livingplanet.panda.org. 2020. https://livingplanet.panda.org/en-us/.
14 Ritchie, Hannah. 2021. "If the World Adopted a Plant-Based Diet We Would Reduce Global Agricultural Land Use from 4 to 1 Billion Hectares." Our World in Data. March 4, 2021. https://ourworldindata.org/land-use-diets.
15 "Heart Disease Starts in Childhood | NutritionFacts.org." n.d. Nutritionfacts.org. https://nutritionfacts.org/video/heart-disease starts-in-childhood/.

infections, and possibly even some neurodevelopmental disorders like ADHD. In the case of asthma, evidence suggests[16] that diets focused on plant-based foods can help protect against the development of asthma and improve asthma symptoms.

Most of us grew up being told to eat our veggies. It wasn't just an annoying suggestion from our parents: plant-based nutrition can be the difference between a comfortable life and a painful one later. And now that **we're** the parents, we can establish a new norm for our kids. If we want to be serious about preventing adulthood illnesses from burdening our children, we can't shy away from educating ourselves about nutrition and teaching it to the youth. Whole-food, plant-based nutrition needs to be a part of our conversations with our littles, and it's clear that the earlier you start, the bigger the impact!

Don't worry. We're going to take a major deep dive into plant-based vegan nutrition for kids in Chapter 3. There's a lot of essential information, so don't skip it.

Important Stats Every Family Should Know

★ Both the American Academy of Pediatrics (AAP)[17] and the Academy of Nutrition and Dietetics (AND)[18] have deemed an appropriately planned vegan diet safe for all stages of the life cycle, including pregnancy, lactation, infancy, childhood, and adolescence.

★ The single biggest dietary predictor of early menarche (first menstrual period) for girls is the consumption of animal protein[19] at a young age. Early age at menarche is associated with the risk of several chronic diseases.

★ Autopsies done[20] on childhood accident victims show the earliest stages of atherosclerosis (hardening of the arteries), called fatty streaks, were found in the arteries of 100 percent of the kids by age ten. If not reversed during adolescence, fatty streaks lead to plaques forming in their twenties, which worsen in their thirties, and can lead to fatal outcomes in middle age. Long-term prevention may be most effective when initiated in infancy.

16 Alwarith, Jihad, Hana Kahleova, Lee Crosby, Alexa Brooks, Lizoralia Brandon, Susan M Levin, and Neal D Barnard. 2020. "The Role of Nutrition in Asthma Prevention and Treatment." **Nutrition Reviews** 78 (11). https://doi.org/10.1093/nutrit/nuaa005.
17 Patel L, Millstein A. Plant-based diets: are they good for kids?. Updated June 2, 2020. Accessed April 6, 2021. https://www.healthychildren.org/English/healthy-living/nutrition/Pages/Plant-Based-Diets.aspx
18 Melina, Vesanto, Winston Craig, and Susan Levin. 2016. "Position of the Academy of Nutrition and Dietetics: Vegetarian Diets." **Journal of the Academy of Nutrition and Dietetics** 116 (12): 1970–80. https://doi.org/10.1016/j.jand.2016.09.025.
19 Nguyen, Ngan Thi Kim, Hsien-Yu Fan, Meng-Che Tsai, Te-Hsuan Tung, Quynh Thi Vu Huynh, Shih-Yi Huang, and Yang Ching Chen. 2020. "Nutrient Intake through Childhood and Early Menarche Onset in Girls: Systematic Review and Meta-Analysis." **Nutrients** 12 (9): 2544. https://doi.org/10.3390/nu12092544.
20 Gregor, Michael. 2014. "Stopping Heart Disease in Childhood." NutritionFacts.org. July 15, 2014. https://nutritionfacts.org/blog/stopping-heart-disease-in-childhood/.

- From 2001 to 2017, the number of American children and adolescents living with type 2 diabetes grew by 95 percent.[21] But studies show[22] that people who consume plant-based diets have a lower risk for developing type 2 diabetes.

- Data has shown[23] that one in five youths already have high cholesterol levels. High blood pressure rates are also increasingly common in children. But well-planned, healthy vegan diets are low in cholesterol and saturated fat.

- Many of the longest-lived populations in the world consume a plant-centered diet.[24]

Why Kids Love Being Vegan

Statistics aside for a moment, let's hear from other families about how a vegan lifestyle has personally impacted their children. I invited my community on social media to ask their kids why being raised vegan matters and what it means to be a vegan superhero. Flip to the next page to read some of the endearing responses.

Raising a Vegan Superhero

21 Lawrence, Jean M., Jasmin Divers, Scott Isom, Sharon Saydah, Giuseppina Imperatore, Catherine Pihoker, Santica M. Marcovina, et al. 2021. "Trends in Prevalence of Type 1 and Type 2 Diabetes in Children and Adolescents in the US, 2001–2017." **JAMA** 326 (8): 717. https://doi.org/10.1001/jama.2021.11165.

22 Jardine, Meghan A, Hana Kahleova, Susan M Levin, Zeeshan Ali, Caroline B Trapp, and Neal D Barnard. 2021. "Perspective: Plant-Based Eating Pattern for Type 2 Diabetes Prevention and Treatment: Efficacy, Mechanisms, and Practical Considerations." **Advances in Nutrition** 12 (6). https://doi.org/10.1093/advances/nmab063.

23 Nguyen, Duong, Brian Kit, and Margaret Carroll. 2015. "Abnormal Cholesterol among Children and Adolescents in the United States, 2011–2014." https://www.cdc.gov/nchs/data/databriefs/DB228.pdf.

24 Buettner, Dan. 2020. "Food Secrets of the World's Longest-Lived People." Blue Zones. July 10, 2020. https://www.bluezones.com/2020/07/blue-zones-diet-food-secrets-of-the-worlds-longest-lived-people/.

What Does It Mean to Be a Vegan Superhero?

"It means I can save animals. My superpower can be super strength so I can use my arms to pick up all the animals who are hurt and put them in the sanctuary so they're safe and have room [to move] and are happy."

—Zarine, age three and a half (daughter of Sara a.k.a. "The Pakistani Vegan" and owner of Punjab Spice Company)

"I'm a superhero because I don't make animals my dinner and I eat superfoods."

—Zuri, age seven

If You Had a Vegan Super Power, What Would It Be?

"To be able to make animals live longer, because dinosaurs are already extinct—we don't need any more animals extinct. Not deers, not fish or any other animals."

—Raia, age eight (daughter of Felicia Cox a.k.a. "Vegan Tastes Good")

"A lot of things we see in the supermarket aren't vegan. If I could have a superpower, it would be to make vegan food out of thin air and put it in the stores so that more people would see vegan food and become vegan."

—Veralina, age seven (daughter of Meredith Marin, CEO of Vegan Hospitality)

Why Are You Vegan?

"I think it's healthy, it's yummy, and because I don't want animals to get hurt."

—Lynora, age six (daughter of Tylar, a vegan blogger)

"Because it's not nice when the farmers take the baby cows away."

—Noa, age four

"I have been vegan my entire life and I am vegan because I want to save animals and vegan food is healthy and delicious."

—Raia, age eight (daughter of Felicia Cox a.k.a. "Vegan Tastes Good")

The Power of a Parent

Given all the sobering statistics coupled with the remarkable emotional connections kids have with animals, avoiding the consumption and exploitation of animals makes sense from both a scientific and ethical viewpoint. So, why do many families continue to uphold the status quo, passing down those consumptive habits to their kids, despite it presenting a sharp conflict with their values? Simply put, the mainstream diets of our society often aren't influenced by science or ethics. They're influenced by marketing, politics, and culture, all of which play significant roles in subconsciously forcing us into ethically compromising situations.

As parents, we can't control the strategic marketing messages that billion-dollar meat and dairy corporations bombard us with daily, which are designed to disconnect us from the living animal their advertised food came from.

As parents, we can't control the politics involved in how nutrition is taught in schools or the billions of dollars in global subsidies paid to animal agriculture industries by governments via taxpayer money, that in turn artificially lower the price of meat and dairy products, making it cheaper to choose a McDonald's Big Mac over a nutrient-dense plant-based meal.

As parents, we can't control the kind of food culture that dominates our societies or the presence of social challenges that accompany going against the norms of our friends, peers, and family members.

However, as parents, we **can** control how we teach our kids about the realities behind what we consume. We can teach them the impact our consumption choices have on our health, the planet, and animals. We can instill within them the knowledge and confidence to decide on their own to choose compassion over cruelty when cruelty isn't a necessity to live and thrive. That is **our** personal superpower as parents.

Whew. That was a lot. At this point, you may be thinking, I thought this was a cookbook. When are we getting to the bomb baby recipes you promised me? If you made it this far though, you have my sincerest gratitude. While this information is heavy, it provides important context into the many layers of a vegan lifestyle.

02

SLAYING COMMON CHALLENGES

Vegan Parenting Myths

After Beyond's first birthday, I began to share videos of what I fed him on social media. There was a dizzying mix of uplifting and gut-punching comments on the first video. While many people loved the content and were curious to follow along, a few onlookers were quick to shame me for my decisions.

Not going to lie—the shaming stung at first. No parent ever wants to feel isolated in their child-rearing choices. I quickly learned not to take it personally, however. I realized the negativity was rooted in two main problems:

1. A general confusion about what being vegan means.
2. A general misunderstanding of plant-based vegan nutrition.

The more I posted, the more I noticed a huge community of parents raising their kids the same way, or at least interested in learning how. And these parents also struggled with society's judgment.

Many stereotypes, myths, and misinformation exist regarding the nutritional benefits and ethical implications of feeding a child a vegan diet. Families adopting a plant-based diet are often accused of being "forceful" and making their children "unhealthy." How many times have you gotten the "But what about protein?!" question. We've all been there.

So, I want to share some reassurance that will help you feel proud and confident in your decisions whenever you run into the challenge of facing misinformed comments from a friend, family member, or online troll.

Slaying Common Misconceptions

Here are some popular fear-based comments directed at vegan parents followed by fact-backed responses you can have on deck.

1. "Kids Need Animal Protein!"

Vegan protein sources can supply all the necessary amounts of protein and essential amino acids (the building blocks of protein) to fuel the growth of your child. You may have even come across the "incomplete protein" myth that suggests the necessity of eating a hefty combination of plant foods throughout the day to compensate for plant foods missing one or more of the essential amino acids. That's not entirely accurate. All plant foods contain all twenty amino acids, including the nine essential amino acids[25] our bodies need. Some plants simply have lower amounts of one or

---

25 Mariotti, François, and Christopher D. Gardner. 2019. "Dietary Protein and Amino Acids in Vegetarian Diets-a Review." **Nutrients** 11 (11): E2661. https://doi.org/10.3390/nu11112661.

more essential amino acids compared to animal protein. By eating a variety of whole plants throughout the day, the higher amounts of amino acids in some plant-based foods will balance out the lower amounts in others.

Furthermore, there is no medical research that shows animal protein is necessary to nourish already well-nourished kids. However, there **are** studies[26] revealing the risks of a diet rich in animal products. Among the risks associated with animal consumption include childhood obesity, type 2 diabetes, heart disease, some cancers, and even early menstruation, to name a few.

2. "A Vegan Diet Will Stunt Your Child's Height!"

This one is particularly grating, because despite knowing better, I catch myself at times unconsciously comparing my son's height to other kids his age in response. While height is more genetic than anything, here is some information to ease your worries. A study[27] examining growth impacts of vegan diets on children revealed vegan children showed normal growth and were less often obese. Another study[28] of 404 mainly vegetarian and vegan children revealed that the

majority fell between the 25th and 75th percentiles for weight and height on US growth charts.

The conversation about height often goes hand in hand with the consumption of cow's milk. Understandably, many associate cow's milk with stronger bones due to the relentless marketing efforts of the dairy industry. Calories, protein, fat, calcium, and vitamin D are all critical nutrients for growth, which are all concentrated in cow's milk. The key here is understanding that it isn't milk that does the body good—it's select nutrients found in milk, which can be obtained elsewhere.

Before the age of one, infants will primarily meet their nutritional requirements through human milk or formula, as well as complementary plant-based foods when they are ready for solids. **After the age of one**, toddlers can then go on to also consume plant-based milks fortified with calcium and vitamin D, ideally fortified soy or pea milk, which are calorie and nutrient-dense to support a toddler's growth. You can also ask your pediatrician about animal-free dairy milk, which is nutritionally similar to cow's milk, but no animals were involved in developing it. Toddlers have smaller appetites, so it is essential to ensure they aren't filling

26 Papier, Keren, Georgina K. Fensom, Anika Knuppel, Paul N. Appleby, Tammy Y. N. Tong, Julie A. Schmidt, Ruth C. Travis, Timothy J. Key, and Aurora Perez-Cornago. 2021. "Meat Consumption and Risk of 25 Common Conditions: Outcome-Wide Analyses in 475,000 Men and Women in the UK Biobank Study." **BMC Medicine** 19 (1). https://doi.org/10.1186/s12916-021-01922-9.

27 Sutter, Daniel Olivier, and Nicole Bender. 2021. "Nutrient Status and Growth in Vegan Children." **Nutrition Research** 91 (May). https://doi.org/10.1016/j.nutres.2021.04.005.

28 O'Connell, J. M., M. J. Dibley, J. Sierra, B. Wallace, J. S. Marks, and R. Yip. 1989. "Growth of Vegetarian Children: The Farm Study." **Pediatrics** 84 (3): 475–81. https://pubmed.ncbi.nlm.nih.gov/2771551/.

up on foods that don't supply them with the nutrients they need to grow.

3. "Soy Causes Cancer!"

If anyone comes for your tofu, not to worry, friend. Just hit them with the facts. Soy is a polarizing topic, thanks to a lot of confusing misinformation out there. It's truly heartbreaking to get comments like this, especially when soy does the exact opposite of causing cancer. In fact, studies show that a lifelong diet rich in soy foods reduces the risk of breast[29] and prostate[30] cancer. There is plenty of medical information and research backing this. If soy caused cancer, then the people of Okinawa, who eat a diet rich in soy, would not have the highest life expectancy[31] in the world.

Rest assured—the latest, most up-to-date research shows no reason to fear soy. An article published in **Critical Reviews in Food Science and Nutrition Researchers**[32] reviewed 417 reports based on human data and concluded isoflavone intake from soy does not adversely affect thyroid function, estrogen levels, ovulation in women, or semen levels in men; nor were there any negative effects identified in children. These results suggest soy

foods, like our beloved tofu, should not be associated with disease and adverse health outcomes.

4. "Vegan Diets Are Dangerous for Kids."

Since sharing my journey online, I've gotten all sorts of theatrical variations of this comment. From disturbing statements such as "this is illegal" or "I reported you to CPS," all the way to cruel bets placed on the lifespan of my child, I have heard it all. Due to a lack of comprehensive nutrition education in schools, many of us grew up with a limited understanding of how to meet our daily nutritional requirements outside of animal products. So unsurprisingly, there are segments of the population who think vegan diets are nutritionally inadequate. However, vegan diets don't cause nutrient deficiencies. Not getting the nutrients you need causes nutrient deficiencies. That can happen on any diet.

Then there are the heartbreaking headlines that surface every once in a blue moon, attributing the tragic death of a child to a vegan diet. In these isolated cases, a lack of animal products isn't to blame; malnutrition is. There have been infuriating situations

29 Hilakivii Clarke, Leena, Juan E. Andrade, and William Helferich. 2010. "Is Soy Consumption Good or Bad for the Breast?" **The Journal of Nutrition** 140 (12): 2326S2334S. https://doi.org/10.3945/jn.110.124230.

30 Applegate, Catherine, Joe Rowles, Katherine Ranard, Sookyoung Jeon, and John Erdman. 2018. "Soy Consumption and the Risk of Prostate Cancer: An Updated Systematic Review and Meta-Analysis." **Nutrients** 10 (1): 40. https://doi.org/10.3390/nu10010040.

31 Mishra, Badrin. 2009. "Secret of Eternal Youth; Teaching from the Centenarian Hot Spots ('Blue Zones')." **Indian Journal of Community Medicine** 34 (4): 273. https://doi.org/10.4103/0970-0218.58380.

32 Messina, Mark, Sonia Blanco Mejia, Aedin Cassidy, Alison Duncan, Mindy Kurzer, Chisato Nagato, Martin Ronis, Ian Rowland, John Sievenpiper, and Stephen Barnes. 2021. "Neither Soyfoods nor Isoflavones Warrant Classification as Endocrine Disruptors: A Technical Review of the Observational and Clinical Data." **Critical Reviews in Food Science and Nutrition** 62 (21): 5824–85. https://doi.org/10.1080/10408398.2021.1895054.

where parents withheld essential nutrients from their children. Read past the misleading headlines and you'll find examples of parents **only** feeding their kids fruits and vegetables, as opposed to a properly planned diet rich in plant-based foods that include fruits, vegetables, whole grains, legumes, nuts, and seeds. Or maybe caregivers inappropriately fed an infant plant-based milk instead of human milk (breast milk) or infant formula. These cases are not reflective of vegan parenting at all, and thankfully you have resources like this book to guide you through your journey.

5. "You Are Forcing Your Kid to Be Vegan."

Ironic, isn't it, how the word "force" is only used when feeding a child plants, but not when feeding a child animals? If a parent offers their kids meat, dairy, and eggs (especially without children fully understanding the origins of those foods), these children aren't being given a choice either. All parents make choices for their little ones, including what food to eat, which holidays to celebrate, or even what color socks to wear that day. That's what you do when you're responsible for a tiny human.

So, let's turn that question around and examine it from a different angle. Instead ask, **why would I "force" my kid to eat animals?** We teach kids to love animals and then turn around and feed them those animals without

them understanding that their food = animals. It's a contradiction. Furthermore, the American Academy of Pediatrics and the Academy of Nutrition and Dietetics agree that appropriately planned vegan diets are nutritionally adequate during pregnancy, lactation, infancy, childhood, and adolescence. If it's not medically necessary to consume animal products, then why do it?

There are a host of reasons that support the decision not to; animal welfare, climate change, environmental degradation, wildlife extinction, world hunger, social justice, and our current health crisis are all perfectly valid motives for raising your children to avoid animal products. With there being enough information today that points to the need to evolve our food systems to reflect the modern times we live in, it is unequivocally irrational to use terms like "force" in reference to raising a kid vegan.

Slaying School, Holidays, and Social Events

Raising a vegan child in a non-vegan world will without a doubt test you. We are social creatures who often seek validation from our families, peers, and communities. A common concern with vegan parenting is whether your kids will be treated like oddballs in a society where they are the dietary minority.

The good news is, although vegans currently comprise a small percentage of the population, the number of people ditching meat and dairy is growing and public perception is shifting. Whether motivated by environmental, health, or ethical reasons, statistics suggest[33] the shift toward a plant-based food system is not only necessary but possible to work toward when barriers are broken at individual and societal levels.

It is no longer out of the ordinary in different places to accommodate requests for vegan options at kids' schools, birthday parties, holiday celebrations, and family events. It may feel overwhelming to think about, but slaying the vegan parenting thing just takes some extra creativity, patience, and persistence. You got this! I'm here to help, friend.

Navigating Schools and Daycares

Choosing the most suitable daycare or early education program for babies and toddlers is no simple task. Our family's list of questions to ask each school we toured was a mile long and still never seemed to be enough. One question made my heart pound: "Does your school support vegan children?" To my surprise, every school we visited was indeed supportive of plant-based meals, although not necessarily in the way we needed. There were key indicators I looked for to help me decide which one would ultimately be the right fit, and it's important to weigh the pros and cons going in.

Our Journey

First Daycare We Toured

The director told me they catered food every day. When I asked if the caterer had vegan options, she confirmed they did. I asked to see the menu and she enthusiastically pointed to the options that said "vegetarian." She was sweet and I knew she meant well, but she didn't know there was a difference between vegan and vegetarian. From what I saw on the menu, there were only vegetarian options available, and they didn't allow parents to bring food. Whomp.

Second Daycare We Toured

We got a little closer to what we wanted with this one. They didn't serve vegan food, but they had a chef who knew how to cook vegan food. She said we could look at the menu and bring in vegan options for the chef to execute.

---

33 Perez-Cueto, Federico J. A., Listia Rini, Ilona Faber, Morten A. Rasmussen, Kai-Brit Bechtold, Joachim J. Schouteten, and Hans De Steur. 2022. "How Barriers towards Plant-Based Food Consumption Differ according to Dietary Lifestyle: Findings from a Consumer Survey in 10 EU Countries." **International Journal of Gastronomy and Food Science** 29 (September): 100587. https://doi.org/10.1016/j.ijgfs.2022.100587.

However, we weren't allowed to pack our lunches and snacks. Not ideal, but doable. We decided to keep looking just in case.

Third Daycare We Toured

Then we toured a school that seemed perfect in every way before we even asked any dietary questions. The vibe was right, so we hoped with all our hearts they would accommodate our needs. Not only could they do it, but this also wasn't new to them. They had other vegan children at the school, and **that** was a huge plus for me. They allowed our family to bring our own meals, as long as they were nut-free, and that was perfect! I felt at peace knowing I would be able to prepare Beyond's food the way we wanted.

Finding the Right Fit for You

We found "the one" through a combination of preparation, persistence, and luck. Here are a few takeaways from our experience to help you navigate your search:

★ Start early, shop around, and tour each facility so you can meet the staff.
★ Know where you're willing to be flexible and where you aren't.
★ Keep a thorough list of questions handy.
★ Be firm and clear (but polite) about your dietary needs.
★ Observe their body language and response. Did they hesitate?

★ Be gracious, approachable, and collaborative.

Here is a list of dietary questions to bring with you on your daycare tours:

1. Does your school accommodate vegan children?
2. Does your facility currently have any vegan children, or have you in the past?
3. How do other vegan families handle food here?
4. What are the biggest challenges you have in supporting vegan families?
5. Does your menu have vegan options?
6. Are parents allowed to bring their own meals?
7. What are your allergen policies?
8. What are some examples of snacks your facility provides?
9. For special occasions where treats are given, do you always have vegan options, or would I be able to provide one?
10. In the event they don't have experience with vegan kids specifically, ask if they have a plan in place to support kids with other types of alternative diets. If not, did they offer to work with you to create one?

When you do find "the one," here are a few tips to help you have a smooth experience:

★ **Build a positive rapport with the caregivers and staff.** I adore

Beyond's teachers and the rest of the staff. They make me feel confident that they are working diligently to ensure Beyond is in a welcoming, safe, nurturing environment. I knew I had nothing to worry about when I got a message asking if he could have some applesauce during a tasting activity in class. It was reassuring to see they chose to ask rather than assume, and I'm sure having a positive relationship helped.

★ **Remind them of your child's needs.** Get a clear understanding of what measures will be in place to ensure your child is supported. In Beyond's school, every child has a card plastered on the classroom wall with their photo and a list of dietary notes, including allergens and preferences. Beyond's dietary card clearly states he is vegan, and his food is brought in from home—which is helpful, especially if there is a substitute teacher.

★ **Get a copy of the menu and activity calendar.** If you are allowed to bring in food, consider trying to mimic what's on their menu. It may be helpful especially for toddlers who don't understand yet why their food looks different from everyone else's. For example, if the class is having cheese pizza, I might whip up a Mushroom Veggie Flatbread Pizza (page 204). Also, if they have an activity calendar, and you see something like "National Ice Cream Sandwich Day" coming up, double-check whether the school will have

a dairy-free option, and if not, you know ahead of time to bring one and store it in their freezer.

Working with the schools in your community is another effective way to advocate for access to healthy, plant-based meals and education in the school system. Parents have found success with this all over the US. Flip to the "Additional Resources" section on page 290 to help you get started.

If there are no vegan options on the school menu, then packing your child's lunch is the way to go. The great thing about this is that plant-based kids often spark discussions amongst their peers when whipping out their delicious lunches. Some kids have never seen hummus, avocado, brussels sprouts, quinoa, tofu, purple sweet potatoes (the list goes on)—and may marvel at the diversity of your child's diet. This could, in turn, lead to productive and educational conversations with the school and other parents.

Navigating Kiddie Holidays

Truthfully, holidays lowkey stress me out. Often, the traditions associated with our holiday celebrations lead to overconsumption, a surge in waste, and animal exploitation of some kind.

Animals who become the symbols of these holidays (think Easter bunny,

Christmas reindeer, Thanksgiving turkey, etc.) end up suffering either for our appetites or entertainment. The cool thing is you can always rethink the way you celebrate and get as creative as you want with it!

As you start families of your own, I challenge you to examine the childhood traditions you plan to pass on to your kids. This is the perfect opportunity to start new ones. Traditions that are sustainable and cruelty-free. We have the power to help future generations break the cycles of our generation's harmful habits.

Holidays can be tricky but remember: you're raising a vegan super kid. You can do **anything**. Here are some ways to slay the holidays.

Valentine's Day

This holiday is all about love, and you can explain to your kids that love isn't just a romantic thing. You love your parents, teachers, friends, animals, and the planet too. They can express their affection using anything from vegan treats to small acts of kindness!

A Few Ideas

★ Is food your love language? Bake vegan sweets together. Try these Fudgy Avocado Brownies on page 256.

★ Or you don't have to use the oven at all. Make some "no-bake" vegan Valentine's treats like Raspberry Coconut Bliss Balls (page 154, but use raspberries instead of blueberries) or Creamy Chocolate Pudding (page 262) that you can dip succulent strawberries into.

★ Use heart-shaped cookie cutters and molds for a twist on meals. You can make heart-shaped dragon fruit, kiwis and pancakes for breakfast that morning and pack star-shaped Sun Butter Jam Sandwiches in their school lunch boxes that day (page 157, but use strawberry chia jam instead of mango).

★ Shop for boxes of vegan candy online. Common non-vegan ingredients in Valentine's Day candy are gelatin and dairy products, so avoid those.

★ Make red or pink smoothies using fruits like strawberries, raspberries, and pink pitaya (dragon fruit). Try the PB&J Smoothie on page 281.

★ Help your child do random acts of love throughout the day. For example, write a love note to a sibling, donate an unused toy, bake a special treat for your fur baby, or plant some winter flowers for wildlife.

★ Help them show love for people and animals in big ways by visiting a farm animal sanctuary, donating to a homeless shelter, or planning a vegan bake sale to raise money for the local animal shelter or charity of choice.

St. Patrick's Day

The theme is green for this one, so vegans are at an advantage here! However, since green is a central focus on St. Patrick's Day, you may notice the use of artificial coloring in desserts, snacks, drinks, and various foods.

Studies have linked[34] artificial food dyes to:

★ Hyperactivity, including ADHD.
★ Behavioral changes like irritability and depression.
★ Hives and asthma.
★ Tumor growth.

Food dyes make food fun, and that's why you'll see them in so many kid-centric food items like candies and other sweets. You can make homemade green food dye using natural foods like green spirulina or the juices of green veggies (see page 143 for food coloring recipes).

A Few Vegan St. Patrick's Day Ideas

★ Make green smoothies, treats, and meals.

★ Veganize a traditional Irish meal.

★ Leprechauns, four-leaf clovers, and rainbows are all animal-friendly, so find creative ways to use these themes.

★ Regrow a green vegetable or herb from food scraps (see page 234 for step-by-step instructions on this project).

★ Where do you live? You can teach your kids to reflect on Irish contributions to your country's culture.

Easter

It's kinda ironic that a religious holiday has become a time of intense distress for animals and the environment. Year after year, there are incidents where parents and grandparents give bunnies and chicks to kids as Easter surprises. Not understanding what it takes to care for these animals, the children abandon these new "friends" after the novelty wears off. According to Nat Geo,[35] around 80 percent of rabbits bought for Easter die or are abandoned within the first year of ownership.

Don't forget the mountains of plastic waste generated along the way—the disposable plastic eggs stuffed with disposable plastic toys and the single-use baskets of shredded plastic Easter grass. So how can we teach our kids some animal and planet-friendly approaches to this holiday? I got you! Ditch the individually wrapped non-vegan candies, dyed animal eggs, and single-use goodies.

34 Cleveland Clinic. 2023. "Is Red Dye 40 Safe?" Cleveland Clinic. March 8, 2023. https://health.clevelandclinic.org/red-dye-40/.
35 Daly, Natasha. 2017. "Here's Why Easter Is Bad for Bunnies." **National Geographic**. April 12, 2017. https://www.nationalgeographic.com/animals/article/rabbits-easter-animal-welfare-pets-rescue-bunnies.

★ Invest in a sturdy reusable basket that can be used every year. You can even search together for one at a second-hand shop or online thrift store.

★ Trying to find a cute Easter outfit for your littles? Shop second-hand or ask other mom and dad friends if they have any pre-loved items they were planning to get rid of.

★ Use eco-friendly basket fillers like Eco Shred made from recycled newsprint or you can make your own using the shredder you have at home.

★ Fill Easter baskets with books, arts and crafts, eco-friendly toys, games, bubbles, accessories, vegan sweets, and healthy snacks.

★ Or you can skip the baskets of goodies and start a new tradition of gifting an experience. Maybe a trip to a farm animal sanctuary or a vegan picnic at a lake. What about going for a hike?

★ Do a spring-themed gardening project together.

★ Have your kids paint rocks with Easter colors and inspirational messages and hide them around your neighborhood for others to find (my neighbor's daughter did this and it was such a sweet surprise).

★ Decorate compostable, wooden, or kraft paper eggs. Use natural dyes (page 143).

★ Do an eco-friendly Easter egg scavenger hunt by filling vegan, plastic-free eggs with puzzle pieces. When they find all the eggs with the puzzle pieces, you can put the puzzle together!

4th of July

Tis the season for grilling and fireworks. Burgers, hot dogs, and other grilled animal products are the norm here, but we can change that in our homes with veggie burgers and veggie hot dogs! If you go to someone else's house, bring your own food items to throw on the grill. Or perhaps you have thoughtful friends, like my neighbors, who let you know in advance they will have vegan options for you and your family (those friends are the real deal, protect them at all costs).

If you're grilling at home, I have a simple experiment for you to try. Remember Tabitha Brown's viral carrot bacon video? Well, here's a secret. You can also use carrots to make vegan, kid-friendly hot dogs too. Okay, I'll admit that might sound a bit unappetizing, but I promise that it can be done and taste phenomenal.

Other Fun 4th of July Treats Include

★ Homemade red, white, and blue popsicles. Try the Watermelon Popsicles on page 254, but use blueberries and blue spirulina powder instead of kiwi to change the green layer to blue.

★ Grilled red, white, and blue kebabs with watermelon, white dragon fruit, and blueberries.

★ A cup of 4th of July parfait with raspberries, blueberries, and vegan yogurt.

★ 4th of July fruit salad with strawberries, blackberries, and star-shaped apple slices.

Leaving the Fireworks Out of It

Also talk to your kids about how fireworks can scare animals, pollute the environment, and even hurt people.

Animals

According to the US Fish and Wildlife Service,[36] "The shock of fireworks can cause wildlife to flee, ending up in unexpected areas or roadways, flying into buildings and other obstacles, and even abandoning nests, leaving young vulnerable to predators."

Planet

Fireworks create a dangerous collection of debris that litters the earth, and many parts of fireworks, firecrackers, and sparklers are not biodegradable. Also, the composition of fireworks creates highly toxic gases when they are lit.

Humans

Those pollutants can poison not only the air but water and soil, threatening both human and animal life. Plus, the explosions are a health hazard that can damage hearing and trigger people with PTSD.

Yikes. So now, what to do with this information? Don't worry—I'm not trying to be the fun police or anything! I wouldn't drop these stats without giving you some other ideas.

Kid-Friendly Fireworks Alternatives Include

★ **Laser shows.** They are popping up more and more.

★ **Glow sticks.** Not all are eco-friendly, so search for ones that are reusable, rechargeable, and nontoxic.

★ **Giant bubbles!** Look for eco-friendly bubble brands.

Halloween

Both vegan and non-vegan parents alike lowkey dread the inevitable sugar rush that follows Halloween

---

36 Celley, Courtney. 2021. "Keeping Wildlife Safe on Independence Day | US Fish & Wildlife Service." FWS.gov. June 10, 2021. https://www.fws.gov/story/keeping-wildlife-safe-independence-day.

candy madness. The anxiety. The stress! Not to worry—as I mentioned earlier, you have the power to make your own traditions or even put a spin on old ones.

Here Are Some Spooky, Cutesy, Vegan, Eco-Friendly Ideas for Celebrating This Holiday

★ For costumes, get creative and use what you already have around your house to make a costume or shop second-hand.

★ Don't waste your pumpkin! You can turn it into an eco-project to do with your kids. Instead of tossing it, you may choose to compost it, bury it, make pumpkin puree, roast the seeds, or donate it to an animal farm sanctuary. Before composting or donating, be sure to remove candles, wax, and any decorations. Don't compost pumpkins with paint or glitter.

★ Buy vegan candy. Some popular ones are even accidentally vegan!

★ Make creepy vegan Halloween treats.

★ Visit a pumpkin patch.

★ Contact local vegan restaurants and businesses to see if any host kid-friendly Halloween events.

★ Make a monster bowling alley! Collect empty, cleaned cans throughout the year and paint Halloween monster faces on six of them with your kids. Once dried,

create a monster bowling alley by stacking the cans in three rows (three on the bottom, two in the middle, one on top) and use a ball small enough for your child to hold (like a tennis ball) as the "bowling ball."

Trick-or-Treat Ideas

★ Have your kids swap their non-vegan candy with friends who aren't vegan at the end of the night.

★ Sort out the non-vegan candy and put it outside for other trick-or-treaters.

★ Reach out to neighbors you have a pleasant relationship with in advance and bring them vegan treats your child can eat. Let them know what time you'll be stopping by to trick-or-treat so they can hand your child those goodies. This could be an endearing, inclusive way to celebrate with your neighbors.

★ Put together a vegan "trunk-or-treat" or find one happening near you.

★ Hop on the Switch Witch bandwagon. The Switch Witch is like the tooth fairy. She's a kind witch who visits your home while your kids sleep. She takes the Halloween candy they left her and switches it for something even more awesome they'll love, like a toy they've been wanting or a fun experience. Get creative with this and make it your own family tradition. Come up with a backstory for the witch. You can even call her something else, like the Candy Fairy.

★ For older kiddos and teens, you can always give them the option of switching out their non-vegan candy for a gift of their choice or cash.

Thanksgiving

This is arguably the most uncomfortable holiday for vegans—and the single worst holiday for animals. My eyes well up just thinking about it. An estimated forty-six million turkeys are killed each year in the US to become the centerpiece for a holiday that is supposed to be about compassion. Turkeys are intelligent animals who enjoy having their feathers stroked and like listening to music (they even often sing along). In their natural environment, they can fly fifty-five miles per hour, run twenty-five miles per hour, and live for up to ten years. But on factory farms, they are killed as babies at three to five months old, and during their short lives, these highly social animals are robbed of the simplest pleasures, such as running, building nests, and forming social bonds. Investigations have even provided undercover footage[37] of workers punching and stomping on living turkeys and slamming them against walls, and that is merely a tiny snapshot of the brutality they experience.

★ Make a beautiful fruit centerpiece.

★ Veganize popular Thanksgiving foods together. When Beyond was ten months old, he demolished some vegan Mac 'n' Geez! (page 226), sweet potato souffle, green bean casserole, and vegan "turkey" from The Very Good Butchers company (they affectionately refer to themselves as "bean butchers").

★ Kids can save a turkey by sponsoring one. Every year, animal sanctuaries rescue as many turkeys as they can from the doom of Thanksgiving, but it costs money to save lives. Search online to support an organization that allows you to symbolically adopt a rescued turkey this holiday season. It will be special and meaningful for both your child and the turkey. Last year we symbolically adopted five turkeys through Farm Sanctuary's Adopt a Turkey Project.

★ Some animal sanctuaries have holiday events you can attend so check with the one closest to you.

★ Paint kindness rocks (similar to Easter inspiration rocks) and place them around your community.

37 "Turkeys Used for Food." 2010. PETA. June 22, 2010. https://www.peta.org/issues/animals-used-for-food/factory-farming/turkeys/.

Hanukkah

Having a green and vegan Hanukkah can be done pretty easily. You mainly need to focus on veganizing traditional recipes, ordering dairy-free gelt, and choosing sustainably made products.

Some Examples

★ Find vegan latke recipes online and in cookbooks and offer to share these with your child's school for their Hanukkah celebrations.

★ Use natural vegan candles instead of paraffin (petroleum byproduct) or beeswax (animal byproduct) candles. Coconut and soy wax candles are examples of plant-based options.

★ Use a rechargeable lighter instead of a disposable one, no fuel required.

★ Planning to get dreidels for the kiddos? Look for options that are made to last, like fair trade wood, bamboo, or stainless steel. Even more fun: you can make them with your kids!

★ Of course, with the game of dreidel comes every kid's favorite prize: gelt! Instead of milk chocolate gelt, you can get dark chocolate or vegan milk-like gelt from companies like No Whey or Paskesz.

Christmas

As a kid, there was always something magical about this time of year! As an adult, I began to look forward to festive Christmas parties with friends and family. Despite it being a season of joy though, 'tis also the season for dairy-filled sweets, meat-centric feasts, and businesses coming for all your coins, prompting a joyless surge in waste.

Here Are Some Ways to Both Veganize Christmas and Generate Less Waste in the Process

★ Santa will adore these Banana Chocolate Chip Oat Breakfast Cookies on page 170, and don't forget to leave him a glass of dairy-free milk. He's probably lactose intolerant anyway, much like a large percentage of the world.

★ Kids love gingerbread houses, but many commercial ones aren't vegan. Thankfully the internet has **everything**, including vegan gingerbread house kits.

★ Itching to throw a vegan-friendly holiday party? See if your mom and dad friends would be open to doing a vegan family potluck. They might enjoy the challenge of coming up with vegan dishes!

★ When gift shopping for kids, keep a lookout for animal ingredients and animal-tested products. Avoid animal materials like wool, leather, fur, and silk.

★ Be mindful of toys, games, and books that normalize animals in oppressive conditions or perpetuate myths that are far removed from the realities of animal exploitation. Old McDonald, I'm lookin' at you! These inaccurate depictions shape the way kids perceive non-human animals more than we realize.

★ Challenge kids to get creative with gift wrap by searching for durable materials around the house they can use, like scarves or cloth bags.

★ Consider spending less on physical gifts overall and making up for it by gifting your kids with experiences they'll never forget. Start your own Christmas gifting tradition!

Navigating Kiddie Birthdays

Last but not least, how can you navigate the challenge of hosting vegan birthday parties and attending non-vegan ones? Is there a way to make it low waste too?

First Let's Talk Hosting

This is an inspiring way to introduce other parents and little ones to what a vegan, environmentally conscious lifestyle can look like and maybe even shatter a stereotype or two. Design a vegan kid's birthday menu that can satisfy even the pickiest of eaters and show how a low-waste party doesn't have to equal buzz kill. Shock the socks off folks and you might motivate others to attempt the same. No pressure or anything.

For a nut-free, vegan menu, keep things simple and tasty. Here's a sample menu:

★ Vegan birthday cake and cupcakes
★ Sun Butter Jam Stars (page 157)
★ Toddler Taquitos (page 200)
★ Dips such as Baby-Friendly Guacamole (page 134) and Mango Salsa (page 135)
★ Tortillas and potato chips
★ Fresh fruit (use cookie cutters for fun shapes)
★ Veggie sticks and hummus
★ Fruit smoothies
★ Chocolate sunflower butter cups in reusable liners
★ Dairy-free ice cream

If you want to impress your guests with vegan ice cream that closely matches what they're accustomed to, you can get animal-free dairy ice cream from a brand like Brave Robot. It's real dairy, so it mimics the creaminess of animal-based ice cream, but it doesn't come from animals. Instead of milking cows, a process called precision fermentation is used to create milk proteins from microflora (like yeast) and plants. It's also lactose-free.

Now Let's Chat Attending

All I can say is—thank you to the old-school vegans who paved the way for our kids to be themselves without feeling like weirdos. Back in the day, it was a lot more challenging to be vegan without getting looked at sideways. Nowadays, between allergies and alternative diets, it is not **as** uncommon to accommodate special dietary requests at birthday parties.

Here's How to Slay Every Birthday Your Child Gets Invited To

1. First contact the host, let them know your child is vegan, and kindly ask if there will be vegan options. If yes, score! Thank them and rejoice. If not, ask what food will be served so you can bring some vegan options that mimic what they'll have. Also, don't take it personally. Not everyone is aware of vegan lifestyles. It'll likely just be pizza and cake anyway, and you can easily pack your own.

2. Find out what flavor cake and/or cupcakes will be served and bring a vegan version to hand to your child.

3. Get an awesome vegan and eco-friendly birthday gift that any kid would love. Etsy has a plethora of creative gift ideas.

4. Get ready to answer questions. Why is your kid vegan? But what about protein? Isn't he/she missing out? Keep your responses short yet informative. Remember what is common

knowledge to you might not be to others, and that's okay! Use it as a teaching moment.

> Okay, that's a wrap for the challenges chapter! If it feels like a lot, that's because it can be. Raising vegan super kids does come with its unique struggles, but nothing you can't slay. We don't live in a vegan society, but hey, that's what this guide is here for. To help you help your kids navigate being vegan in a non-vegan world. Plus, saving the world is a breeze, said no superhero ever.

03

NUTRITION GUIDE

Take a Deep Breath

You can do this. That's the first thing you need to know. If your partner or other adults are involved in your child's upbringing, they need to hear this too. Everyone, just take a beat and **breathe**. Rest assured, this **can** be done—and read this chapter to understand how.

"Competence Breeds Confidence."

Understanding nutritional needs can boost a parent's confidence in raising a vegan child. Perhaps the biggest barrier to getting started is the lack of access to comprehensive nutrition education. I'm a millennial mom. I didn't grow up in an era where the idea of leaving meat, dairy, and eggs off my plate was even fathomable. As a child with limited knowledge of nutrition in general, I did what my parents told me to do. I ate what all my friends ate. I believed what my teachers taught me, food pyramid and all. I trusted the adults in my life to guide my eating decisions without question—until I became an adult and became responsible for my lifestyle choices.

Despite the acceptance of plant-based diets in many cultures, in the US, abstaining from animal products has often been seen as extreme. With archaic, misleading headlines portraying vegans as nutrient-deficient and deterring people from doing further research, it's no surprise that parents are greeted with pushback from their loved ones. Thankfully, the perception is rapidly changing as access to education and options increases—and now a global transition toward a plant-based food system isn't even as "out there" as it sounds.

So, how do we kick any nagging doubts that we and our loved ones have and feel confident that a plant-based vegan diet is safe and healthy for our littles?

What's a parent to do when plant-based nutrition was never taught to us in school?

When our kids' dusty school textbooks still haven't caught up either?

When their school menus today still look the same as ours did?

It's time to take charge of our learning, educate ourselves, and then share that knowledge with our children.

Those of you from my generation and older were raised by parents who didn't have the same access to the information we have today. Our parents' generation didn't have the internet, but we do. At the click of a button, we can easily access clinical studies, science-backed research, health professionals to follow, published material to sift through, courses to take, communities to join, documentaries to watch, and a plethora of other tools and resources to educate us on plant-based nutrition and vegan lifestyles. So, trust me when I say **you can do this.**

When wanting to learn the specific nutritional requirements for kids, I read books, spoke with experts, took courses, and even got a certificate in plant-based nutrition, all while I was pregnant with my first vegan super baby, Beyond. This chapter, reviewed by a pediatric health professional, consolidates all that I've learned about plant-based nutrition for children.

Read it, share it with your loved ones, and feel empowered knowing you have the knowledge you need to raise a thriving vegan superhero.

Nutritional Guidelines for Vegan Kids

Dr. Yami Cazorla-Lancaster, a board-certified pediatrician, certified lifestyle medicine physician, certified health and wellness coach, author, and speaker, has medically reviewed this chapter for accuracy.

As a passionate promoter of healthy lifestyles, Dr. Yami champions the power of plant-based diets to prevent chronic disease.

Dr. Yami is a fellow of the American Academy of Pediatrics and a diplomate of the American College of Lifestyle Medicine. She also holds a certificate in plant-based nutrition, is a certified Food for Life Instructor, and has her own pediatric practice, Nourish Wellness.

In 2013, Dr. Yami founded VeggieFitKids.com to educate families about the importance of healthy food choices and show them how easy it can be—even with today's busy schedules. Her podcast, Veggie Doctor Radio, explores diet and nutrition, healthy habit formation, behavior change, and motivation.

As the Academy of Nutrition and Dietetics notes, a vegan diet can provide adequate nutrition at all stages of life, including childhood.[38]

---

38 Melina, Vesanto, Winston Craig, and Susan Levin. 2016. "Position of the Academy of Nutrition and Dietetics: Vegetarian Diets." **Journal of the Academy of Nutrition and Dietetics** 116 (12): 1970–80. https://doi.org/10.1016/j.jand.2016.09.025.

> **Definitions to Know:**[39] **Recommended Dietary Allowance (RDA):** The average daily dietary intake level sufficient to meet the nutrient requirement of nearly all healthy individuals in a group.
>
> **Adequate Intake (AI):** A value based on observed or experimentally determined approximations of nutrient intake by a group (or groups) of healthy people—this is used when an RDA cannot be determined.

Infants 0–6 Months

First, let's talk about your baby's special needs for the first six months of life.

The Power of Human Milk or Infant Formula

Human milk: Not all families are the same, and we should celebrate them all! When it comes to feeding children human milk, some lactating parents feed their babies directly at the chest/breast ("chest/breastfeeding"), while others express their milk ("pumping" or "hand expressing"). Parents may even choose to utilize donor milk.

If you have a choice between chest/breastfeeding and expressing/pumping, then ideally, chest/breastfeed if you are able and want to. The nutrients in human milk match your baby's needs better when your body directly interacts with your baby. Your chest/breast responds to the baby's saliva, producing antibodies for viruses and bacteria. However, both chest/breastfeeding and expressing/pumping milk are beneficial because human milk is the gold standard[40] for feeding an infant.

While the benefits of human milk are undeniable, not everyone can or wants to chest/breastfeed or pump or has access to donors, so human milk is not an option for every family. Not to fret—there is an alternative for you: infant formula.

Infant formula: If human milk is not an option, infant formula is recommended. Although cow's milk dominates the infant formula category, vegan families have other options, though they may be difficult to find. When human milk is not an option, plant-based infant formula can be an alternative. However, always consult your healthcare provider first to determine which one to choose.

---

39 Institute of Medicine (US) Food and Nutrition Board. 2014. "What Are Dietary Reference Intakes?" Nih.gov. National Academies Press (US). 2014. https://www.ncbi.nlm.nih.gov/books/NBK45182/.

40 Zhang, Shunhao, Tianle Li, Jing Xie, Demao Zhang, Caixia Pi, Lingyun Zhou, and Wenbin Yang. 2021. "Gold Standard for Nutrition: A Review of Human Milk Oligosaccharide and Its Effects on Infant Gut Microbiota." **Microbial Cell Factories** 20 (May): 108. https://doi.org/10.1186/s12934-021-01599-y.

It is important to note that infant formula is strictly regulated around the world, and depending on where you live, you may not be able to access completely vegan infant formula. In the United States, most plant-based infant formulas, such as soy formula, may still contain animal-derived ingredients. For example, vitamin D is required in all US-made baby formula, and although vitamin D can be plant-based, it is typically sourced from sheep's wool for infant formula. I understand this might be disappointing news for vegan parents.

The bottom line is, though, if human milk is not an option for your family, then infant formula is the way to go. I know it can be discouraging to learn of the lack of access to vegan baby formulas available on the market for infants under age one—but I want to remind you that veganism is not about being perfect. It is not always possible or practicable to avoid the use of animals. It's about doing your best. When formula is your only option, go with the best plant-based formula available and ensure your healthcare provider supports that!

PS: **The good news** is the vegan food market is booming, and big changes are coming. The world's first 100 percent plant-based, organic, and **vegan-certified** infant formula launched in Australia!

In 2021, Sprout Organic became the world's first 100 percent plant-based, organic, and vegan-certified infant formula sold in Australia! It was developed with pea and rice protein as an alternative for babies with dairy and soy allergies.

Bite-sized Recap: **Human milk (frequently referred to as breastmilk) or infant formula is 100 percent required for all infants in their first year of life. While human milk is recognized as the gold standard, when that's not an option or preference, go with a plant-based infant formula approved by your pediatrician.**

One crucial aspect to be aware of in the early stages of a child's life is the need for vitamin D supplementation. Vitamin D helps to strengthen your baby's bones, and special attention will need to be given if your child's primary food source is human milk.[41]

Human milk-fed infants: When I started breastfeeding Beyond, I was surprised to learn that human milk alone does not provide infants with adequate vitamin D. Experts recommend that **all** exclusively breastfed (human milk-fed) babies supplement with 400 IU of vitamin D daily, beginning shortly after birth. Vitamin D2 is animal-free. Vitamin D3 is often sourced from sheep's wool, but you can find plant-based vitamin D3 drops derived from a vegan-friendly source called lichen.

Formula-fed infants: If your baby is formula-fed, vitamin D supplementation is typically not needed because infant formula contains vitamin D. As always, double-check with your pediatrician.

Bite-sized Recap: **Vitamin D is essential for strong bones. All exclusively human milk-fed babies need a daily 400 IU vitamin D supplement from birth, while formula-fed babies typically do not.**

Infants 6–12 Months & Toddlers 1–3 Years

Time flies, and before you know it, your baby is growing and reaching new milestones. Six months is when the real fun begins! This is around the time many families begin introducing solid foods **in addition to** continuing human milk or formula. This is an important step in helping babies learn to eat, giving them the experience of new tastes and textures, developing their teeth and jaws, building skills they'll need later for language development, and supporting their growing nutritional needs. So, let's dive into some daily nutrients to pay attention to from six months on.

---

41 Domenici, Raffaele, and Francesco Vierucci. 2022. "Exclusive Breastfeeding and Vitamin D Supplementation: A Positive Synergistic Effect on Prevention of Childhood Infections?" **International Journal of Environmental Research and Public Health** 19 (5): 2973. https://doi.org/10.3390/ijerph19052973.

The Power of Calories

First up, let's shift our attention to calories, which play a key role in your baby's growth.

During the first twelve months of life, babies are in a rapid state of growth, which requires a lot of energy, so they must get adequate calories.[42] Growth then slows after the first year; however, toddlers are typically more active and exploring their environment, so their energy needs remain high. Plant-based diets tend to be lower in calories than typical Western diets, and since children have tiny tummies, you'll want to focus on the following to maximize calorie intake:

1. Feeding on demand until twelve months of age (human milk or formula) and;

2. Ensuring they get adequate calories from healthy fats and energy-dense foods when they are ready for solids, typically beginning around six months of age. However, some babies (like mine) may start as early as four months if showing signs of readiness.

Don't worry. You'll learn an easy method for structuring your child's meals in a balanced way that meets their needs in Chapter 4 and how to introduce solids in Chapter 6.

Human milk FAQ: How long should I breastfeed or pump milk for my baby?

I breastfed Beyond for two years, but recommendations vary globally. The World Health Organization (WHO) recommends[43] exclusive breastfeeding for the first six months of life and continued breastfeeding for up to two years or more, along with the introduction of nutritionally adequate and safe complementary solid foods at six months.

The American Academy of Pediatrics (AAP) recommends[44] exclusive breastfeeding for approximately six months after birth and supports continued breastfeeding, along with appropriate complementary foods introduced at about six months, as long as mutually desired by breastfeeding parent and child for two years or longer.

Bite-sized Recap: **Babies and toddlers need adequate calories to support their rapid growth, so feed them human milk or formula on demand during their first twelve months of life and provide energy-dense foods once they are ready for solids.**

---

42 Patel, Jalpa K., and Audra S. Rouster. 2020. "Infant Nutrition Requirements and Options." PubMed. Treasure Island (FL): StatPearls Publishing. 2020. https://www.ncbi.nlm.nih.gov/books/NBK560758/.

43 World Health Organization. 2021. "Infant and Young Child Feeding." Who.int. World Health Organization: WHO. June 9, 2021. https://www.who.int/news-room/fact-sheets/detail/infant-and-young-child-feeding.

44 Meek, Joan Younger, and Lawrence Noble. 2022. "Policy Statement: Breastfeeding and the Use of Human Milk." **Pediatrics** 150 (1). https://doi.org/10.1542/peds.2022-057988.

Hey, super parents! When introducing solid foods, remember to continue providing human milk or infant formula until your baby is at least 12 months old.

The Power of Protein

Recommended Daily Allowance (RDA):[45]

0–6 months	9 g *Needs met exclusively through human milk or formula.
7–12 months	11 g *Needs met primarily through human milk or formula, along with complementary foods
1–3 years	13 g (or 0.5g per pound of body weight)
4–8 years	19 g
Pregnancy	An adult who is *not* pregnant and not physically active should get about 0.36 g of protein per pound of body weight (or 0.8 g of protein per kilogram of body weight). An adult who *is* pregnant should eat an additional 25 g.
Lactation	71 g

Next on the list is protein, an important nutrient for an infant's growth and development, especially during their first year.

Human milk or infant formula provides the total protein and essential amino acids an infant needs in their early months. Then begin including complementary food sources of protein when your child is ready for solids. At age one and onward, food will become the primary source of protein.

---

45 Lauri, Stephanie. 2021. "How Much Protein Does My Child Need?" CHOC—Children's Health. July 1, 2021. https://health.choc.org/how-much-protein-does-my-child-need/.

Vegans are no strangers to the frequently asked **"But where do you get your protein from?"** question. When thinking about protein, many people automatically think of meat—but plenty of plant-based sources are packed with protein. If you provide your child with a balanced diet that includes varied sources of plant protein throughout the day, you should provide all the protein and essential amino acids needed.[46] Protein needs can easily be achieved with nuts, seeds, legumes, and grains. Even fruits and vegetables contain small amounts of protein!

FOODS RICH IN PROTEIN
Legumes: Black beans, navy beans, kidney beans, pinto beans, chickpeas (a.k.a. garbanzo beans), lima beans (a.k.a. butter beans), lentils, peas
Seitan & Soy Legumes: Tofu, tempeh, soybeans, edamame, seitan
Nuts & Seeds: Shelled hemp seeds, pumpkin seeds, flax seeds, chia seeds, almonds, peanut butter, almond butter, sunflower seed butter
Grains: Oats, spelt, teff, amaranth, quinoa, millet, farro, whole wheat pasta, couscous
Plant-based Milks: Fortified pea or soy milk (suitable after age one as a beverage)

Bite-sized Recap: **Protein, a critical nutrient needed to support your child's growth and development, can be found in legumes, seitan, soy, nuts, seeds, grains, and fortified plant-based milks. Provide a balanced diet with varied plant-based protein sources to meet their needs.**

46 Baroni, Luciana, Silvia Goggi, Roseila Battaglino, Mario Berveglieri, Ilaria Fasan, Denise Filippin, Paul Griffith, et al. 2018. "Vegan Nutrition for Mothers and Children: Practical Tools for Healthcare Providers." **Nutrients** 11 (1): 5. https://doi.org/10.3390/nu11010005.

The Power of Healthy Fats

Recommended Daily Allowance (RDA):[47]

0–6 months	30 g *Needs met exclusively through human milk or formula.
7–12 months	31 g *Needs met primarily through human milk or formula, along with complementary foods
1–3 years	30–40 percent of daily intake
4–8 years	25–35 percent of daily intake
Pregnancy	25–35 percent of your daily intake
Lactation	20–35 percent of your daily intake

Now let's move on to fat, which promotes the development of your child's brain and nervous system, aids in wound healing, allows for the absorption of nutrients, and provides padding for organs.

Babies and toddlers need lots of fat! This is not the time to choose a low-fat approach to diet. There is no need to restrict fat consumption, especially before age two. In fact, about two-thirds of your child's brain is composed of fat.

Fat accounts for about 50 percent of the calories in human milk and infant formula;[48] therefore, during your baby's first twelve months of life, human milk or formula will be the primary source of fat. When ready, offer solid foods that provide additional sources of healthy fats to complement your infant's overall diet. From age one onward, food will be the primary source of fat.

Despite the negative perception often associated with dietary fats, it's important to understand that not all fats are detrimental to health. There are healthy fats, like those found in whole plant foods, and unhealthy fats, like animal fats and trans fats. Omega-3 fatty acids are of particular importance, so we'll dive into that next.

First, here are some examples of healthy fats.

---

47 "Dietary Fat and Children: MedlinePlus Medical Encyclopedia." n.d. Medlineplus.gov. https://medlineplus.gov/ency/article/001979.htm.
48 Mazzocchi, Alessandra, Veronica D'Oria, Valentina Cosmi, Silvia Bettocchi, Gregorio Milani, Marco Silano, and Carlo Agostoni. 2018. "The Role of Lipids in Human Milk and Infant Formulae." **Nutrients** 10 (5): 567. https://doi.org/10.3390/nu10050567.

FOODS RICH IN HEALTHY FATS
Avocados, chia seeds, flax seeds, shelled hemp seeds, nuts, nut and seed butters, hummus, sesame tahini, olive oil, avocado oil

Bite-sized Recap: Include an ample amount of healthy plant-based fats in your child's diet, like avocados, nuts, and seeds, to aid brain and nervous system development, wound healing, nutrient absorption, and organ padding.

The Power of Omega-3 Fatty Acids

Speaking of healthy fats, let's talk about omega-3 fatty acids, which are crucial to cell, brain, and eye health.

There are three main types of omega-3 fatty acids:

★ **ALA (alpha-linolenic acid):** This is an essential omega-3 fatty acid found in plants such as chia seeds, flax seeds, shelled hemp seeds, and walnuts.

★ **DHA (docosahexaenoic acid):** This is a "marine omega-3" that non-vegans typically get from fish. However, fish get their DHA from algae, so vegans can go straight to the source by getting DHA from algae-based foods or supplements.

★ **EPA (eicosapentaenoic acid):** EPA, like DHA, is also a marine omega-3.

When we get ALA from food, our bodies can convert some ALA into EPA and DHA; however, the conversion rate is low. So, dietary sources of EPA and DHA, like algae-based foods or supplementation, are needed.

Is DHA supplementation necessary? DHA accumulates quickly in a baby's brain from the third trimester of pregnancy through age two, so it is vital both in pregnancy and after birth.[49] DHA is paramount to brain and eye development. Infants receive DHA through human milk, provided the lactating parent is consuming adequate DHA, or through infant formulas fortified with DHA. Beyond that, infants and toddlers can consume DHA through supplementation.

I began giving my son omega-3 DHA and EPA algal oil drops around nine months of age and have continued through toddlerhood. Perhaps I'm biased, but he's a brilliant kid, and my husband and I often joke that it must be the DHA. Though anecdotal, our experience aligns with research suggesting the importance of DHA for brain health.

49 Lauritzen, Lotte, Paolo Brambilla, Alessandra Mazzocchi, Laurine Harsløf, Valentina Ciappolino, and Carlo Agostoni. 2016. "DHA Effects in Brain Development and Function." **Nutrients** 8 (1): 6. https://doi.org/10.3390/nu8010006.

*Experts have not established recommended amounts for omega-3 fatty acids, except for ALA.

Bite-sized Recap: Provide your child with plant foods like nuts, seeds, and oils to get enough ALA, an omega-3 fatty acid essential to cell health. DHA, an omega-3 fatty acid critical to brain and eye development, should be given as a supplement once a toddler is weaned.

The Power of B12

Recommended Daily Allowance (RDA):[50]

0–6 months	0.4 mcg *Needs met exclusively through human milk or formula.
7–12 months	0.5 mcg *Needs met exclusively through human milk or formula.
1–3 years	0.9 mcg *Due to the low absorption rate of B12, it is recommended to exceed the RDA and supplement with at least 5 mcg once a toddler is weaned.
4–8 years	1.2 mcg *Due to the low absorption rate of B12, it is recommended to exceed the RDA and supplement with at least 25 mcg.
Pregnancy	2.6 mcg *Due to the low absorption rate of B12, it is recommended to exceed the RDA and supplement with 100–250 mcg.
Lactation	2.8 mcg *Due to the low absorption rate of B12, it is recommended to exceed the RDA and supplement with 100–250 mcg.

Now let's dive into vitamin B12, an often-discussed topic in the vegan community. Vitamin B12, produced by bacteria, is essential to prevent anemia and irreversible nervous system damage.

For the first twelve months of life, vegan infants receive B12 through human milk, provided the lactating parent is consuming enough, or infant formula. Once a toddler is weaned, they will need to receive a daily B12 supplement or multivitamin that contains B12.

50 National Institutes of Health. 2021. "Office of Dietary Supplements—Vitamin B12." Nih.gov. July 7, 2021. https://ods.od.nih.gov/factsheets/VitaminB12-Consumer/.

Despite its presence in fortified foods like nutritional yeast flakes, breakfast cereals, and plant-based milk products, a supplement remains the most reliable source for both vegan toddlers and adults. The reason for this is daily intake from fortified B12 foods can be difficult to calculate, and due to bioavailability factors, we don't want to become overly reliant on fortified products for our kids when a high-quality supplement is much easier to measure and track. Given the extreme importance of B12, this is the best and safest approach.[51]

As shown in the RDA chart, due to the low absorption rate of B12, it is recommended to take doses much higher than the RDA. For example, although 0.9 mcg is the RDA for toddlers ages one to three, plan to give them a B12 supplement or multivitamin with at least 5 mcg. There is no upper limit for vitamin B12, so there's no need to worry about toxicity.[52] Look for vitamin B12 supplements or multivitamins in liquid form as they have flexible doses and are easier for toddlers to take.

Bite-sized Recap: **Vitamin B12 plays a critical role in preventing anemia and irreversible nervous system damage. Providing a toddler with a B12 supplement once weaned is nonnegotiable.**

The Power of Calcium

Recommended Daily Allowance (RDA):[53]

0–6 months	200 mg *Needs met exclusively through human milk or formula.
7–12 months	260 mg *Needs met primarily through human milk or formula, along with complementary foods
1–3 years	700 mg
4–8 years	1,000 mg
Pregnancy	18 years old or younger: 1,300 mg 19–50 years old: 1,000 mg
Lactation	18 years old or younger: 1,300 mg 19–50 years old: 1,000 mg

51 Baroni, Luciana, Silvia Goggi, Roseila Battaglino, Mario Berveglieri, Ilaria Fasan, Denise Filippin, Paul Griffith, et al. 2018. "Vegan Nutrition for Mothers and Children: Practical Tools for Healthcare Providers." **Nutrients** 11 (1): 5. https://doi.org/10.3390/nu11010005.
52 National Institutes of Health. 2022. "Office of Dietary Supplements—Vitamin B12 Fact Sheet for Health Professionals." Nih.gov. March 9, 2022. https://ods.od.nih.gov/factsheets/VitaminB12-HealthProfessional/.
53 National Institutes of Health. 2019. "Office of Dietary Supplements—Calcium." Nih.gov. December 6, 2019. https://ods.od.nih.gov/factsheets/Calcium-Consumer/.

Now, let's cover calcium, a vital mineral that fosters the development and strengthening of your baby's bones and teeth.

During the first six months of life, human milk or formula will provide all the calcium your infant needs and will likely supply most of their calcium needs until age one or when they begin eating solid foods exclusively. From ages one to three, calcium needs jump significantly and can be met through a combination of whole plant foods[54] and calcium-fortified foods.

Excellent sources of calcium are green leafy vegetables and legumes, or an easy way to remember it—"greens and beans." The exceptions to this are certain greens like spinach, Swiss chard, rhubarb, and beet greens, which contain lots of calcium but are harder to absorb.

The dairy industry has misled many to believe cow's milk is needed to meet calcium needs, especially for growing children; however, that simply is not true. More on that at the end of this chapter, but for now, here are some examples of how to get calcium for your little one.

FOODS RICH IN CALCIUM
Fruits & Vegetables: Dried figs, oranges, kale, broccoli, bok choy, sweet potato, butternut squash, collard greens, mustard greens, okra, arugula
Legumes: Chickpeas (a.k.a. garbanzo beans), white beans, pinto beans, black beans, navy beans
Soy Legumes: Tofu, tempeh, edamame, soybeans
Nuts & Seeds: Chia seeds, sunflower seeds, sesame tahini, almonds
Fortified products: Fortified pea or soy milk (suitable after age one as a beverage), fortified dairy-free yogurt, fortified orange juice

Bite-sized Recap: **Calcium, a vital mineral for the development of your baby's bones and teeth, is adequately supplied through human milk or infant formula for the first twelve months of life. After age one, their needs nearly triple, so provide calcium-rich foods like green leafy vegetables, legumes, nuts, seeds, and calcium-fortified vegan products.**

54 Baroni, Luciana, Silvia Goggi, Roseila Battaglino, Mario Berveglieri, Ilaria Fasan, Denise Filippin, Paul Griffith, et al. 2018. "Vegan Nutrition for Mothers and Children: Practical Tools for Healthcare Providers." **Nutrients** 11 (1): 5. https://doi.org/10.3390/nu11010005.

The Power of Choline

Adequate Intake (AI):[55]

0–6 months	125 mg *Needs met exclusively through human milk or formula.
7–12 months	150 mg *Needs met primarily through human milk or formula, along with complementary foods
1–3 years	200 mg
4–8 years	250 mg
Pregnancy	450 mg
Lactation	550 mg

Choline, a nutrient akin to B vitamins, plays a pivotal role in your baby's brain development.

Many Americans, regardless of diet, do not consume enough choline. Supplementation during pregnancy and lactation, when the demand for choline is particularly high,[56] is recommended for those who are unable to meet their needs through diet. For children, however, routine supplementation is **not** recommended. Focus on regularly providing sources of choline from plant-based foods in your child's diet once solids are introduced and especially after weaning.

FOODS RICH IN CHOLINE
Soy milk, soybeans, tofu, wheat germ, cruciferous vegetables, quinoa, shiitake mushrooms, red potatoes, green peas, almonds, peanut butter

Bite-sized Recap: **Include choline-rich foods in your child's diet, like soy, cruciferous vegetables, quinoa, and peanut butter, for healthy brain development.**

55 National Institutes of Health. 2017. "Office of Dietary Supplements—Choline." Nih.gov. 2017. https://ods.od.nih.gov/factsheets/Choline-Consumer/.
56 Zeisel, Steven H, and Kerry-Ann da Costa. 2009. "Choline: An Essential Nutrient for Public Health." **Nutrition Reviews** 67 (11): 615–23. https://doi.org/10.1111/j.1753-4887.2009.00246.x.

The Power of Iodine

Recommended Daily Allowance (RDA):[57]

0–6 months	110 mcg—Adequate Intake (AI) *Needs met exclusively through human milk or formula.
7–12 months	130 mcg—Adequate Intake (AI) *Needs met exclusively through human milk or formula.
1–8 years	90 mcg
Pregnancy	220 mcg
Lactation	290 mcg

Now, let's talk about iodine, an important nutrient for brain health, metabolism, and thyroid function.

If you didn't learn much about iodine needs growing up, you're not alone. Interestingly, people will constantly ask how vegans get their protein, but what they should ask is where vegans get their iodine. It's not discussed as much but needs to be. Iodine deficiency in young children has been linked[58] to a lower IQ and stunted growth and can cause thyroid gland enlargement.

Because iodine deficiency was so common in the United States and in Europe, manufacturers began adding iodine to salt.[59] However, processed foods are not typically made using iodized salt, and nowadays people don't always choose to buy iodized salt from the store. While it can be found in small amounts in plant foods, depending on the soil conditions, it isn't enough. Sea vegetables also supply iodine, but the amount can sometimes be too much, which is just as bad as getting too little! Non-vegans typically get iodine through sources such as seafood, dairy, and eggs. Still, even with dairy, the amount is not naturally high and is only a result of iodine-based chemicals being used to disinfect cows' udders during production. Disheartening to even imagine what those mama cows endure for their milk.

Is iodine supplementation necessary? Vegan adults and children who don't cook with iodized salt are at a higher risk of iodine deficiency. Before age one, babies receive all of the iodine they need from human milk, provided the lactating parent has adequate intake, or infant formula. After age one, it is recommended that vegan

57 National Institutes of Health. 2017. "Office of Dietary Supplements—Iodine." Nih.gov. 2017. https://ods.od.nih.gov/factsheets/Iodine-Consumer/.
58 World Health Organization. 2013. "Nutrition: Effects of Iodine Deficiency." Www.who.int. May 24, 2013. https://www.who.int/news-room/questions-and-answers/item/nutrition-effects-of-iodine-deficiency.
59 Leung, Angela, Lewis Braverman, and Elizabeth Pearce. 2012. "History of US Iodine Fortification and Supplementation." **Nutrients** 4 (11): 1740–46. https://doi.org/10.3390/nu4111740.

kids receive a supplement containing iodine and/or receive appropriate iodine intake through a fortified option like iodized salt. If your family cooks with iodized salt, you can supplement with only half of the RDA. Following this approach, part of your child's intake will come from a fortified option (iodized salt), and part of your child's intake will come from a supplement. If your family does **not** cook with iodized salt, provide your child with the full RDA of an algal-derived iodine supplement.[60]

Bite-sized Recap: Once your child is weaned, consider providing an iodine supplement, especially if your family doesn't cook with iodized salt. Iodine is crucial for brain health, metabolism, and thyroid function.

The Power of Iron

Recommended Daily Allowance (RDA):[61]

0–6 months	0.27 mg *Needs met through human milk or formula; however, the AAP recommends an iron supplement at ages 4–6 months for human milk-fed babies, as human milk does not supply enough during this stage.
7–12 months	11 mg *Needs met through a combination of complementary foods + human milk or formula.
1–3 years	7 mg
4–8 years	10 mg
Pregnancy	27 mg
Lactation	18 years old or younger: 10 mg 19 years old or older: 9 mg

Next, let's shift gears and dive into the significance of iron, a mineral needed for brain development and to make hemoglobin, which carries oxygen in red blood cells to all parts of the body.

If you are a chest/breastfeeding or pumping parent, you may be surprised to learn that human milk does not provide enough iron, regardless of your diet. Most newborns have iron reserves for the first four to six months of life. By the age of six months, they need an external source of iron apart from human milk. Human milk is

60 Baroni, Luciana, Silvia Goggi, Roseila Battaglino, Mario Berveglieri, Ilaria Fasan, Denise Filippin, Paul Griffith, et al. 2018. "Vegan Nutrition for Mothers and Children: Practical Tools for Healthcare Providers." **Nutrients** 11 (1): 5. https://doi.org/10.3390/nu11010005.
61 National Institutes of Health. 2022. "Office of Dietary Supplements—Iron." Nih.gov. April 5, 2022. https://ods.od.nih.gov/factsheets/Iron-Consumer/.

undeniably phenomenal but low in iron.[62] Around six months, their iron needs can be met by introducing iron-rich and iron-fortified foods. Your pediatrician may even recommend liquid iron drops if needed.

Here are two important tips for increasing iron absorption:[63]

1. Eating vitamin C-rich food with your iron-rich food can increase iron absorption by two to four times! Try squeezing some lime or lemon juice into an iron-rich dish to add some vitamin C. For example, black beans are rich in iron, so if you make black bean tacos, include lime juice in the seasoning. Or you can serve those black bean tacos with mango salsa.

2. Calcium competes with iron for absorption, and calcium always wins. Imagine two people trying to get through a narrow doorway at the same time, but there's only room for one at a time. So, try eating calcium-heavy foods, like fortified plant-based milks, separately from your iron-rich foods. For example, instead of serving plant-based milk with a meal, offer it as a snack between meals.

FOODS RICH IN IRON
Chickpeas, tofu, lentils, beans, tempeh, leafy greens, dried fruit, legume pasta, bread, almond butter, canned tomatoes, and iron-fortified foods.

Bite-sized Recap: Human milk is low in iron, so begin providing complementary iron-rich and iron-fortified foods at four to six months if ready for solids. Boost iron absorption by serving iron foods with vitamin C-rich foods. Try to avoid serving calcium-rich foods with iron foods, as calcium inhibits iron absorption.

62 Friel, James, Wafaa Qasem, and Chenxi Cai. 2018. "Iron and the Breastfed Infant." **Antioxidants** 7 (4): 54. https://doi.org/10.3390/antiox7040054.
63 Piskin, Elif, Danila Cianciosi, Sukru Gulec, Merve Tomas, and Esra Capanoglu. 2022. "Iron Absorption: Factors, Limitations, and Improvement Methods." **ACS Omega** 7 (24): 20441–56. https://doi.org/10.1021/acsomega.2c01833.

The Power of Vitamin A

Recommended Daily Allowance (RDA):[64]

0–6 months	400 mcg *Needs met exclusively through human milk or formula.
7–12 months	500 mcg *Needs met primarily through human milk or formula, along with complementary foods.
1–3 years	300 mcg
4–8 years	400 mcg
Pregnancy	18 years old or younger: 750 mcg 19 years old or older: 770 mcg
Lactation	18 years old or younger: 1,200 mcg 19 years old or older: 1,330 mcg

Next, let's go over vitamin A, which plays a variety of roles in your baby's health. Vitamin A is important for growth, development, and immune function. It also supports healthy vision, reproduction, and communication between your baby's cells for proper organ functioning.

During infancy, babies get enough vitamin A through human milk or infant formula. Once weaned off of human milk or formula, your child will need to consume vitamin A through food.

Have you ever heard that plant-based sources of vitamin A are not as good as animal sources? Let me reassure you that's not factual. Our bodies do not require the consumption of animals to meet our vitamin A needs. As long as our kids eat enough plant-based provitamin A,[65] which includes the phytochemical beta-carotene, then their bodies can make enough active vitamin A to meet their needs and thrive. Since kids might not always get enough vitamins from food alone due to selective eating phases, a daily multivitamin containing vitamin A can also help fill any gaps.

How can you tell which vegan foods contain vitamin A? An easy way to remember vitamin A foods is to think of colors. Focus on orange, yellow, and dark green fruits and vegetables.

64 National Institutes of Health. 2021. "Office of Dietary Supplements—Vitamin A." Nih.gov. January 14, 2021. https://ods.od.nih.gov/factsheets/VitaminA-Consumer/.

65 Institute of Medicine (US) Panel on Micronutrients. 2015. "Vitamin A." Nih.gov. National Academies Press (US). 2015. https://www.ncbi.nlm.nih.gov/books/NBK222318/.

FOODS RICH IN VITAMIN A
Carrots, kale, spinach, red peppers, orange sweet potato, pumpkin, butternut squash, dried apricots, cantaloupe, mango, papaya

Bite-sized Recap: Include vitamin A-rich foods in your child's diet, like orange, yellow, and dark green fruits and vegetables, to support their growth, development, organs, and immune functioning.

The Power of Vitamin D

Recommended Daily Allowance (RDA):[66]

0–12 months	10 mcg (400 IU) *Supplementation is needed for human milk-fed babies, as human milk does not supply enough.
1–8 years	15 mcg (600 IU)
Pregnancy	15 mcg (600 IU)
Lactation	15 mcg (600 IU)

Now let's circle back to vitamin D, a key nutrient babies and toddlers need to help their bodies absorb calcium and develop and strengthen bones.

Supplementation for infants: As mentioned earlier in the "Babies 0–6 Months" section, human milk is low in vitamin D, regardless of the lactating parent's diet, so the AAP advises[67] chest/breastfeeding and pumping parents to provide their infants with a daily supplement containing 10 mcg (400 IU) of vitamin D for the first twelve months of life. Look for vegan-friendly vitamin D in liquid form that you can easily administer using your finger, a dropper, placed on your nipple before chest/breastfeeding, or mixed in with your expressed milk in a bottle. Formula-fed infants do not need extra supplementation.

Is vitamin D supplementation necessary for toddlers? After twelve months of age, toddlers may be able to meet their vitamin D needs with vitamin D-fortified pea or soy milk. Always check the nutrition label to ensure the milk you choose has enough and what the serving amount would be to meet the requirement. If it isn't enough, consider supplementing.[68] My toddler's daily multivitamin contains vitamin D, which gives me peace of mind knowing his needs are being met.

66 National Institutes of Health. 2017. "Office of Dietary Supplements—Vitamin D." Nih.gov. 2017. https://ods.od.nih.gov/factsheets/VitaminD-Consumer/.

67 National Institutes of Health. 2022. "Vitamin D Fact Sheet for Health Professionals." Nih.gov. August 12, 2022. https://ods.od.nih.gov/factsheets/VitaminD-HealthProfessional/.

68 Baroni, Luciana, Silvia Goggi, Roseila Battaglino, Mario Berveglieri, Ilaria Fasan, Denise Filippin, Paul Griffith, et al. 2018. "Vegan Nutrition for Mothers and Children: Practical Tools for Healthcare Providers." **Nutrients** 11 (1): 5. https://doi.org/10.3390/nu11010005.

Bite-sized Recap: Human milk is low in vitamin D, a nutrient needed for calcium absorption and healthy bones, so all breastfeeding and pumping parents, regardless of diet, should provide their infants with a 10 mcg (400 IU) supplement. After twelve months of age, their needs may be met through vitamin D-fortified pea or soy milk; however, if it's not enough, consider supplementing.

The Power of Zinc

Recommended Daily Allowance (RDA):[69]

0–6 months	2 mg *Needs met through human milk or formula.
7–12 months	3 mg *Needs met primarily through human milk or formula, along with complementary foods.
1–3 years	3 mg
4–8 years	5 mg
Pregnancy	18 years old or younger: 12 mg 19 years old or older: 11 mg
Lactation	18 years old or younger: 13 mg 19 years old or older: 12 mg

Lastly, let's discuss the importance of zinc, an essential mineral for your baby's proper growth and development, wound healing, immunity, and senses of smell and taste.

Zinc requirements can be met through human milk or infant formula the first several months of life. Like iron, surprisingly human milk is relatively low in zinc.[70] Fortunately, many of the iron-rich foods you feed your child also supply zinc. Protein can help boost zinc absorption,[71] so eating these nutrients together can be advantageous. Routine supplementation is not recommended for babies and toddlers.

FOODS RICH IN ZINC
Wheat germ, bran flakes, oatmeal, tahini, chickpeas, lentils, peanut butter, quinoa, pumpkin seeds

69 National Institutes of Health. 2016. "Office of Dietary Supplements—Zinc." Nih.gov. 2016. https://ods.od.nih.gov/factsheets/Zinc-Consumer/.

70 Aumeistere, Līva, Inga Ciproviča, Dace Zavadska, Konstantīns Bavrins, and Anastasija Borisova. 2018. "Zinc Content in Breast Milk and Its Association with Maternal Diet." **Nutrients** 10 (10). https://doi.org/10.3390/nu10101438.

71 Saunders, Angela V., Winston J. Craig, and Surinder K. Baines. 2013. "Zinc and Vegetarian Diets." **Medical Journal of Australia** 199 (S4). https://doi.org/10.5694/mja11.11493.

Bite-sized Recap: Zinc helps with your baby's growth and development, wound healing, immunity, and senses of smell and taste. Human milk is low in zinc, so offer zinc-rich foods, like beans, lentils, and oatmeal, once your baby is ready for solids.

Cow's Milk Alternatives for Toddlers One to Three Years Old

We've gone over some key nutrients to know about for babies and toddlers. Lastly, I dedicate a section to answering a commonly asked question about "milk" consumption once your child turns one. A commonly held belief is that dairy milk is needed to make a kid's body strong. Let's dive into this further and break down why this isn't accurate.

Why do parents feed their kids cow's milk? If you made it through the nutrition guidelines, then you may have noticed the following nutrient needs are challenging to meet through food alone: calcium, vitamin D, B12, and iodine. All four of these are found in cow's milk, so non-vegan parents often turn to cow's milk as the easiest way to ensure their kids get these nutrients, especially given the selective eating phases many toddlers go through. However, while cow's milk can provide these nutrients, that doesn't mean it's necessary or the healthiest choice.

PS: Did you know cow's milk doesn't naturally have vitamin D?[72] Manufacturers began adding vitamin D to cow's milk in the 1930s as a public health initiative to reduce rickets, a condition that causes poor bone development in children. Vitamin D helps the body absorb calcium, which cow's milk naturally has, so by adding vitamin D to it, their goal was for those two nutrients to work together to strengthen people's bones.

What are cow's milk alternatives for vegan families? For vegan families, a simple alternative to meet calcium and vitamin D needs is to choose a fortified dairy-free option. Fortified pea and soy milk brands typically ensure their calcium, vitamin D, and protein content are comparable to cow's milk. You can find fortified pea or soy milk at most grocery stores, depending on where you live. They are usually fortified with B12 as well; however, as mentioned earlier, a supplement is the most reliable source of B12.

The only nutrient of concern that is found in cow's milk but **not** found in fortified dairy-free milk is iodine (at least in the US). Iodine is essential for your toddler's brain health, metabolism, and thyroid function, so ensure their iodine needs are being

---

72 Institute of Medicine (US) Committee on Use of Dietary Reference Intakes in Nutrition Labeling. 2015. "Overview of Food Fortification in the United States and Canada." Nih.gov. National Academies Press (US). 2015. https://www.ncbi.nlm.nih.gov/books/NBK208880/.

met through iodized salt and/or supplementation if iodine is not present in their fortified dairy-free milk.

You may be wondering why pea and soy milk are recommended[73] by dieticians over other forms of plant-based milks. The main reason is pea and soy milk are both calorie- and nutrient-dense. Toddlers have tiny tummies, so we want to focus on maximizing the nutritional content of what we give them. Pea milk may be a particularly ideal option for families with soy or nut allergies, as it is soy, nut, and gluten-free.

Can't I make dairy-free milk? I often hear concerns from parents wanting to avoid store-bought dairy-free milks and make their own from scratch instead. You technically can do that, but it is imperative to ensure your child has an alternative way to consume the nutrients they would typically get from a store-bought option. For example, while calcium is found in plant-based foods, toddlers need 700 mg of it, and the easiest way to reach that amount daily is with the help of calcium-fortified pea or soy milk. Additionally, because vitamin D helps the body absorb calcium, the balance of calcium and vitamin D in store-bought fortified dairy-free milk is an easy way to ensure your child's needs are being met.

If you are determined to make plant-based milk for your toddler, you could potentially fortify it yourself by adding calcium carbonate powder and vitamin D drops. Discuss it with your pediatrician for further guidance. Make sure your toddler is getting enough protein and fat from other food sources as well.

You Made It Through!

Remember that deep breath you took in the beginning? Take another, but this time, let it out as a sigh of relief. You got through it all. You are empowered with the nutrition knowledge you need to feel confident about raising your child vegan. You. Got. This.

Onward to some lighthearted stuff! In the next chapter, you will learn how all of this comes together practically. We'll dive into how to structure a balanced vegan meal, my go-to meal prep strategy, and look at some sample menus. Rest your eyeballs if necessary, and then turn the page for some fun meal prep and menu planning 101!

73 Gomez, Gina Hudley, and Jennifer Anderson. 2022. "The Best Non-Dairy Milk for Toddlers and Kids." Kids Eat in Color. May 12, 2022. https://kidseatincolor.com/best-non-dairy-milk-for-toddlers/.

04

MEAL PREP & MENU PLANNING

How It All Comes Together

Whether you're a newbie to vegan eating or a seasoned pro, nailing down an effective strategy for meal prepping and menu planning is essential. Even people who have been vegan for years might feel confused about how to structure a nutritious vegan plate when a child enters the picture.

Not all vegans are whole-food, plant-based vegans, after all. Some (like me at the beginning of my journey with zero guidance) might survive off cereal for breakfast, Tofurky sandwiches for lunch, and frozen vegan pizzas for dinner—because it is easier to settle for the ultra-processed options when you only have yourself to worry about. It happens!

When a person becomes pregnant, however, it is often a wake-up call to the necessity of paying closer attention to our nutrient intake. It can be the perfect opportunity to reexamine our eating habits and strategize a more whole-food, plant-based approach, one that can help us feel our best during pregnancy and healthily nourish our kids once their vegan foodie journeys begin.

In the previous chapter, you got a crash course in plant-based nutrition. You learned about the various vitamins, minerals, nutrients, and nourishing foods that will help your little one thrive. In this chapter, I'm going to walk you through how to bring it all together as wholesome meals!

Time-saving Tip: Make menu planning and meal prepping easier by serving your child smaller portions of your family's healthy vegan meals!

How to Structure Meals

Have you heard of the Plant-Based Juniors™ PB3 Plate? Developed by registered dieticians Whitney English, MS RDN, and Alexandra Caspero, MA RDN, the creators of Plant-Based Juniors,™ this method[74] is designed to simplify meal planning while ensuring your little one hits their nutrition targets. It's pure **brilliance**. This approach has been my ultimate menu planning tool for Beyond. Let's break down the components of the wondrous PB3 Plate.

In a nutshell, ideally each meal should have foods from these three important categories:

- ★ One-third of the meal: Fruits and Vegetables (F/V)
- ★ One-third of the meal: Grains and Starches (G/S)
- ★ One-third of the meal: Legumes, Nuts, and Seeds (L/N/S)

Also, try to incorporate healthy fats into every meal; you can easily work fats into any of the three above categories. For example:

- ★ Avocado is in the fruits and veggies (F/V) category, and it is also a healthy fat.
- ★ Chia and hemp seeds are in the legumes, nuts, and seeds (L/N/S) category, and they are also healthy fats.
- ★ Roasting starchy butternut squash in olive oil fits into the grains and starches (G/S) category, and olive oil is also a healthy fat.

The three categories are equally important!

- ★ The F/V category is important because fruits and vegetables are a major source of fiber, minerals, and vitamins that can help protect against numerous diseases.
- ★ The G/S category is important because grains and starches are packed with energy and nutrients like protein, fiber, B vitamins, and minerals that support metabolism, muscle building, and a healthy microbiome.
- ★ The L/N/S category is important because legumes, nuts, and seeds typically contain some of the richest sources of protein. On top of that, they provide fiber, healthy fats, carbohydrates, and tons of key micronutrients like calcium, folate, iron, zinc, selenium, and vitamin E.

One thing I love about the PB3 Plate is that it moves away from the traditional concept of a meal we grew up on of having "one main dish and sides." When I was a little girl, a typical dinner would be something like a giant pork chop (protein) as the

74 English, Whitney, and Alexandra Caspero. 2021. **The Plant-Based Baby & Toddler: Your Complete Feeding Guide for 6 Months to 3 Years with More than 50 Recipes**. New York: Avery.

main dish, along with some buttered rice (grain) and broccoli (veggie) as side items. With the PB3 Plate, children get variety in equal amounts. Fruits and veggies aren't just sides; they take up as much space as the other categories. It's also helpful to remember that while the bulk of protein will usually be in the L/N/S category, it can be found in all three categories! So never fear your child isn't getting enough protein. Our society is so hyper-focused on protein that people often forget about the plethora of other essential nutrients our bodies need.

Following this simple three-part structure, while being mindful of including healthy fats, means every meal is nutritious and diverse. The authors recommend aiming to include each of these three categories at meals and at least two of these with snacks. Of course, not every meal and snack needs to follow this perfectly, but the more you stick to this as a guideline, the better.

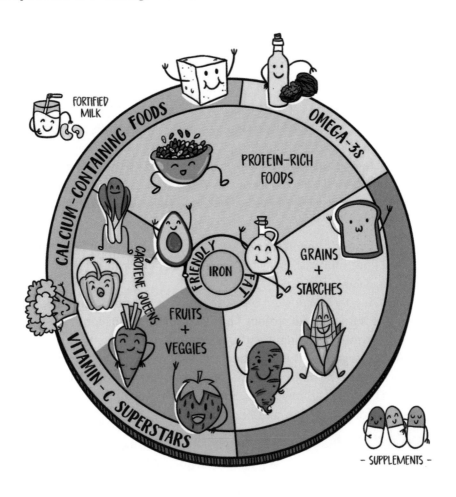

PB3 Plate method developed by Plant-Based Juniors™

The PB3 Plate method doesn't mean a meal must always look like a perfectly divided plate. Remember, the goal is simply to include foods from the main categories. For example, let's take a breakfast bowl with oat yogurt, ground flax seeds, banana slices, and almond butter drizzled on top:

The oat yogurt fits into the G/S category.

The ground flax seeds and almond butter fit into the L/N/S category and double as healthy fats.

The banana slices fit into the F/V category.

Here are some examples of meals I've put together using the PB3 Plate method:

Example 1: This kimchi grilled sandwich with carrot fries has sesame seeds (L/N/S and healthy fats), carrots (F/V), and whole grain bread (G/S).

Example 2: This vegan yogurt bowl has chia and hemp seeds (L/N/S and healthy fats), raspberries (F/V), and oat yogurt (G/S).

Example 3: This healthy lunchbox is packed with tofu bites (L/N/S and healthy fats), sautéed greens (F/V), and starchy roasted sweet potatoes (G/S).

Here is a handy snapshot of foods that fit into each of these categories:

This is not an all-encompassing list but rather a general idea of foods we tend to build our meals with. Use this as a reference to help inspire your menu planning and grocery shopping. Notice how some foods fit into multiple categories!

FRUITS AND VEGETABLES (F/V)	GRAINS AND STARCHES (G/S)	LEGUMES, NUTS, AND SEEDS (L/N/S)	HEALTHY FATS (NOTICE MANY OF THESE ARE ALSO IN THE L/N/S CATEGORY)
Apples	Amaranth	Chickpeas	Avocado
Applesauce	Barley	Lentils	Coconut
Asparagus	Buckwheat	Black beans	Edamame
Avocado	Bulgur wheat	Kidney beans	Tofu
Bananas	Corn	Pinto beans	Chia seeds
Bell pepper	Couscous	Cannellini beans	Shelled hemp seeds
Blackberries	Farro	Edamame	Pumpkin seeds
Blueberries	Green peas	Tofu	Flax seeds
Broccoli	Oatmeal	Tempeh	Sesame seeds
Butternut squash	Oat flour	Quinoa	Pecans
Carrots	Oat yogurt	Chia seeds	Macadamia nuts
Cauliflower	Potatoes	Shelled hemp seeds	Walnuts
Celery	Pumpkin	Pumpkin seeds	Cashews
Cucumber	Spelt flour	Flax seeds	Almonds
Dates	Squash	Sesame seeds	Peanut butter
Kale	Sweet potatoes	Pecans	Almond butter
Lemon	Teff	Macadamia nuts	Cashew butter
Lime	Tortillas	Walnuts	Sunflower seed butter
Mandarin	Whole grain bread	Cashews	Tahini
Mango	Whole wheat bread	Almonds	Hummus
Onion	Whole wheat flour	Peanut butter	Almond yogurt
Peaches	Whole wheat pasta	Almond butter	Cashew yogurt
Pears		Cashew butter	Coconut yogurt
Pineapple		Sunflower seed butter	Soy yogurt
Squash		Tahini	Extra-virgin olive oil
Strawberries		Hummus	Coconut oil
Sweet potatoes		Almond yogurt	Fortified pea or soy milk
Tomatoes		Cashew yogurt	
Watermelon		Soy yogurt	
Zucchini		Fortified pea or soy milk	

Meal Prep 101

Every parent is different in their approach to meal planning. Some cook throughout the week, while others might pick one day to batch-cook everything for the week. Batch cooking simply means you make multiple portions of a recipe or specific food to eat as leftovers throughout the week or freeze for later use. In our house, we do both and follow a solid system that works for our family.

Our Meal Prep Routine

Meal prep is a team effort for us. We each have our roles, and my husband and I even split up the meals. He might do lunches and dinners one week, while I do breakfasts and snacks—or vice versa. Here's the routine we love that we finally fell into after several chaotic months of winging it.

SATURDAY: The Menu Planner. I design the menu for our whole family. Usually, the menu I come up with is three or four main recipes to cook for the family as well as specific food items to prep for Beyond from the PB3 Plate categories. I write out a grocery list on our shared Note app with all the ingredients needed for each recipe. Additionally, I create a list of the recipes we plan to follow so my husband and I can both easily access it when we're ready to cook.

SUNDAY: The Batch Cooker. My husband takes Beyond to the store, and they do all the grocery shopping for the week (see next chapter for grocery guide). When they come back home, I take over the parental duties and spend time with Beyond while my husband spends a few hours cooking our lunches and dinners for the week in batches. During Beyond's afternoon nap, I step in to do some quick batch cooking too. I pick three simple foods to meal prep for Beyond that we can store in jars and freeze for later. For example: I might cook a simple pot of pasta, steam some frozen mixed veggies, and pan-fry some tofu. I do this once a week to build up a diverse freezer stash of prepped foods we can easily grab whenever we need.

MONDAY–FRIDAY: The On-the-Go Chef. With lunch and dinner out of the way, I focus on whipping up breakfast and snacks throughout the week. Additionally, every night, I pack Beyond's morning snack, lunch, and afternoon snacks into his lunchbox and store it in the fridge so it's ready for me to grab on the way out the door the next day. It's one less thing I have to worry about when getting him ready for school in the morning. After bringing him home in the afternoon, I clean the containers from his lunchbox so they are ready for me to pack his next day's meals later that night.

Why This Works for Us

My husband and I are complete opposites, but it works! He meal preps one day and I cook throughout the week. He washes dishes as he cooks on Sunday, while I load the dishwasher throughout the week when I cook. He loves batch-cooking multiple servings of a few meals and organizing them neatly in containers in the fridge. I love whipping up fewer servings of a wide variety of meals daily and presenting them to Beyond in creative ways. He's a Virgo; I'm a Pisces. We're perfectly opposite on the zodiac, right down to the month and day, and while that sounds like it should be a recipe for chaos, we have learned to make our differences complement each other.

Choose What Works for You

Ultimately, how you decide to meal prep will depend on your lifestyle and schedule. I am an early riser with a flexible work schedule on weekdays, so waking up earlier to make meals throughout the week is suitable for my schedule. If your weekends are busy, and you have more flexibility during the week like me, then cooking on weekdays may be feasible for you. My husband has a packed morning and evening self-care routine and a fixed work schedule on weekdays, so cooking throughout the week isn't practical for him. If your weekday schedule is firmer like his, then batch-cooking on weekends may be perfect for you.

Batch Cooking & Freezing

As I mentioned above, one effective strategy we use to ensure Beyond always has a diverse range of foods to choose from each week is batch cooking and freezing. We build up a freezer stash of prepped foods that we can thaw overnight in the refrigerator and serve weekly. Using the PB3 Plate as our guide, we pick a few foods each week that we can easily batch cook and store for later use.

Here are some examples of easy meal prep foods from the PB3 Plate food categories to batch and freeze.

- ★ Week 1: Pasta (G/S), sautéed mixed veggies (F/V), refried beans (L/N/S)
- ★ Week 2: Oatmeal (G/S), strawberry applesauce (F/V), pan fried tofu (L/N/S)
- ★ Week 3: Roasted sweet potatoes (G/S), steamed broccoli (F/V), lentils (L/N/S)
- ★ Week 4: Couscous (G/S), roasted carrots (F/V), quinoa porridge (L/N/S)

When you batch-cook these foods, set aside enough in the fridge to use that week and freeze any extras for later use. Following this strategy, you will build up an arsenal of different foods to pull out of your freezer that you can mix and match.

Thawing Tip: Slowly thawing your frozen leftovers in the refrigerator often results in the least change to texture and taste.

Sample Menus

0–6 Months

Human milk or infant formula.

6–9 Months

If your pediatrician says so, you can begin introducing solids as early as four months. We started introducing solids at four and a half months. Here's a fourteen-day sample menu for parents following either the "traditional" feeding method or the "baby-led weaning" feeding method (see Chapter 6 for more information on feeding methods and recipes). You can also combine these methods to see what works for your baby. Some babies like purees, while others enjoy exploring appropriately prepared finger foods. Simply continue introducing a new food every other day until you are comfortable moving on to more complex food combinations and textures.

	PRIMARY FOOD SOURCE	INTRODUCE OPTION 1: TRADITIONAL FEEDING METHOD	OR OPTION 2: BABY-LED WEANING METHOD
Days 1–2	Human milk or infant formula	Banana Puree (page 117)	Banana sliced in half (page 124)
Days 3–4	Human milk or infant formula	Baby Oatmeal (page 115)	Banana Oat Pancakes (page 186, omit the maple syrup)
Days 5–6	Human milk or infant formula	Avocado Puree (page 117)	Sliced avocado (page 124)
Days 7–8	Human milk or infant formula	Bean Puree (page 117)	Smashed bean toast (page 123)

Days 9–10	Human milk or infant formula	Sweet Potato Puree (page 116)	Roasted sweet potato (page 164)
Days 11–12	Human milk or infant formula	Quinoa puree	Coconut Quinoa Porridge (page 182, omit the maple syrup)
Days 13–14	Human milk or infant formula	Carrot puree	Roasted carrots (page 125)

9–12 Months

We started out with two solid meals a day and then worked our way up to three.

	Primary Food Source	Solid Meal 1	Solid Meal 2
Mon	Human milk or infant formula	Chia Strawberry Applesauce (page 118), No-Bake Chewy Fruity Snack Bars (page 165)	Saucy Chickpea Balls (page 206), Carrot Fries (page 160)
Tue	Human milk or infant formula	Apple Pumpkin Muffin (page 268), Savory Chickpea Scramble (page 192)	F'sh Sticks (page 202), quinoa salad
Wed	Human milk or infant formula	Peaches 'n' Cream Overnight Oats (page 184), almond butter toast strips	Three-Bean-Chili (page 244), Mango Salsa (page 135)
Thu	Human milk or infant formula	Chia Strawberry Applesauce, Chewy Fruity Snack Bar	Saucy Chickpea Balls, Carrot Fries
Fri	Human milk or infant formula	Apple Pumpkin Muffin, Savory Chickpea Scramble	F'sh Sticks, quinoa salad
Sat	Human milk or infant formula	Dragon Mango Bowl (page 285)	Three-Bean-Chili, Mango Salsa
Sun	Human milk or infant formula	Breakfast Banana Split (page 197)	Saucy Chickpea Balls, Carrot Fries

1–3 Years

Daily beverage: water and fortified soy or pea milk (and/or human milk)

	BREAKFAST	AM SNACK	LUNCH	PM SNACK	DINNER
Mon	Speedy Scrambled Tofu (page 176), Chia Pudding (page 178), mandarin slices	Chickpea "Not Tuna" Salad (page 148) and crackers	Curried Lentil Soup (page 250)	Blueberry Coconut Bliss Balls (page 154)	Mushroom Penne Pasta (page 222)
Tue	Apple Pie Porridge (page 180)	Maple Roasted Chickpeas (page 153), sliced grapes	Corn and Potato Chowder (page 248), Cumin Lime Avocado (page 166)	Green Pea Patties and Lemony Sauce (page 214)	Refried Mixed Beans (page 216), steamed garlic broccoli, farro
Wed	Garlic Hummus (page 137) on toast, sliced strawberries	Almond Butter Banana Bites (page 152)	Toddler Taquitos (page 200), Baby-Friendly Guacamole (page 134)	Cinnamon Roasted Sweet Potatoes (page 164)	Pasta, mixed veggies, pan-fried tofu
Thu	Speedy Scrambled Tofu, Chia Pudding, mango chunks	Smashed Avocado Chickpea Toast Sticks (page 150)	Chickpea of the Sea "Not Tuna" Salad, carrot slices	Blueberry Coconut Bliss Balls	Mushroom Pesto Flatbread (page 204)
Fri	Vegan yogurt bowl with hemp seeds and berries	Maple Roasted Chickpeas, raspberry applesauce	Curried Lentil Soup	Green Pea Patties and Lemony Sauce	Mushroom Penne Pasta
Sat	Banana Oat Pancakes (page 186) topped with vegan yogurt and granola	Silly Animal Toast (page 174)	Corn and Potato Chowder, Cumin Lime Avocado	Cinnamon Roasted Sweet Potatoes	Refried Mixed Beans, steamed garlic broccoli, farro
Sun	Apple Pie Porridge	PB&J Smoothie (page 281)	Toddler Taquitos, Baby-Friendly Guacamole	Hummus and crackers	Pasta, mixed veggies, pan-fried tofu

Balance Is Key

Batch-cooking full meals and single-ingredient foods can help you provide your baby or toddler with a variety of options every week. Using the Plant-Based Juniors™ PB3 Plate method as your guide will ensure these options are well-balanced and optimized to meet your child's nutritional needs. For convenience, setting aside smaller kid-friendly portions of your family's meals can make this practical for busy schedules.

Feeling confident in your ability to build healthy vegan meals for your child? Go you! Let's move on to the next chapter where you'll learn how to shop for vegan groceries and stock your kitchen.

05

KITCHEN AND GROCERY GUIDE

Stocking Up on Vegan Essentials

Understanding how to shop for vegan groceries and efficiently stock your kitchen is a valuable skill, particularly for families transitioning to a vegan lifestyle. It's not only about the foods you choose but also about creating a vegan-friendly environment that makes meal prep easy and fun. As you read this chapter, do an inventory check. What items do you already have? What items do you need? For those who are transitioning, you may be surprised to see you have more vegan ingredients in your kitchen than you realize. Do you need to go out and buy everything listed in this chapter? Absolutely not. Use this as a general guide to help you identify what to try and what to avoid. You can build your kitchen as you go!

Let's Go Shopping!

Here are some of my go-to vegan staples to have on hand for my little one. These are simply the items I reach for the most—so neither limit yourself nor feel pressured to get all these at once! Explore the aisles of your favorite grocery store and have fun experimenting with whatever yummy vegan foods pique your interest.

Activity Idea: Mark the items you're familiar with and highlight the ones you're interested in trying!

BAKING	HERBS, SPICES, & SWEETENERS	PANTRY	FRIDGE & FREEZER
Apple cider vinegar	Basil leaves	Amaranth	Dairy-free milks (fortified soy or pea, for over-one year olds if used as a beverage)
Arrowroot powder	Black pepper	Barley	
Baking powder	Cardamom, ground	Beans (black, garbanzo/chickpeas, kidney, navy, pinto, etc.)	Dairy-free yogurt (almond, soy, coconut, cashew, etc.)
Baking soda	Ceylon cinnamon, ground		
Breadcrumbs (authentic Japanese style)	Coriander, ground	Bread	Frozen fruits
	Cumin, ground	Buckwheat	Frozen vegetables
Coconut oil	Curry powder	Coconut aminos or low-sodium soy sauce	Lemon juice
Cacao powder	Dill weed		Lime juice
Cocoa powder, unsweetened	Fortified nutritional yeast seasoning	Coconut milk, canned	Tempeh
		Couscous	Tofu
Coconut sugar or raw cane sugar	Garlic powder	Farro	Vegetable stock (or you can make your own—page 237)
Extra-virgin olive oil	Ginger, ground	Heart of palm, canned (vegetable with a seafood-like texture used as meat replacement in vegan cooking)	
Flour of choice (oat, whole wheat, spelt tapioca, etc.)	Iodized sea salt		
	Italian seasoning		
Pitted dates (unpitted are fine too)	Kala Namak (also called black salt and used to add an egg-like taste to vegan egg dishes)	Lentils	
		Nuts (almonds, cashews, pecans, walnuts, etc.)	
Unsweetened applesauce (or you can make your own)	Maple syrup	Nut butters, unsweetened (peanut, almond, cashew, etc.)	
	Nutmeg, ground		
	Onion powder	Pasta (experiment with different kinds, like lentils, chickpeas, whole grain, etc.)	
	Oregano leaves		
	Paprika powder		
	Pure vanilla extract	Pasta sauce	
	Rosemary, ground	Pure pumpkin puree	
	Sage, ground	Quinoa	
	Thyme, ground	Rolled oats	
	Turmeric, ground	Seeds—large (sunflower, pumpkin, etc.)	
		Seeds—small (chia, ground flax, hemp hearts, sesame, etc.)	
		Seed butters, unsweetened (sunflower seed, pumpkin seed, watermelon seed, etc.)	
		Tahini	
		Tomato paste	
		Tomatoes, canned	
		Tortillas	

Understanding Food Labels

You learned in the first chapter that being vegan is a whole lifestyle, not a fad diet. It's a way for you and your family to take a stance against animal exploitation, take control of your consumption choices, and contribute to a healthier planet. So, what does that mean when it comes to grocery shopping? In a nutshell—no meat, no dairy, no eggs, no animal-derived ingredients. Sounds easy enough to look out for, right? Well, it should be, but that's not always the case, thanks to a lack of transparency in the naming conventions of ingredients. There are many ingredients whose names don't clarify what they mean or where they come from. Is it plant-based? Is it animal-based? Is it synthetically made? Unfortunately, ingredient names often aren't descriptive of their source.

These Are Some Common (Sometimes Sneaky) Non-Vegan Ingredients to Avoid

INGREDIENT	DESCRIPTION
Beeswax	Wax produced by bees to build their hives
Bone meal	Crushed or ground animal bones
Butter	Dairy product made from churned cow's milk or cream
Carmine	Red food dye derived from the crushed female cochineal insect
Casein	Protein derived from cow's milk
Confectioner's glaze or Shellac	Resin secreted by the female lac insect
Curds	Byproduct of coagulating cow's milk
Gelatin	Protein made from boiling the bones, hides, and connective tissues of animals
Ghee	Form of highly clarified butter typically derived from cow's milk
Honey	Food source created by bees that enables the hive to get through winter
Lactose	Milk sugar from milk of mammals
Lard	Fat that has been separated from the bellies of pigs
Milk protein	Protein derived from cow's milk
Ovalbumin	Main protein found in egg white
Surimi	Minced fish flesh
Tallow	Made by rendering suet which is the fat of cows or sheep
Whey	Liquid remaining after cow's milk has been curdled and strained

Avoiding Harmful Artificial Food Dyes

While we are on the subject of ingredients to avoid, let's talk about artificial food coloring. Growing up I never paused to wonder how my favorite snacks and drinks were all so perfectly vibrant. Various brightly colored drinks, cereals, candy, and "fruit-flavored" snacks are often strategically designed to capture the attention of children, from the kid-centric packaging to the actual food exhibiting every brilliant shade of the rainbow.

Unlike colorful fruits and vegetables that acquire their vivid plant pigments **naturally** from disease-fighting phytonutrients, many colorful processed foods marketed to kids achieve these hues through the application of artificial food dyes, **petroleum-derived** substances that give color to food. Artificial coloring is a low-cost way for food manufacturers to boost the aesthetic appeal of their products; however, it comes at the expense of the public's health, particularly our kids.

Studies over the years have linked[75] artificial food dyes to:

★ Hyperactivity, including ADHD.
★ Behavioral changes like irritability and depression.
★ Hives and asthma.
★ Tumor growth.

Adding to the years of mounting evidence, a recent 2023 study by scientists at Cornell and Binghamton University found[76] that nanoparticles frequently used in food coloring may cause damage to certain sections of the human intestine.

Despite available research that has been raising alarms since the 1970s,[77] the US and Europe have reacted quite differently to the information:

In Europe, measures were taken to address the concerns of synthetic dyes after a 2007 study[78] in the United Kingdom uncovered a connection between artificial food colorings and hyperactivity in children, even those **without** ADHD. While artificial food coloring was not outright banned, the European Union issued a requirement for products containing certain dyes to have a warning label displaying the potential adverse effects on children's activity and attention spans, which triggered an

75 Cleveland Clinic. 2023. "Is Red Dye 40 Safe?" Cleveland Clinic. March 8, 2023. https://health.clevelandclinic.org/red-dye-40/.
76 Cheng, Jacquelyn, Nikolai Kolba, Alba García-Rodríguez, Cláudia N. H. Marques, Gretchen J. Mahler, and Elad Tako. 2023. "Food-Grade Metal Oxide Nanoparticles Exposure Alters Intestinal Microbial Populations, Brush Border Membrane Functionality and Morphology, in Vivo (Gallus Gallus)." **Antioxidants** 12 (2): 431. https://doi.org/10.3390/antiox12020431.
77 Miller, Mark D., Craig Steinmaus, Mari S. Golub, Rosemary Castorina, Ruwan Thilakartne, Asa Bradman, and Melanie A. Marty. 2022. "Potential Impacts of Synthetic Food Dyes on Activity and Attention in Children: A Review of the Human and Animal Evidence." **Environmental Health** 21 (1). https://doi.org/10.1186/s12940-022-00849-9.
78 McCann, Donna, Angelina Barrett, Alison Cooper, Debbie Crumpler, Lindy Dalen, Kate Grimshaw, Elizabeth Kitchin, et al. 2007. "Food Additives and Hyperactive Behaviour in 3-Year-Old and 8/9-Year-Old Children in the Community: A Randomised, Double-Blinded, Placebo-Controlled Trial." **The Lancet** 370 (9598): 1560–67. https://doi.org/10.1016/s0140-6736(07)61306-3.

important shift in the way food manufacturers made their products. Many European food companies opted to replace synthetic dyes with natural colorings to avoid branding their products with an unappealing warning.

In the United States, however, the Food and Drug Administration (FDA) continues to stand firm in its belief[79] that color additives are safe when they are used in accordance with FDA regulations. In 2008, the Center for Science in the Public Interest (CSPI) petitioned the FDA[80] to ban artificial food dyes given the evidence of their links to behavioral changes in children. Two years later the CSPI released a new report, **Food Dyes: A Rainbow of Risks**,[81] concluding the nine artificial dyes approved in the US were likely to be carcinogenic, cause hypersensitivity reactions and behavioral problems, or are inadequately tested.

The report mentions three dyes in particular, Red 40, Yellow 5, and Yellow 6, which account for 90 percent of the dyes used in foods, contain benzidine, a manufactured chemical that The Department of Health and Human Services (DHHS), the World Health Organization (WHO), and the Environmental Protection Agency (EPA) have all deemed to be a human carcinogen.

Artificial Dyes to Look for on Ingredient Labels

★ Blue 1
★ Blue 2
★ Citrus Red 2
★ Green 3
★ Orange B

★ Red 3
★ Red 40
★ Yellow 5
★ Yellow 6

Here are some examples of how brands will use plant-based food colorings for a specific food product in Europe, while needlessly using artificial dyes for that same food product in the US.

79 Center for Food Safety and Applied Nutrition. 2018. "Color Additives Questions and Answers for Consumers." US Food and Drug Administration. 2018. https://www.fda.gov/food/food-additives-petitions/color-additives-questions-and-answers-consumers.
80 Potera, Carol. 2010. "DIET and NUTRITION: The Artificial Food Dye Blues." **Environmental Health Perspectives** 118 (10). https://doi.org/10.1289/ehp.118-a428.
81 Center for Science in the Public Interest. 2010. "Food Dyes a Rainbow of Risks." https://www.cspinet.org/sites/default/files/media/documents/resource/food-dyes-rainbow-of-risks.pdf.

UNITEDA KINGDOM PLANT-BASED COLORING	UNITED STATES OF AMERICA ARTIFICIAL COLORING
Fanta Orange Soda is colored with pumpkin and carrot extracts.	Fanta Orange Soda is colored with Red 40 and Yellow 6.
Sour Patch Kids is colored with anthocyanins, vegetable carbon, paprika extract, lutein, and curcumin.	Sour Patch Kids is colored with Blue 1, Red 40, Yellow 5, and Yellow 6.
Doritos Tangy Cheese is colored with paprika extract, annatto, and caramel.	Doritos Nacho Cheese is colored with Red 40, Yellow 5, and Yellow 6.
Tic Tac Fruit Adventure is colored with beet red, curcumin, and beta-carotene.	Tic Tac Fruit Adventure is colored with Blue 1, Red 40, Yellow 5, and Yellow 6.

While the US does not require a warning label for these dyes as Europe does, their presence is required to be listed in the ingredients list of food labels. When shopping for food, be sure to check labels for any of the above artificial food colorings, which the CSPI has determined should have no place in our food supply.

Activity Idea: While grocery shopping, show your kids how to outsmart food marketers and point out artificial dyes listed on food labels. Teach them fun facts about the colorful fruits and vegetables they enjoy and explain how they get their vibrant colors naturally.

Meat, Dairy, & Egg Replacements

If you're a parent or caregiver new to vegan eating, one of the biggest challenges is figuring out what to replace the animal products you've been eating your whole life with. One tip I often give families going vegan for the first time is to continue making all their favorite dishes but replace the non-vegan ingredients with a vegan substitute. For example, if you love spaghetti and meatballs, make your meatballs with a plant-based ingredient like lentils or chickpeas (page 206) instead of, well, cows.

My husband switched over to a plant-based diet in late 2019 after watching the documentary **The Game Changers**. Years before making that transition, he stopped drinking cow's milk after learning he could easily replace it with dairy-free milk that tasted just as great with his morning cereal. Though it was a simple swap at the time, it is an example of how straightforward it can be to replace animal products, especially nowadays when options have considerably expanded.

Understanding how to swap animal ingredients with plant-based ingredients will help make grocery shopping a smoother experience. Here is a handy cheat sheet for replacing meat, dairy, and eggs for your child's meals.

Meat Replacements

Jackfruit

The texture and taste of this tropical fruit make it a useful stand-in for meat. It can especially mimic pulled pork and is often used for mouthwatering vegan barbecue sandwiches and stir-fries.

Mushrooms

Cremini, portobello, and oyster mushrooms are some of my faves. They have robust, earthy flavors with tender, hearty textures. They are great for pizzas, wraps, sandwiches, breakfast dishes, and more.

Lentils

Lentils are hearty, low-cost, and fast-cooking! They can easily replace ground beef and create juicy fillings for dumplings, tacos, and pot pies.

Beans

Beans are another low-cost option. Black beans and garbanzo beans (chickpeas) are popular picks. Use them in burgers, stews, tacos, chilis, soups, and more.

Eggplant

Eggplant is super rich and multi-purpose—you can make eggplant 'meat'balls, fries, noodles, burgers, and gyros.

Cauliflower

When I first saw cauliflower as a main dish on a menu, I was skeptical. Shockingly, it was flavorful and filling! It is often used as a substitute for chicken, steaks, and ground meat in tacos.

Sweet Potato

Roasted, boiled, baked, mashed, or fried—its versatility means plenty of options. Use sweet potatoes in patties, scrambles, savory cakes, and pies to add substance and texture.

Beets

Sweet and detoxifying, use beet slices on pizzas and sandwiches. You can also make beet patties, veggie bowls, burgers, and more.

Coconut

No, not coconut oil. I mean fleshy coconut meat. Did you know you can use it to make crispy, sweet vegan bacon?

Tofu/Tempeh

These come from soybeans and are excellent sources of protein and calcium.

Seitan

This is a chewy, mildly flavored, high-protein meat substitute made from wheat gluten. Sometimes called "wheat meat," it has become a popular meat replacement for vegans. It's great in veggie bowls, stir-fries, and curries. You can usually find it in the refrigerated section of the grocery store near the tofu and tempeh.

Dairy Replacements

★ **Milk (as a beverage):** store-bought fortified pea or soy milk **after** the age of one (***from 0–12 months, infants need human milk or infant formula**)

★ **Milk (for recipes):** any dairy-free milk of your choice (soy, pea, oat, flaxseed, etc.)

★ **Butter (for cooking):** oils (extra-virgin olive, coconut, avocado, etc.)

★ **Butter (as a condiment):** nut or seed butters, tahini, hummus, jams, jellies, plant-based butter

★ **Cheese:** fortified nutritional yeast, nut-based cheese, tofu cheese

★ **Cottage cheese or Ricotta:** silken tofu

★ **Yogurt:** store-bought dairy-free yogurt (you could also make your own, but one advantage of store-bought is many brands have additional fortifications, such as live active cultures for gut health).

My favorite dairy-free yogurt has 17g of protein!

Examples of Replacing Dairy for Kids

1. Instead of buttered toast, top their toast with Sweet Chia Fruit Jam (page 131), nut or seed butters, smashed chickpeas and avocado (page 124), or cinnamon banana (page 172).

2. Instead of cheese and crackers, try topping those crackers with tofu ricotta, Chickpea of the Sea 'Not Tuna' Salad (page 148), nut or seed butters, or Garlic Hummus (page 137).

3. Try fortified nutritional yeast seasoning as a replacement for sprinkling cheese on top of food. It adds that umami flavor and works especially well as a seasoning for pasta, casseroles, soups, stews, and chili. Try using it to add a savory, cheesy flavor to sauces like Every Day Basil Pesto (page 132) or dressings.

4. Instead of using butter for cooking, let's sauté with oils like coconut, extra-virgin olive, or avocado—these oils can help your vegan child add more healthy fats to their meals.

5. Make desserts fun with dairy-free toppings like coconut whipped cream or vegan sprinkles—you can even make them yourself (page 143)!

Egg Replacements

Traditionally, eggs are used to help baked goods rise, bind ingredients together, add moisture for softness, and even aid in browning. Of course, they are also used outside of baking—think scrambled eggs for breakfast or egg salad for lunch; but after reading this book, you'll be able to make Speedy Scrambled Tofu (page 176) or a Tofu 'Egg' Salad Sandwich (page 208) instead!

So how can you skip eggs in baking and still make delicious recipes? While vegan egg replacements are available in many grocery stores, you likely have a replacement hiding in plain sight in your kitchen already.

REPLACEMENT FOR ONE EGG	BEST USED FOR
Chia egg: Mix 1 tablespoon of chia seeds with 3 tablespoons of water. Let it sit for 5 minutes until it becomes gel-like.	Pancakes, cookies, biscuits, quick breads
Flax egg: Mix 1 tablespoon of ground flaxseeds with 3 tablespoons of water. Let it sit for 5 to 10 minutes until it thickens.	Pancakes, waffles, cookies, bread, muffins
Baking soda & apple cider vinegar: Mix 1 tablespoon of apple cider vinegar with 1 teaspoon of baking soda.	Cakes, brownies, quick breads, muffins
¼ cup (4 tablespoons) of unsweetened applesauce	Muffins, quick breads, brownies, cakes, bars
1 mashed ripe banana	Muffins, quick breads, cakes
¼ cup (4 tablespoons) of plain dairy-free yogurt	Muffins, cakes, cupcakes, quick breads, bars
¼ cup (4 tablespoons) of silken tofu: Whirl in a blender and add water until it's smooth.	Muffins, pies, quick breads, cheesecake
3 tablespoons of Aquafaba: This is the thick leftover liquid of canned chickpeas (garbanzo beans). It's a magical vegan ingredient that most people discard, not knowing it can be used as a free egg replacement.	Whipped toppings, frostings, meringue

Equip Your Kitchen

While you **technically** don't need a bunch of fancy kitchen tools and appliances to cook vegan meals—a few have made my life easier. Here are the ones I find the most helpful for cooking, baking, and storing—and I've tried my best to choose kitchen tools made from more sustainable and nontoxic materials whenever possible. I have a mix of stainless steel, glass, silicone, and wooden kitchenware and storage items.

Appliances

Essential

- ★ High-speed blender
- ★ Food processor
- ★ Toaster

Nice to Have

- ★ Hand blender ("immersion blender")
- ★ Air fryer

Bakeware

- ★ Baking sheet set
- ★ Baking dish set
- ★ Silicone baking mats (or parchment paper)
- ★ Muffin/cupcake pan
- ★ Silicone cupcake liners
- ★ Loaf pan
- ★ Cake pan
- ★ Popsicle molds

Cookware

★ Stockpot with lid or Dutch oven
★ Saucepan with lid
★ Sauté pan with lid
★ Frying pan
★ Steamer pot with lid

Basic Utensils

★ Can opener
★ Cutting board
★ Chef's knife
★ Measuring cups
★ Measuring spoons
★ Mixing bowls
★ Potato masher
★ Slotted spoon
★ Solid spoon
★ Spatula
★ Spoon ladle
★ Tongs

Storage Containers

★ Freezer bags (reusable or disposable)
★ Lidded glass containers
★ Lidded glass baby food jars
★ Silicone refillable pouches
★ Silicone zip-top kid snack containers

Extra Tools

★ **Cookie scoop:** used to scoop uniform sizes of dough and batter.
★ **Lemon squeezer:** used to extract juice from lemons, limes, and other citrus fruits.
★ **Peeler:** helpful for quickly removing the peels or skins from fruits and vegetables.
★ **Tofu press:** used to extract excess water from tofu, improving its texture and ability to absorb flavors.
★ **Zester:** used to shave (zest) bits or strands from the outer layer of citrus fruits, adding a tangy flavor to recipes.

Cooking Materials to Avoid if Possible

Nonstick/Teflon

Reasons to avoid: While Teflon cookware is an undeniably convenient choice due to its magical nonstick capabilities, the surface is easily compromised. Scientists have estimated[82] that thousands to millions of ultrasmall Teflon plastic particles may be released during cooking as nonstick cookware loses its coating over time. Chemicals used in nonstick cookware like Teflon, such as polytetrafluoroethylene (PTFE) or perfluorooctanoic acid (PFOA), may cause damage to the thyroid, kidneys, and reproductive organs. These chemical coatings can break down and lead to problems as cooking temperatures rise.

Replacement options: We primarily use stainless steel cookware and have some cast-iron pans.

Plastic

Reasons to avoid: We all know plastic pollution is wreaking havoc on the planet, but plastic can also be detrimental to our health. It has been shown to leach[83] endocrine-disrupting chemicals into food and beverages. BPA (bisphenol-A) is one of the most well-researched of these chemicals, and has been linked to[84] developmental issues and a higher risk of chronic illnesses, including cancers. It's not always possible to avoid plastic, so remember that it's not about being perfect but rather doing the best you can.

Replacement options: Plastic containers can be replaced with glass containers. Swap plastic cooking utensils with steel, wooden, or silicone utensils. Opt for wooden cutting boards over plastic ones. Plastic storage bags can be swapped with silicone ones. You can even cut down on plastic waste when grocery shopping by bringing reusable shopping and produce bags.

82 Luo, Yunlong, Christopher T. Gibson, Clarence Chuah, Youhong Tang, Ravi Naidu, and Cheng Fang. 2022. "Raman Imaging for the Identification of Teflon Microplastics and Nanoplastics Released from Non-Stick Cookware." **Science of the Total Environment** 851 (December): 158293. https://doi.org/10.1016/j.scitotenv.2022.158293.

83 Rubin, Beverly S. 2011. "Bisphenol A: An Endocrine Disruptor with Widespread Exposure and Multiple Effects." **The Journal of Steroid Biochemistry and Molecular Biology** 127 (1–2): 27–34. https://doi.org/10.1016/j.jsbmb.2011.05.002.

84 Hafezi, Shirin A., and Wael M. Abdel-Rahman. 2019. "The Endocrine Disruptor Bisphenol a (BPA) Exerts a Wide Range of Effects in Carcinogenesis and Response to Therapy." **Current Molecular Pharmacology** 12 (March). https://doi.org/10.2174/1874467212666619030616 4507.

Final Thoughts

Remember not to let the pursuit of perfection inhibit your progress. Profit-driven societies can be challenging to navigate when you open your eyes to the plethora of injustices littering our world. Education is the gateway to positive change, and you should be proud of yourself for taking that step by picking up this book. If you've made it through all of Part I, you now have the knowledge, skills, and motivation to make that change happen—and I have confidence you will!

Now that your kitchen is equipped and ready to go, your super vegan parent powers are ready to activate. Are you excited to get started? I hope so, because I don't want to be alone here. It's the moment you have been patiently waiting for. Drum roll, please.

No seriously. Pick up your phone and find some drumroll sound effects on the internet to set the tone. This is your moment.

Ready? Now turn the page and enter the Vegan Super Kid Recipes section. Time to make magic.

Part II

VEGAN SUPER KID RECIPES

06

INTRODUCING SOLIDS

Essential Food Guidelines to Know Before We Get Started

Food Allergies

Food allergy advice for babies has changed over time in light of updated research.[85] Delayed introduction of food allergens was once recommended by professional institutions, and it was discovered later on that this guideline may have **contributed to** the development of food allergies in children, rather than prevented them as intended. Allergists and pediatricians now recommend introducing many common food allergens before a baby's first birthday, in some cases between four to six months of age, to minimize the risk of food allergy development.

Before introducing food allergens, it is important to know if your baby is at high risk of developing food allergies, such as having severe eczema or existing allergies. Seek guidance from your pediatrician or pediatric allergist about the latest recommendations for early food allergen introduction.

Some of the recipes in this book contain ingredients that are common food allergens, such as peanuts, tree nuts, soy, and wheat. Be sure to review the ingredients list of the recipes in this book and ensure you have introduced any allergen foods before cooking and serving dishes that contain allergen ingredients.

For parents whose children attend nut-free daycares and schools or have known peanut and/or tree nut allergies, I have listed peanut-free and nut-free alternatives for any recipes containing peanuts and tree nuts.

Leftover Food Safety

When you follow a whole-food, plant-based vegan diet, many of the dishes you prepare can be refrigerated or frozen for later use, allowing you to save time and money by batch-cooking large portions. Some dishes can be stored in the refrigerator for four to five days or even up to a week.

For those who may be new to cooking, particularly batch cooking, it may be helpful to review your country's guidelines on food storage safety. I live in the United States,

85 Trogen, Brit, Samantha Jacobs, and Anna Nowak-Wegrzyn. 2022. "Early Introduction of Allergenic Foods and the Prevention of Food Allergy." **Nutrients** 14 (13): 2565. https://doi.org/10.3390/nu14132565.

and here is a quick summary of what the US Department of Agriculture (USDA) recommends[86] for handling leftovers:

1. **Storing in the fridge and freezer:** Generally, leftovers can be stored in the refrigerator for three to four days or frozen for three to four months. Refrigerate all leftovers within two hours of cooking food or after it is removed from an appliance keeping it warm.

2. **Thawing:** The ideal way to thaw frozen leftovers is in the refrigerator. This method takes the longest, but the leftovers stay safe the entire time. After thawing, consume the food within three to four days or refreeze it.

3. **Reheating without thawing:** If time is short, you can safely reheat frozen leftovers in a saucepan, oven, or microwave without thawing first.

4. **Reheating safety tips:**

   ★ **Saucepan:** Reheat sauces, soups, and gravies by bringing them to a boil. Cover leftovers to reheat, which helps with moisture retention and ensures that food will heat all the way through.

   ★ **Microwave:** Cover and rotate the food for even heating. Use microwave-safe dishes, add some liquid if needed, and vent the lid or wrap to allow steam to escape. The moist heat that is created can help destroy harmful bacteria and ensure uniform cooking.

Remember, these are general food storage guidelines you can refer to as you navigate cooking different recipes from this book. They are not necessarily strict rules you must abide by. For most of the recipes in this book, you can store leftovers in an airtight container in your fridge or in freezer-safe containers and bags in your freezer, for either the recommended amount of time your country advises or using your personal judgment.

Added Salt and Sugar

The Dietary Guidelines of Americans (DGA)[87] for 2020 to 2025 recommend that for kids under two:

1. Foods with added sugar should be avoided; and

2. Foods higher in sodium should be avoided.

86 "Leftovers and Food Safety | Food Safety and Inspection Service." n.d. www.fsis.usda.gov. https://www.fsis.usda.gov/food-safety/safe-food-handling-and-preparation/food-safety-basics/leftovers-and-food-safety.

87 US Department of Agriculture and US Department of Health and Human Services. "Dietary Guidelines for Americans, 2020–2025." 9th Edition. December 2020. https://www.dietaryguidelines.gov/sites/default/files/2020-12/Dietary_Guidelines_for_Americans_2020-2025.pdf.

While these are the recommended guidelines to follow, this is a judgment-free zone, so I want to acknowledge that different families have different views on the topic of added salt and sugar for infants and toddlers. Some will allow limited amounts of added salt and sugar, while others omit it completely. Some will omit it completely for infants and allow limited amounts for toddlers, while others avoid it completely for both. Some are fine with certain added sugars like maple syrup and coconut sugar, while others prefer to naturally sweeten dishes with fruits only, like mashed bananas, grated apples, and dates.

The recipes in this book are customizable to what works best for your family. I refrained from listing specific amounts of salt, because you should be in control of what goes into your family meals. I'll usually recommend you to "salt to taste," omit it completely for infants, or salt your portion separately from your infant's portion. I provided many recipes that can work for everyone in your household. Older family members may want some salt and sugar in their portions, so salting or sweetening portions separately from your baby's portion is a feasible strategy. I welcome you to adjust the recipes to suit your family's preferences.

Practical Example

Let's say you want to bake the Apple Pumpkin Muffins on page 268 and omit added sugar for your baby, while including it for older members of your family. Here are two approaches you can choose from:

> **Option 1: Sweeten the batter separately during the baking process.** Omit maple syrup in the batter initially and pour half of the sugar-free batter into some muffin liners. Then, add maple syrup to the remaining batter, and pour that half of the batter into the rest of the muffin liners. With this approach, one-half of the batch is infant-friendly, and the other half of the batch is adult-friendly.

> **Option 2: Sweeten individual servings after the baking process.** Instead of adding maple syrup to half the batter, proceed with baking it sugar-free and let the older family members control the sweetness of their portions afterward. They can do so by drizzling maple syrup on top of their muffins (just as they would a pancake).

The same example can be applied to added salt. You can salt the adult portion separately from your baby's portion during the cooking process or allow adults to sprinkle some salt onto their individual portions after the cooking process is over, when they are ready to eat.

Your Family, Your Choice

As always, do what works for your family and when in doubt, seek professional guidance. When it comes to food allergens, food storage safety, and the added sugar and salt debate, it is essential to make informed decisions. I hope the guidelines I listed provide valuable insights that help you navigate this new and exciting world of feeding your littles.

A Whole New World of Food

Are you feeling excited, nervous, or a mix of both at the thought of introducing solids to your little one? As a first-time mom, I felt both of those emotions. I was enjoying my body being my baby's only food source. But alas, part of the deal of having kids is that **just** when you feel confident you've found your parenting groove, it's time to step out of your comfort zone and learn how to adapt to a brand new, unknown child-rearing phase.

My husband and I had many questions, and the internet had even more opinions. Ultimately, we decided to introduce solids to baby Beyond at the tender age of 4.5 months. He showed all the signs of readiness and got the green light from our first pediatrician (we later switched to a plant-based pediatrician).

Here's a Quick Rundown of What We Did

1. **4–6 months:** We started with mashed banana mixed with my pumped breastmilk, which he gobbled right up! We continued introducing a new fruit, vegetable, legume, or grain every two days, which we would puree in a blender and serve to him with my pumped breastmilk mixed in. ***Breastfeeding on demand continued to be his primary food source.**

2. **6–9 months:** We started feeding him two different foods at a time, twice a day. For example, banana and oatmeal for breakfast and avocado and beans for lunch. We didn't shy away from adding seasonings or experimenting with food combinations. ***Breastfeeding on demand continued to be his primary food source.**

3. **9–12 months:** His meals started looking like ours. We served him breakfast, lunch, and dinner, and the food was often smaller portions of what we cooked for ourselves. We also began giving him a liquid multivitamin and omega-3 DHA drops per the recommendation of the plant-based pediatrician

we switched to. ***Breastfeeding on demand continued to be his primary food source.**

4. **1 year+:** We added snacks to his daily routine. We were now serving him breakfast, a morning snack, lunch, an afternoon snack, and dinner. ***Food became his primary food source, while I continued breastfeeding on a schedule until age two.**

There are different approaches to introducing solids, but this is the route we chose as first-time parents. Some people follow the "traditional" method of introducing food in pureed form as we did. In contrast, others follow the "baby-led weaning (BLW)" method, where purees and spoon-feeding are skipped in favor of finger foods that babies feed themselves. The BLW method is the approach we will use for our second baby, Wonder, now that we have a firm understanding of its benefits and how to do it properly, which you will learn about in this chapter.

Regardless of your path, feel confident knowing it's the one you are most comfortable with and works the best for your family! However, I understand the sea of questions that can arise during this time. It led me to seek professional guidance to ensure we're making the best choices for our little ones. With this aim, I reached out to plant-based pediatrician Dr. Shayna Smith. She has been an invaluable resource to us and to my online community of families, providing expert advice and answers to frequently asked questions. Let's delve into our enlightening conversation and see what Dr. Smith had to say.

FAQ with a Plant-Based Pediatrician: Starting Solids, Allergen Exposure, Supplements, and More

Shayna Smith, MD, DipABLM, is board-certified in Pediatrics, Pediatric Emergency Medicine, and Lifestyle Medicine. Dr. Smith is the owner and Medical Director of Flourish Pediatrics, a US-based pediatric medical office focusing on a whole-body approach to pediatric health and wellness. She promotes a plant-positive diet and healthy lifestyle and was honored as Best Pediatrician in Atlanta by **Atlantan** magazine in 2021.

Dr. Smith focuses on providing evidence-based pediatric care and implementing lifestyle medicine principles such as sleep, diet, exercise, stress management, and social connectedness. She works to provide whole-family nutrition counseling, educational classes, and programs to support their needs.

Dr. Smith recognizes that there is mounting evidence of the beginning of chronic disease conditions in childhood and strong evidence that poor nutrition is a significant contributing factor. She has found an increased incidence of hypertension, high cholesterol, and pre-diabetes indicators among incoming patients, with children as young as ten years old already on type 2 diabetes medication and being assessed for heart disease risk levels by cardiologists. She utilizes lifestyle medicine and an emphasis on nutrient-dense plant-based foods to address the root causes of illnesses as a tool for preventing and/or treating chronic diseases and other conditions.

Is a plant-based vegan diet healthy for babies and toddlers?

Absolutely! When done correctly, children can thrive off of a plant-based or vegan diet. As with all parents, they have to make sure that they are giving their child a balanced nutritious diet.

When should I begin feeding my baby solids?

Babies can be offered solids as early as four to six months. Starting solids is usually based on a child's readiness such as when they can hold up their head, show interest in food, open their mouth when food is offered, and move food from the spoon to their mouth.

Are there specific foods I should start out with?

There is no rule that you must start with a specific food. Just think about how many cultures there are and how many differences there have to be with the introduction of food and look around at restaurants—everyone is eating! Because I am a pediatrician and I am attempting to develop the palate of fresh human beings, I suggest fresh foods over processed foods and starting with vegetables first. But there is no evidence that shows that starting with fruits will make babies not like vegetables. It just seems like that is the case at the office!

Does it matter if I do the traditional (pureed) vs. baby-led weaning (finger food) method?

The type of method can vary from family to family. Every child's preference is different. As a pediatrician, I have seen that a child does not prefer purees but will often take "table food" vigorously.

In all cases, safety first. As long as the baby is sitting upright with adult supervision and doesn't have any food that is a choking hazard then I am okay with it.

What foods should I avoid and how can I avoid choking hazards if I go the baby-led weaning route?

Some foods to avoid include raw vegetables, nuts, popcorn, hard fruit, uncut grapes, hot dogs, and seeds. The Centers for Disease Control and Prevention (CDC) has a great reference list!

As a pediatric ER doctor, I saw patients come in with food stuck in their airways, so I suggest that parents are always present when their infant or toddler is eating.

Is there a window for introducing allergens to my baby?

According to the LEAP study,[88] it is best to introduce allergens to babies early. Early introduction of allergens has been shown to decrease the chance of food allergy in the future. Introducing peanut protein starting at four months of age vs. waiting like we did in the past has been shown to promote peanut tolerance.

Can babies eat spicy food?

Babies can enjoy a wide range of herbs and spices in their food. Think of all of the babies and children around the world. Flavors are often passed through the placenta and breastmilk, so infants often enjoy foods the mom consumes during pregnancy or while breastfeeding.

Note: Intense spices, such as hot spices, may upset the stomach. Parents should consider these in small doses or offer later after the first birthday.

When I start feeding my baby the same meals I feed the rest of my family, do I need to modify the salt and sugar amounts?

Yes, it is awesome if your child eats the same meals as the rest of the family. I highly suggest that this is the goal as early as possible. Well, the child will eventually throw his food on the floor and want to eat off the parent's plate, so the parents must always remember that you must practice what you preach when it comes to salt and sugar amounts. If the food is oversalted, definitely, make another slightly salted or unsalted dish for the infant/toddler.

88 Du Toit, George, Graham Roberts, Peter H Sayre, Henry T Bahnson, Suzana Radulovic, Alexandra F Santos, Helen A Brough, et al. 2015. "Randomized Trial of Peanut Consumption in Infants at Risk for Peanut Allergy." **The New England Journal of Medicine** 372 (9): 803–13. https://doi.org/10.1056/NEJMoa1414850.

What supplements should I pay attention to, and when should I start giving them?

It is important that plant-based or vegan parents discuss their diet/lifestyle with their doctor and ensure that their child is growing and developing as expected at their regular appointments. While there are nutrients that every child needs to thrive, we must ensure that vegan children are getting enough vitamin D and B12.

What can I do if my pediatrician doesn't support my decision to raise my child vegan?

Feel confident that you can raise a healthy vegan child. Social media will make it easy to find someone in the community to lead you in the right direction. There are even websites that have directories with plant-based health providers. Check to see if you have one near you.

See page 290 in the Additional Resources section for information on finding plant-based health providers closest to you!

See page 290 in the Additional Resources section for information on finding plant-based health providers closest to you!

I enjoyed this conversation with Dr. Smith and hope her professional insights helped ease any apprehensions you may be experiencing. Parenting is often a learn-as-you-go rollercoaster ride, and we are continuously evolving along the way. Looking back, our journey was a mix of trials, triumphs, and more than a few "messy" meals. But remember, it's all part of the process, and there's no one-size-fits-all. Don't hesitate to ask for help when you need it.

Feeding Methods: Traditional vs. Baby-Led Weaning

As Dr. Smith mentioned in the Q&A, the method you choose for introducing complementary solid foods will depend on you and your baby. Some families find comfort in the tradition of pureeing and spoon-feeding their babies, while others prefer to flip the script and put babies in charge at mealtime. Some babies feast merrily on pureed foods, while others reject them entirely and show favor to finger foods. Some folks successfully combine these approaches by spoon-feeding and self-feeding with finger foods!

Important reminder: Regardless of which route you choose, remember that solids are complementary and should never be used to replace human milk or infant formula until age one.

Let's dive a little deeper into these two popular feeding methods.

Traditional Feeding Approach

With the traditional feeding approach to introducing solids to babies, food is offered in a pureed form and typically spoon-fed by the parent or caregiver. This method is based on a graduated exposure to solid foods with different textures, which means infants are given pureed foods before advancing to mashed and chopped foods and eventually graduating to family foods.

Some families buy jarred baby food from the grocery store, while others make pureed food at home. Ironically, although this feeding approach is labeled "traditional," it wasn't always standard practice. Here's a brief look at how this became popularized in American households, giving important context into how cultural norms aren't always influenced by what is best but rather what has been **marketed** as best.

The Eye-Opening History of Pureed Baby Food

According to Amy Bentley, author of **Inventing Baby Food**, commercially made baby food was popularized in the 1930s after father and son team Frank and Dan Gerber began experimenting with strained food at their cannery and produced more than two million cans of baby food.[89] While their line of baby

---

89 Bentley, Amy. 2014. **Inventing Baby Food: Taste, Health, and the Industrialization of the American Diet**. Oakland, California: University of California Press.

food was a big success amongst consumers, they ramped up their marketing efforts to win over those still hesitant to try it. Gerber created advertising campaigns to convince parents and the medical community that their processed baby food was "nutritionally superior and safer" than homemade baby food. The impact of industrial baby food on American food culture contributed to a societal shift away from homemade foods and table foods. Before this era, babies were often exposed to a wider variety of textures.

This little glimpse into history exemplifies how capitalism and marketing can heavily influence cultural norms and behaviors. Making informed parenting decisions often requires us to dig a little deeper to find sound advice that is designed to genuinely benefit our children, not corporations. Thankfully, if you choose to go the "traditional" route of pureed foods, you don't have to buy baby food from the store. Homemade pureed baby food is simple to whip up and offers more control over what goes into your baby's belly. We made all of Beyond's infant food at home and stored leftovers in glass jars.

Here are some easy puree recipes and basic guidelines to help get you started.

Basic Guide to Steaming

If you don't have a fancy baby food maker that steams and blends, don't worry. You can use a pot and steamer basket for steaming and a blender for pureeing.

For all of the puree recipes below that require steaming, when noted, refer back to this basic steaming method:

★ **Step 1:** Prep your fruit or vegetable appropriately by washing (if needed), peeling (if needed), coring or pitting (if needed), and chopping (if needed) into small pieces. The smaller the pieces are, the quicker they will cook.

★ **Step 2:** Fill a small pot with about one inch of water. Insert a steamer basket and bring the water to a boil.

★ **Step 3:** Add the fruit or vegetable to the steamer pot, cover it, and reduce the heat to a simmer.

★ **Step 4:** Check on the food periodically to prevent overcooking. Once the food is steamed and softened, add whatever herbs and spices you want to elevate the taste, thus exposing your baby's palate to even more flavors.

Blending, Storing, Thawing, and Food Safety

Blending: After steaming, allow the food to cool and then transfer it to a blender. Blend it until it's smooth and add in water, expressed human milk, or infant formula until your desired consistency is reached.

Storage: In most cases, you can store homemade purees in an airtight container in a refrigerator for up to three days. If you won't be using it within those three days, freeze it for up to three months. Baby food freezer trays work well for this, or if you don't have one, you can portion them into ice cube trays and place them in a resealable freezer bag. Label the freezer bag with the date and name of the puree.

Thawing: To thaw frozen baby food, try using one of these two methods:

1. **Overnight thaw:** Pop the frozen portions you plan to feed your baby out of the ice cube trays or baby food freezer trays and place them in an airtight glass container. Refrigerate overnight for eight to twelve hours and serve the next day.

2. **Quick thaw:** If you need a more immediate approach, thaw them using your stove. Put your frozen food cubes in a small pot over medium-low heat and gently cook the puree until warm, stirring occasionally. Remove the pot from the heat when thawed and allow the food to cool before serving.

Once thawed, if you feel the texture is too watery, thicken it by adding an unsweetened dairy-free yogurt of your choice.

Food safety: When feeding, avoid serving food directly from a storage container that has baby food you plan to refrigerate. Bacteria from your baby's mouth can be transferred to the spoon and into the baby food where that bacteria can grow. Instead, transfer your desired serving of baby food from the storage container into your baby's serving dish and serve the food from there. After the meal, discard all uneaten food from that serving dish. Only store baby food that has not come in contact with your baby's saliva.

Tip: Add extra healthy fats and protein to your purees with chia seeds or hemp seeds.

Sunflower Seed Butter Puree

Ingredients: 2–3 tablespoons of unsweetened creamy sunflower seed butter and preferred liquid (water, expressed human milk, or infant formula)

Instructions: Into a small bowl, add the sunflower seed butter and stir in enough of your preferred liquid until it forms the consistency you want. Serve it immediately.

Green Pea Puree

Ingredients: 2 cups (290 g) frozen peas, a pinch of rosemary, and preferred liquid (water, expressed human milk, or infant formula)

Instructions: Follow steps 2 through 4 of the steaming guide on page 113 to steam the peas and add the pinch of rosemary. Transfer the steamed peas to a blender and add just enough of your preferred liquid to reach your desired consistency. Blend until it's smooth. For storage, thawing, and food safety tips, see page 114.

Baby Oatmeal

Ingredients: ½ cup (45 g) rolled oats, 1–2 tablespoons preferred liquid (water, expressed human milk, or infant formula), and a pinch of nutmeg or cinnamon (Ceylon if possible)

Instructions: Add the oats to a blender and blend into a powder. Add 2 tablespoons of the oat powder to your baby's serving bowl. Stir in 1–2 tablespoons of your preferred liquid and a pinch of nutmeg or cinnamon. Mix it and serve it immediately. Store the remaining blended oat powder in an airtight container in the refrigerator. When preparing another serving of baby oatmeal, repeat these instructions, starting with taking out 2 tablespoons of oat powder.

Introducing Solids

Peachy Puree

Ingredients: 1 cup sliced peaches (225 g), a pinch of ground ginger, and preferred liquid (water, expressed human milk, or infant formula)

Instructions: If the peaches are super firm, steam them first using the steaming guide on page 113, and then proceed to blend. If they are ripe and soft enough, go ahead and add them to the blender, along with the pinch of ginger, and just enough of your preferred liquid to reach your desired consistency. Blend until smooth. For storage, thawing, and food safety tips, see page 114.

Sweet Potato Puree

Ingredients: 2 small sweet potatoes, a pinch of ground clove, 1 teaspoon extra-virgin olive oil, and preferred liquid (water, expressed human milk, or infant formula)

Instructions: Peel the sweet potatoes. Dice and steam them using the steaming guide on page 113 and add a pinch of ground clove. Transfer the steamed sweet potatoes to a blender and add just enough of your preferred liquid to reach your desired consistency. Blend until it's smooth. For storage, thawing, and food safety tips, see page 114.

Cauliflower or Broccoli Puree

Ingredients: 2 cups (170 g) fresh or frozen cauliflower or broccoli florets, a pinch of garlic, and preferred liquid (water, expressed human milk, or infant formula)

Instructions: Steam the broccoli or cauliflower using the steaming guide on page 113 and add the pinch of garlic. Transfer the steamed broccoli or cauliflower to a blender and add just enough of your preferred liquid to reach your desired consistency. Blend until it's smooth. For storage, thawing, and food safety tips, see page 114.

Raspberry Puree

Ingredients: 1 cup (125 g) fresh raspberries and preferred liquid (water, expressed human milk, or infant formula)

Instructions: Rinse your raspberries and pat them dry. In a bowl, mash them until smooth. Stir in enough of your preferred liquid until it forms the consistency you want. For storage, thawing, and food safety tips, see page 114.

Bean Puree

Ingredients: 1 (15 oz/425 g) can of preferred beans (drained and rinsed), pinch of ground cumin, and preferred liquid (water, expressed human milk, or infant formula)

Instructions: Add the beans and cumin to a blender and blend until smooth. Then, add in just enough of your preferred liquid until you reach your desired consistency. For storage, thawing, and food safety tips, see page 114.

Banana Puree

Ingredients: ¼ ripe banana, sprinkle of cardamom, and preferred liquid (water, expressed human milk, or infant formula)

Instructions: In a small bowl, use a fork to mash the banana until smooth. Add a sprinkle of cardamom. Stir in enough of your preferred liquid until it forms the consistency you want. Serve it immediately.

Avocado Puree

Ingredients: 1 ripe avocado, pinch of ground coriander, preferred liquid (water, expressed human milk, or infant formula), and a squeeze of lemon

Instructions: Cut the avocado in half, scoop out the flesh, and discard the pit and peel. Use a fork to mash the avocado in a small bowl until smooth. Add a pinch of coriander. Stir in enough of your preferred liquid until it forms the consistency you want. Serve your desired amount. To store in the refrigerator or freezer, place the puree in an airtight container or freezer tray and squeeze fresh lemon juice on top to prevent browning. Refrigerate it for up to three days or freeze it for up to three months.

Traditional Recipes: Ten Puree Power Combos

There are two easy ways to make puree combos. You can mix and match from the single-ingredient purees you have stored in the refrigerator or freezer. Or you can make fresh batches of combo purees by blending multiple new ingredients together.

Sweet Potato and Bean Puree

Ingredients: Sweet Potato Puree (page 116) and Bean Puree (page 117)

Instructions: Using either the overnight thaw or quick thaw method (page 114), thaw one serving of each of these two purees together and serve to your baby. Alternatively, you can make a fresh batch by following the cooking instructions for each of these and blending them together.

Chia Strawberry Applesauce

Ingredients: 1 unpeeled medium apple, 2 or 3 strawberries, ½ tablespoon chia seeds, 6 tablespoons water (or expressed human milk or infant formula)

Instructions: Add all of the ingredients to a blender and blend until it's smooth. Add more liquid, if needed. For storage, thawing, and food safety tips, see page 114.

Banana Sunflower Seed Butter Puree

Ingredients: Banana Puree (page 117) and Sunflower Seed Butter Puree (page 115)

Instructions: In your baby's serving dish, combine the Banana Puree and Sunflower Seed Butter Puree and serve it immediately.

Spinach Pineapple Puree

Ingredients: 1 cup (225 g) fresh chopped pineapple, 1 cup (30 g) fresh chopped spinach, and preferred liquid (water, expressed human milk, or infant formula)

Instructions: Add the pineapple and spinach into a blender and blend until it's smooth, adding your preferred liquid until you reach your desired consistency. For storage, thawing, and food safety tips, see page 114.

Raspberry Oatmeal

Ingredients: 1 serving of Baby Oatmeal (page 115) and 1 serving of Raspberry Puree (page 116)

Instructions: In your baby's serving dish, combine the Baby Oatmeal and Raspberry Puree and serve it immediately.

Blueberry Mango Puree

Ingredients: ½ cup (83 g) fresh blueberries, ½ fresh mango (peeled and sliced), and preferred liquid (water, expressed human milk, or infant formula)

Instructions: Place all the ingredients into a blender and blend until it's smooth, adding your preferred liquid until you reach your desired consistency. For storage, thawing, and food safety tips, see page 114.

Peachy Green Pea Puree

Ingredients: Peachy Puree (page 116) and Green Pea Puree (page 115)

Instructions: Using either the overnight thaw or quick-thaw method (page 114), thaw one serving of each puree together and serve to your baby. Alternatively, you can make a fresh batch by following the cooking instructions for each and blending them together.

Coconut Quinoa Puree

Ingredients: 1 cup water (237 mL), ½ cup quinoa (90 g), ¼ cup (59 mL) coconut milk, a pinch of cardamom

Instructions: In a small saucepan, bring the water and quinoa to a boil over high heat. Reduce the heat to low, cover with a lid, and cook for about fifteen minutes, or until water is absorbed. Remove it from the heat and allow it to cool. Transfer the quinoa to a blender and add the coconut milk and cardamom. Blend until it's smooth. For storage, thawing, and food safety tips, see page 114.

Cauliflower Avocado Puree

Ingredients: Cauliflower Puree (page 116) and Avocado Puree (page 117)

Instructions: Using either the overnight thaw or quick-thaw method (page 114), thaw one serving of each puree together and serve to your baby. Alternatively, you can make a fresh batch by following the cooking instructions for each and blending them together.

Carrot Pear Puree

Ingredients: 4 carrots (peeled and chopped), 2 pears (cored and chopped), a pinch of allspice, and preferred liquid (water, expressed human milk, or infant formula)

Instructions: Steam the chopped carrots and pears together using the steaming guide on page 113. Transfer the steamed carrots and pears to a blender and blend until it's smooth, adding your preferred liquid until you reach your desired consistency. For storage, thawing, and food safety tips, see page 114.

Baby-Led Weaning Feeding Approach

Now, let's explore the other feeding method that has gained popularity in the United States due to its hands-on approach and potential developmental benefits. As you learned in the brief history lesson from the previous section, the baby-led weaning (BLW) feeding method isn't anything new. It's more of a return to what once was. With this method, you feed your baby finger foods from the start rather than altering the texture into a pureed form. In addition, you allow them to independently self-feed, under your supervision, of course, rather than spoon-feeding them. This puts your baby in the driver's seat and allows for greater exploration of foods at mealtime.

The idea behind this method is that once a baby is developmentally ready for the introduction of solids, they intuitively understand their bodies, know when they are hungry or full, and can get food into their mouths without assistance. This approach can empower your baby, giving them autonomy over their eating experience and fostering a sense of curiosity and exploration.

According to the BLISS (Baby-Led Introduction to SolidS) study,[90] a large research study that analyzed health outcomes of baby-led weaning:

★ By six to seven months of age, most infants can chew, sit unsupported, and bring food to their mouths.

★ A gradual transition from purees to finger foods may not be necessary.

★ Introducing complementary solids utilizing the BLW approach may have beneficial effects on their development and eating habits, including a positive relationship with food and a lower risk of obesity, as this method allows babies to self-regulate their intakes.

90 Daniels, Lisa, Anne-Louise M. Heath, Sheila M. Williams, Sonya L. Cameron, Elizabeth A. Fleming, Barry J. Taylor, Ben J. Wheeler, Rosalind S. Gibson, and Rachael W. Taylor. 2015. "Baby-Led Introduction to SolidS (BLISS) Study: A Randomised Controlled Trial of a Baby-Led Approach to Complementary Feeding." **BMC Pediatrics** 15 (1). https://doi.org/10.1186/s12887-015-0491-8.

Some parents hesitate to try the BLW method out of fear of choking hazards and doubts concerning a baby's ability to chew without teeth. These fears are natural, and doing your own research and consulting with a professional can help build your confidence.

★ Regarding choking, an article published in the American Academy of Pediatrics concluded[91] that infants following a modified version of baby-led weaning did not choke more than babies following traditional feeding approaches.

★ Regarding chewing, rest assured that infants do not need teeth to eat solid food. Their gums are tough enough to chew a variety of textures.

Admittedly, for our first son, my husband was terrified by the idea of BLW, and I also had reservations. However, with education and guidance from our pediatrician, we are more informed this time around, so we can implement BLW for our second baby. Consulting professionals or seeking advice from experienced parents can help assuage these fears and provide practical tips.

It can be reassuring to know some BLW guidelines to follow before you begin:

1. **Only begin when they are developmentally ready.** They should be able to hold their head up well, sit upright with minimal support, pick up objects while seated and easily bring them to the mouth, and exhibit signs of being interested in food (such as watching what you eat or reaching for your food).

2. **Seat your baby in a fully upright highchair.** This ensures that your baby is in a safe and stable position to handle food themselves. Adjust the straps and footrest as needed.

3. **Know how to cut foods appropriately.** Cut foods should be big enough that it would be difficult to fit the entire thing into their mouths. Generally, finger foods should be roughly the size of your finger and easy enough to pick up and hold on to. It's also important to choose foods that are soft enough for your baby to handle without teeth but still provide resistance for their gums.

4. **Supervise your baby at all times.** Do not leave them alone while they are eating.

5. **Model healthful eating behaviors.** Shared mealtimes are a great opportunity for your baby to learn healthy eating habits, so it can be helpful to dine with them. Remember, your baby learns by watching you, so your approach to food can greatly influence theirs.

91 Fangupo, Louise J., Anne-Louise M. Heath, Sheila M. Williams, Liz W. Erickson Williams, Brittany J. Morison, Elizabeth A. Fleming, Barry J. Taylor, Benjamin J. Wheeler, and Rachael W. Taylor. 2016. "A Baby-Led Approach to Eating Solids and Risk of Choking." **Pediatrics** 138 (4). https://doi.org/10.1542/peds.2016-0772.

6. **Offer a variety of foods.** Don't limit your baby to only fruits and vegetables. Provide iron-rich foods like quinoa and mashed beans, and energy-rich foods like toast strips with hummus or seed butters smeared on top. Serve iron-rich foods with vitamin C–rich fruits and vegetables because vitamin C helps boost iron absorption.

7. **Remove distractions.** Create a pleasant eating environment, make it fun, and stay present!

8. **Understand the difference between gagging and choking.** True choking is when the airway is obstructed. Signs of choking include difficulty breathing, inability to cry, a look of terror, skin tugging at the chest, high-pitched sounds, and skin color changes. Gagging, however, is a protective reflex that causes the contraction of the back of the throat and protects your baby from choking.

9. **Learn infant CPR.** It's one of the most important skills you can learn to help protect your baby.

10. **Check your emotions.** Your baby is new to the world of food, and it would be unfair to expect them to eat everything you put in front of them. Refrain from pressuring your baby. Your job is to offer safe, healthy foods for your baby to eat. Your baby's job is to decide if and how much of it they will eat.

Foods to Avoid

Earlier, Dr. Smith mentioned that the CDC website has a helpful list of foods that should be avoided while implementing the baby-led weaning approach. Below are the potential choking hazards the CDC listed,[92] both vegan and non-vegan. I have included both since non-vegan foods can also technically be veganized (e.g., vegan cheese, vegan hot dogs, vegan sausage, vegan meat replacements, and I've even been to restaurants that serve vegan wings with "bones" inside made from plants).

While this list might seem overwhelming, remember that with proper preparation and supervision, introducing solids can be a safe and enjoyable experience.

Choking Hazards: Fruits/Vegetables

- ★ Cooked or raw whole corn kernels
- ★ Uncut cherry or grape tomatoes
- ★ Pieces of hard raw vegetables or fruit, such as raw carrots or apples
- ★ Whole pieces of canned fruit
- ★ Uncut grapes, berries, cherries, or melon balls
- ★ Uncooked dried vegetables or fruit, such as raisins

---

92 CDC. 2020. "Choking Hazards." Centers for Disease Control and Prevention. March 30, 2020. https://www.cdc.gov/nutrition/InfantandToddlerNutrition/foods-and-drinks/choking-hazards.html.

Choking Hazards: Proteins

- ★ Whole or chopped nuts and seeds
- ★ Chunks or spoonfuls of nut and seed butters, such as peanut butter
- ★ Tough or large chunks of meat
- ★ Hot dogs, meat sticks, or sausages
- ★ Large chunks of cheese, especially string cheese
- ★ Bones in meat or fish
- ★ Whole beans

Choking Hazards: Grain Products

- ★ Cookies or granola bars
- ★ Potato or corn chips, pretzels, popcorn, or similar snack foods
- ★ Crackers or breads with seeds, nut pieces, or whole grain kernels
- ★ Whole grain kernels of cooked barley, wheat, or other grains
- ★ Plain wheat germ

Choking Hazards: Sweetened Foods

- ★ Round or hard candy, jelly beans, caramels, gum drops, or gummy candies
- ★ Chewy fruit snacks
- ★ Chewing gum
- ★ Marshmallows

There are several characteristics that increase the risk of choking. The more small, round, hard, and slippery a food is, the greater the choking risk. Prepare food appropriately to counteract these characteristics. For example, small and round food like blueberries can be quartered. Hard fruits and vegetables can be steamed until soft. Slippery foods like kiwi can be coated to add texture—roll it in ground flax, ground seeds, coconut flakes, etc., to make it easier to grip.

Foods to Try

Now that you have an idea of what types of food to avoid, let's look at ten BLW food ideas to get you started. Every baby is unique, and part of the fun of baby-led weaning is discovering your child's personal tastes and preferences. Don't be afraid to get creative and mix things up!

Smashed Bean Toast

Benefits: Beans are legumes full of protein, zinc, iron, and an array of other vital nutrients for a growing infant.

Preparation: If using dry beans, cook them thoroughly first. If using canned beans, drain and rinse them. Mash or puree the beans, squeeze with lemon juice (the vitamin C will aid in iron absorption), sprinkle on your favorite seasoning, and spread it on an appropriately sliced piece of toast.

Sliced Avocado

Benefits: Avocado is a beloved fruit that serves as an excellent source of healthy fats, an energy-dense nutrient critical to the growth of an infant's brain, eyes, and other vital organs.

Preparation: Make sure the avocado is ripe and soft. Slice it into a thick strip, squeeze a little lime juice onto it, sprinkle it with a spice of your choice, dip it into hemp hearts or ground flax for a better grip, and offer it to your baby.

Cooked Sweet Potato

Benefits: Sweet potatoes are delicious vegetables exceptionally high in beta-carotene—a nutrient that the body converts into vitamin A, which supports a baby's eyesight, skin health, and immune system.

Preparation: Peel and cut the sweet potato into finger-length strips. Cook the sweet potato until soft by roasting it in the oven or steaming it on the stovetop. Season it with your herb of choice and serve it to your baby.

Tofu

Benefits: Tofu is strong but soft and packed with protein, iron, zinc, and healthy fats. It is also one of the best plant-based sources of choline, an essential nutrient for brain development and liver function. Tofu is made of soybeans, a common allergen, so keep that in mind when introducing.

Preparation: Whip up some flavorful Speedy Tofu Scramble (page 176) without any added salt or slice some firm tofu into thick strips and bake it in the oven with some extra-virgin olive oil and seasoning of choice.

Sliced Banana

Benefits: Bananas are packed with energizing carbohydrates and other vital nutrients like potassium, folate, vitamin B6, and antioxidants.

Preparation: Bananas are easy to hold and require minimal effort to serve. Peel it, slice it in half, and present it to your baby. You can even roll it in ground flax for a nutrient boost and better grip.

Roasted Carrots

Benefits: Carrots are another vitamin A powerhouse, like sweet potatoes. Additionally they contain fiber to aid bowel movements and vitamin K, which helps with blood clotting.

As you may have learned during pregnancy, newborns have little vitamin K in their bodies at birth and there is little of it in human milk. This is why health experts strongly recommend[93] that parents give permission to their medical providers to give their babies vitamin K injections at birth. This helps to protect them from severe bleeding until around six months, when infants are typically introduced to solids and can eat vitamin K-containing foods, like carrots, broccoli, and pumpkin.

Preparation: Raw, uncooked carrots are a choking hazard, so prepare them appropriately. Start by peeling your carrots, drizzling them with a little olive oil and season them with your herb of choice. Then, roast them until they are completely soft and can be easily pierced with a fork. Lastly, cut one in half lengthwise and offer it to your baby.

Penne Pasta

Benefits: Pasta can be packed with nutrients, particularly legume-based ones, like chickpea, lentil, and black bean pasta. Thick, textured pastas are great as a first food for babies, especially penne pasta, which has ridges that make it easier for your baby to grip and self-feed.

Preparation: Cook your pasta according to the instructions on the box and experiment with adding flavors and sauces. Some jarred pasta sauces have added sugar and salt, so try making your own. Check out my Sneaky Roasted Veggie Pasta Sauce recipe (page 138) and omit the salt.

Tempeh Strips

Benefits: Tempeh is a high-protein legume made from fermented soybeans. Fermented foods contain probiotic microorganisms that support a baby's gut health. You can help build a child's immunity by fueling the good bacteria in their gut with probiotic foods like tempeh, sauerkraut, vegan kimchi, dairy-free yogurts labeled as having "live and active cultures," and miso.

Preparation: Tempeh's firm texture poses a choking hazard if not prepared appropriately for an infant. To soften it, you will need to cook it well. Tempeh easily

93 CDC. 2019. "Protect Your Baby from Bleeds." Centers for Disease Control and Prevention. December 26, 2019. https://www.cdc.gov/ncbddd/vitamink/vitamin-k-fact-sheet-general.html.

absorbs flavors, so first start out by cutting it into thick strips and marinating it in a savory or sweet sauce of your choice—like lime juice or coconut milk. Then, heat some extra-virgin olive oil in a pan, add the marinated tempeh, sprinkle with any additional spices you like, and sauté it until softened.

Sautéed Cinnamon Apples

Benefits: Apples offer a variety of nutrients that help a growing infant thrive, including fiber, antioxidants, vitamin C, and vitamin B6. This naturally sweet fruit can even be blended with water to make applesauce, which can be used as a nutritious replacement for processed sugar in recipes.

Preparation: Raw apple is a choking hazard, so prepare it in a safe way. Core and chop your apple into thick slices. Heat some extra-virgin olive oil in a pan, pour the apple slices in, and sprinkle them with cinnamon (Ceylon if possible). Cook the apples until they are soft enough to be pierced with a fork.

Oat Pancakes

Benefits: Oats are a nutritious grain packed with energy-providing carbohydrates. They also contain zinc, which plays an important role in immune functioning, DNA synthesis, and your baby's senses of smell and taste. Oatmeal also offers a safer alternative to baby rice cereals. Rice and rice products contain higher levels of arsenic,[94] a known human carcinogen, than other grains.

Preparation: Try my scrumptious Banana Oat Pancakes recipe (page 186) and omit the maple syrup. Slice the pancake into finger-width slices to allow for your baby to pick it up more easily. For a boost of healthy fats, top it with a thin layer of unsweetened creamy seed or nut butter and then sprinkle hemp seeds on top.

> Remember, baby-led weaning is about fostering independence and exploration in your baby. It's an exciting journey, and armed with these guidelines and tips, you can introduce a variety of foods safely and confidently.

94 Davis, Matthew A., Antonio J. Signes-Pastor, Maria Argos, Francis Slaughter, Claire Pendergrast, Tracy Punshon, Anala Gossai, Habibul Ahsan, and Margaret R. Karagas. 2017. "Assessment of Human Dietary Exposure to Arsenic through Rice." **Science of the Total Environment** 586 (May): 1237–44. https://doi.org/10.1016/j.scitotenv.2017.02.119.

Choose What Works for Your Family

The milestone of introducing solids can bring out strong emotions in parents. It's important not to get caught up in the heated debates about which method is better. This phase should bring more joy than stress, so do what you are comfortable with and allow your baby to enjoy the adventure. No matter which route you go, know that both are perfectly fine and safe, as long as you talk to your pediatrician and follow recommended safety precautions. Both the traditional feeding methods and the baby-led weaning method come with their own sets of comforts, fears, pros, and cons, and you can find support for either route. I hope you gained helpful insights from this chapter to feel empowered in your ability to make an informed decision. This is a whole new world for both you and your baby. Are you ready to embark on this feeding journey? What's the first food you're excited to introduce to your baby?

07

SUPERCHARGED SAUCES, TOPPINGS, AND DIPS

SWEET CHIA FRUIT JAM

Ages: 6 months+ (makes 1 baby jar)

Ingredients:

1 cup (150 g) frozen fruit of choice (or fresh fruit)

½ tablespoon black or white chia seeds

Optional: 1 teaspoon maple syrup (omit for infants)

Equipment:

Small saucepan

Cooking spoon

Heat-safe glass jar (for storage)

Optional: Potato masher

This recipe won't have all the sugar or preservatives of store-bought jams and jellies. It's fresh, sweet, and can be used in many ways! Toast, pancakes, waffles, thumbprint cookies, you name it. The chia seeds thicken the jam and add protein and other superstar nutrients. This is a weekly staple in our home.

Health highlights: Chia seeds are packed with omega-3 ALA for a dose of heart-healthy fats, antioxidants to help protect against cellular damage, and fiber to aid digestion. Fruit is an excellent source of vitamin C that helps kids form and repair red blood cells, bones, and tissues.

INSTRUCTIONS:

1. Pour the fruit into a small saucepan over low heat. Cook it uncovered while stirring occasionally until the fruit breaks down and releases its juices.

2. Mash the fruit with a spoon or potato masher until you reach your desired consistency—it can be as smooth or chunky as you want!

3. Once mashed, remove the pot from the heat and stir in the chia seeds and optional maple syrup until well combined.

4. Transfer it to a heat-safe glass jar and allow it to cool completely in the refrigerator. It will thicken as it cools, and the chia seeds will expand.

Tip: This recipe works for many juicy fruits. Try it with raspberries, strawberries, blackberries, blueberries, peaches, or mango!

EVERYDAY BASIL PESTO

Ages: 6 months+ (makes 1 baby jar)

Ingredients:

1 cup (20 g) fresh basil leaves

1 tablespoon fortified nutritional yeast seasoning

juice of half a lemon (or 1½ tablespoons of lemon juice)

¼ cup (28 g) walnuts (or make it nut-free: see note below)

1 tablespoon shelled hemp seeds

1 garlic clove, peeled

salt to taste (omit for infants)

¼ cup (59 mL) extra-virgin olive oil

Nut-free option: Replace walnuts with pumpkin seeds or sunflower seeds

Equipment:

Food processor or blender

Bring a burst of fresh flavor to your little one's meals with this Everyday Basil Pesto! Packed with the vibrant goodness of basil, the heartiness of walnuts, and the zesty tang of lemon, this versatile pesto is perfect for perking up pasta, sandwiches, and more. With an easy-to-make recipe and a nut-free option, you'll find yourself turning to this delightful condiment time and time again.

Health highlights: Walnuts and shelled hemp seeds offer omega-3 ALA for a dose of heart-healthy fats, as well as protein for growth and muscle-building. Fortified nutritional yeast is packed with energy-boosting B vitamins. Basil is a source of vitamin K, a nutrient that plays a vital role in blood clotting.

INSTRUCTIONS:

1. Add the basil leaves, nutritional yeast seasoning, lemon juice, walnuts (or a nut-free alternative), shelled hemp seeds, garlic, and salt to a food processor or blender. Close the lid and begin to process.

2. Use the small opening at the top of your device to slowly pour in the olive oil. Process it until smooth. Taste it and adjust the seasonings, if desired. Store it in the fridge in an airtight container.

PAPRIKA-DIJON AIOLI

Ages: 6 months+ (makes ¼ cup)

This mayo-free aioli uses dairy-free yogurt as the star creamy ingredient! Use it as a topping in various dishes, including tacos, burgers, fries, and fritters. Beyond loves it drizzled on Saucy Chickpea Balls (page 206).

Health highlights: Store-bought dairy-free yogurt is often fortified with probiotics that help your child maintain a healthy gut microbiome. Lemon juice supplies vitamin C, which powers your baby's immune system.

Ingredients:

¼ cup (61 g) plain dairy-free yogurt of choice, unsweetened

1 tablespoon vegan Dijon mustard

1 tablespoon lemon juice

1 teaspoon garlic powder

1 teaspoon ground paprika

1 teaspoon Italian seasoning

Equipment:

Small bowl

Spoon

INSTRUCTIONS:

1. Place all the ingredients into a small bowl and mix.
2. Taste it and adjust the seasonings, if needed. Store the sauce in an airtight container in your refrigerator.

BABY-FRIENDLY GUACAMOLE

Ages: 6 months+ (makes 1 large family-sized serving)

Ingredients:

2 avocados, peeled and pitted

1 garlic clove, peeled and minced

Juice of 1 lime (or 2 tablespoons of lime juice)

¼ cup (4 g) cilantro, finely chopped

Salt to taste (**Tip:** omit for infants and salt your portion separately)

Optional: Think your child will enjoy some extra flavor and texture? Dice half a small tomato and chop ¼ a small red onion for older infants and toddlers.

Equipment:

Small mixing bowl

Potato masher or fork

While I typically love using chopped onions and tomatoes for classic guacamole, I want to share a straightforward, flavorful baby-friendly guac you can quickly whip up on busy days. This recipe is a little less chunky and smoother for your little one.

 Health highlights: Hello, healthy fats! Avocado is a nutritious and delicious concentrated source of brain-supporting fat, as well as fiber for digestive health, vitamin K to help with blood clotting, and vitamin E for a healthy immune system.

INSTRUCTIONS:

1. Place the avocado flesh into your bowl and mash it with a potato masher or fork to an appropriate consistency for your child.

2. Season the mashed avocado with minced garlic, lime juice, cilantro, and salt. If desired, add the optional ingredients as well. Stir the mixture until combined.

Tip: Serve this on its own, with chips, on toasted bread, or in tacos and burritos!

MANGO SALSA

Ages: 6–12 months with modifications, 12 months+ as is
(makes 1 large family-sized serving)

This vibrant mix of sweet mango, tangy onion, lime, earthy avocado, flavorful garlic, and tart tomatoes makes this mango salsa a family fave! The rainbow of colors creates the perfect opportunity to engage your child in conversation about the food. Ask questions like, "What colors do you see?" or "How many colors can you find?" to make it an interactive experience.

 Health highlights: Between the mango, avocado, tomato, onions, and lime juice, this salsa packs a heavy vitamin C punch for immune health and iron absorption.

Ingredients:

1 mango, peeled, pitted, and diced

1 large avocado, peeled, pitted, and diced

1 large tomato, diced

⅓ large red onion, finely diced

1 garlic clove, peeled and minced

1 tablespoon lime juice

salt to taste (**Tip:** omit for infants and salt your portion separately)

Equipment:

Small mixing bowl

Spoon

INSTRUCTIONS:

1. Combine all the ingredients in a small mixing bowl and mix well.
2. Taste it and adjust the seasonings, if needed. Serve this immediately—it tastes amazing fresh!

Tips:

★ **Storage:** Store any leftovers in an airtight container for up to three days. Avocado browns quickly, so I prefer to finish this within a few days.

★ **Serving ideas:** Add it to tacos, use it as a dip for chips, or try serving it to your little one as a salad in a baby bowl!

★ **Infant modification:** Puree it to an appropriate consistency for six- to twelve-month-olds.

GARLIC HUMMUS

Ages: 6 months+ (makes 1 large family-sized serving)

Ingredients:

1 (15.5 oz/439 g) can garbanzo beans (also called chickpeas), drained and rinsed

¼ cup (60 g) tahini

1–2 garlic cloves, peeled and roughly chopped

juice of half a lemon (or 1½ tablespoons of lemon juice)

3 tablespoons extra-virgin olive oil

½ teaspoon ground cumin

½ teaspoon mild chili powder

3 tablespoons water

salt to taste (**Tip:** omit for infants and salt your portion separately)

Optional garnish: Pinch of chili powder or paprika, dried parsley, or chives

Equipment:

Food processor or high-speed blender

There is nothing quite like making your own rich and creamy hummus. This recipe has some fun seasonings to help expand your little one's palate. As Dr. Smith said in our Q&A in Chapter 6, **"Babies can enjoy a wide range of herbs and spices in their food."** So, don't be shy! Give it a try.

 Health highlights: Chickpeas and tahini are both excellent sources of brain-supporting healthy fats, muscle-building protein, and iron for neurological development. The vitamin C in the lemon juice will help your baby's body absorb the iron from the chickpeas and tahini.

INSTRUCTIONS:

1. Combine all the ingredients, except the optional garnishes, in a food processor or high-speed blender and blitz until smooth and creamy. Add more water if needed.

2. Taste it and adjust the seasonings, if desired. We love garlic, so we use two garlic cloves, but depending on your child's preference, one might be enough.

3. Serve with one of the optional garnish options and store the hummus in an airtight container in the fridge.

Tip: Beyond's two favorite ways to eat hummus are slathered on pita bread for a nutritious snack or smeared on toasted sourdough bread for breakfast.

SNEAKY ROASTED VEGGIE PASTA SAUCE

Ages: 6 months+ (makes 1 large jar of pasta sauce)

Ingredients:

For Roasting

1 head of garlic, unpeeled, top sliced off

1 zucchini, roughly chopped into large chunks

1 bell pepper, any color, sliced in half

1 large onion, peeled, sliced in half

1 large tomato, sliced in half

2 carrots, sliced in half

salt to taste (omit for infants, if desired)

extra-virgin olive oil, for baking sheet and drizzling

For Sauce

juice of half a lemon (or 1½ tablespoons of lemon juice)

½ cup (118 mL) fortified dairy-free milk of choice, unsweetened (or canned coconut milk)

½ cup (30 g) fortified nutritional yeast seasoning

1 tablespoon shelled hemp seeds

1 teaspoon onion powder

1 teaspoon garlic powder

1 teaspoon Italian seasoning

pinch of black pepper

salt to taste (**Tip:** omit for infants and salt your portion separately)

Equipment:

Baking sheet

High-speed blender

I know, I know. The word **sneaky** sounds deceptive, but hear me out. You're not **hiding** veggies. You're finding tasty, creative ways to **incorporate** them into your dishes. My toddler is old enough to help me prep and he can watch everything that goes into his pasta sauce. There's no deception, and there's no hiding. Just transparent, nutrient-dense results that the whole family can get down with!

Health highlights: This pasta sauce is a powerhouse of fruits and vegetables, offering a super source of vitamin C, which helps kids form and repair red blood cells, bones, and tissues. Fortified nutritional yeast is a complete protein source packed with energy-boosting B vitamins. Shelled hemp seeds provide muscle-building protein and heart-healthy omega-3 ALA.

INSTRUCTIONS:

1. Preheat the oven to 400°F (200°C). Lightly grease your baking sheet with oil and place the veggies (listed under "**For Roasting**") onto the sheet. Drizzle with oil and add a pinch of salt.

2. Place it in the oven for 35 minutes until the veggies are roasted.

3. Remove it from the oven. Squeeze out the garlic cloves and discard the skin.

4. Add all the roasted veggies, any leftover juices from the tray, and all the sauce ingredients (listed under "**For Sauce**") to a blender and blend until smooth. Pour it over your favorite pasta and serve it to the whole family!

PASTA
SAUCE

WHITE BEAN WONDER DIP

Ages: 6 months+ (makes 1 large family-sized serving)

Ingredients:

1 tablespoon extra-virgin olive oil, for cooking

1 garlic clove, peeled and minced

1 teaspoon ground sage

1 teaspoon ground rosemary

1 teaspoon onion powder

1 (15 oz/425 g) can cannellini beans, drained and rinsed (or any canned white beans)

1 tablespoon lemon juice

salt to taste (**Tip:** omit for infants and salt your portion separately)

pinch of black pepper

2 tablespoons water, if needed

Equipment:

Small pan

Food processor or high-speed blender

Sometimes, all you need is a fuss-free dip that you can whip up in no time and enjoy with friends and family. This White Bean Wonder Dip is exactly that—a laid-back, flavorful dip made with simple ingredients that's perfect for any occasion. Give it a try and see how this humble dip can become a go-to in your snack rotation!

 Health highlights: White beans are the superstar here, offering protein for growth support, zinc for metabolism and immune function, and iron for neurological development and blood health.

INSTRUCTIONS:

1. Heat 1 tablespoon of oil in a small pan over medium heat. Add the garlic, sage, rosemary, and onion powder. Cook the spices, stirring, until fragrant, for about a minute. Add the cannellini beans and stir until the spices evenly coat the beans. Cook for another 1 or 2 minutes and then remove the pan from the heat.

2. In a food processor or blender, pulse the seasoned cannellini beans, lemon juice, salt, and black pepper until combined. Add the water only if needed and process it until you have a wonderfully smooth, creamy dip.

Tips:

★ **Serving Ideas:** For infants, add some human milk or infant formula to thin it out and spread it on a thick piece of toasted bread. For toddlers, this is great with pita chips, crackers, and fresh crunchy veggies.

★ **No-cook method:** Cooking the canned beans and spices first is completely optional and only intended to optimize the flavor! You can skip the first step and add all the ingredients as is to the food processor or blender.

OOEY GOOEY MOZZARELLA CHEEZE

Ages: 9 months+ (makes 1 cup)

Say hello to your baby's new go-to vegan cheeze! Ready in under ten minutes, this Ooey Gooey Mozzarella Cheeze is stretchy, flavorful, and oh-so-easy to make. Many vegan cheeses have a nut base, but I created an allergy-friendly version that you can pack and take to nut-free daycares and schools. The star ingredient here is sunflower seed kernels! Use this cheeze on Cheezy Pizza Bagel Bites (page 156), make some nachos, whip up a grilled cheese sandwich, or use it as a dipping sauce for chips.

Ingredients:

½ cup (60 g) raw sunflower seed kernels (also called hulled sunflower seeds)

1 cup (237 mL) water

4 tablespoons tapioca flour (also called tapioca starch)

1 tablespoon fortified nutritional yeast seasoning

1 teaspoon apple cider vinegar

¼ teaspoon garlic powder

½ teaspoon lemon juice

salt to taste (omit for infants, if desired)

Equipment:

High-speed blender

Small saucepan

Whisk

Health highlights: Sunflower seeds are an excellent source of brain-supporting healthy fats, fiber for digestion, muscle-building protein, vitamin E for immune function, and iron for blood health. The vitamin C in lemon juice helps your baby's body absorb iron. Fortified nutritional yeast seasoning is packed with energy-boosting B vitamins, including vitamin B12, which is essential for brain development.

INSTRUCTIONS:

1. Add all the ingredients to a high-speed blender and blend until smooth. The mixture will be watery.

2. Pour the mixture into a small saucepan over medium heat and continually whisk for 3 to 5 minutes until it's thick and stretchy. **Note:** After a minute, it will start to thicken, and after about 3 minutes, it will get super stretchy. It is important to stir constantly.

3. Remove the saucepan from the heat and let it cool.

4. Taste it and adjust as needed. Serve it fresh or store it in a tightly sealed container in the refrigerator.

Tip: This mozzarella cheeze gets its stretchy texture from the tapioca starch. It is a key ingredient in this recipe, so please don't skip it!

RAINBOW COCONUT SUPER SPRINKLES

Ages: 6 months+ (makes 1 cup of sprinkles)

Ingredients:

Pink:

¼ teaspoon beetroot powder

2 tablespoons water

¼ cup (18 g) unsweetened
shredded coconut

Yellow:

¼ teaspoon ground
turmeric powder

2 tablespoons water

¼ cup (18 g) unsweetened
shredded coconut

Green:

¼ teaspoon green spirulina or
chlorella powder

2 tablespoons water

¼ cup (18 g) unsweetened
shredded coconut

Blue:

¼ teaspoon blue
spirulina powder

2 tablespoons water

¼ cup (18 g) unsweetened
shredded coconut

Equipment:

1 small mixing bowl

Spoon

Baking sheet lined with
reusable baking mat (or
parchment paper)

Add a pop of color and fun to your family treats with these vibrant Rainbow Coconut Super Sprinkles! Made with all-natural superfood ingredients, these homemade sprinkles are beautiful and a healthier alternative to store-bought ones. Perfect for topping cakes, brownies, or even smoothie bowls, these sprinkles will make any dessert stand out. So, unleash your creativity and brighten your child's day with these simple dye methods!

 Health highlights: Flip to page 89 in Chapter 5 for a breakdown of the harmful impacts of artificial food dyes. The dyes in this recipe utilize natural ingredients rich in vitamins and antioxidants that help protect your baby's cells from damage.

INSTRUCTIONS:

Step 1: Color Your Sprinkles

1. In a small bowl, mix 1 powder with 2 tablespoons of water.
2. Add the shredded coconut and stir to coat it fully with the color.
3. Add it to the prepared baking sheet in a single row and aim to keep all the colors separate.
4. Rinse out the small bowl and repeat steps 1–3 with the rest of the colors.

Step 2: Dry Your Sprinkles

1. Bake these at your oven's lowest temperature for an hour or leave the tray somewhere cool and dry overnight until the sprinkles have completely dried.
2. Store it in a sealed jar or airtight container for up to three months.

Infant tip: When introducing solids to an infant, finely shredded coconut can be used to add texture to slippery foods like mango, making it easier to grip.

08

SNACKS ARE MY SUPERPOWER

A Reflection on Marine Animals and Recreating Seafood Flavors

Growing up I remember a phase of being obsessed with tuna sandwiches. I didn't know how to cook back then, so it was an easy snack to prepare with a can of tuna, some mayo, and cracked black pepper. Of course, now I recognize tuna, and all fish, as sentient sea creatures who don't wish to be turned into sandwiches.

Sentience is the capacity of a being to experience feelings and sensations, which fish have, yet every year around the globe, fish are traded, caught, farmed, experimented on, and killed in the trillions. The welfare of fish is often neglected, and their sentience is rarely acknowledged. According to an in-depth study[95] on the evidence of fish sentience, while scientific knowledge of fish sentience is widely available, public attitudes toward fish and legislation do not reflect these facts. How society treats fish is often dependent on the type of fish in question. As an example, the study highlights how shark finning is viewed by Western societies as cruel and inhumane; however, commercial and leisurely fishing practices, such as allowing fish to die of suffocation when pulled out of the water, are regarded as acceptable and overlooked by society and legislators, despite it also being a cruel and inhumane practice.

Tuna is one example of commercially caught fish whose sentience is constantly disregarded—and they aren't the only ones affected when they are captured. Certain tuna fishing gear is also a cause of the bycatch and slow deaths of other species such as turtles, seabirds, sharks, and even dolphins—and ultimately contributes to the degradation of our sea friends' homes, disrupting the balance of marine ecosystems and impacting the future of our oceans.

If you grew up having a fondness for seafood, fear not, friends. There are ways to replicate those flavors to recreate similar culinary experiences for our kids. So what are some common ingredients that can help us emulate those aromas and flavor profiles?

★ Capers
★ Celery salt, celery seeds, or chopped celery
★ Dill
★ Lemon juice and zest
★ Mustard
★ Old Bay seasoning

★ Parsley
★ Seaweed flakes, such as dulse, kelp, or nori, provide a briny taste that can remind one of the sea, and you can find these at local health food stores and online.

---

95 Lambert, Helen, Amelia Cornish, Angie Elwin, and Neil D'Cruze. 2022. "A Kettle of Fish: A Review of the Scientific Literature for Evidence of Fish Sentience." **Animals** 12 (9): 1182. https://doi.org/10.3390/ani12091182.

While plant-based recreations might not be exactly like their original animal-based versions, they can still be delicious and satisfying.

Remember: All the animal-based foods we considered to be irresistibly mouthwatering growing up would have been utterly bland without the herbs, spices, and condiments that accompanied them. Most of the flavors in animal-based dishes come from plant-based seasonings! It's the **seasonings** we crave, **not the animal.**

CHICKPEA OF THE SEA "NOT TUNA" SALAD

Ages: 6 months+ (makes a large family-sized serving)

Ingredients:

1 (15.5 oz /439 g) can garbanzo beans (also called chickpeas), drained and rinsed

1 small celery stalk, minced

¼ large red onion, minced

2 tablespoons lemon juice

1 tablespoon tahini, unsalted (or vegan mayo or plain dairy-free yogurt)

1 tablespoon vegan Dijon mustard (or regular mustard)

½ teaspoon garlic powder

¼ teaspoon celery salt (**Tip:** omit for infants and salt your portion separately)

pinch of black pepper

Optional: 1 tablespoon capers

Equipment:

Medium mixing bowl

Fork or potato masher

Spoon

This is one of the first vegan baby recipes I shared on social media! Beyond was about thirteen months old when he first tried it. He smiled and clapped cheerfully with each bite. It's savory, tangy, and fluffy, and pairs flawlessly with crackers for a bit of kid-friendly crunch. As mentioned on the previous page, this is a veganized version of a childhood favorite, tuna salad. Tuna are sentient sea creatures who want to live as we do, so let's serve this beloved classic dish with hearty, nutritious chickpeas instead. Your child won't miss a thing because this recipe boasts a few flavors found in traditional seafood dishes, including zesty lemon, savory celery salt, and tangy capers, making this an oh-so-yummy plant-based recreation of the original dish.

Health highlights: Chickpeas and tahini are both magnificent sources of brain-supporting healthy fats, muscle-building protein, and iron for neurological development. The vitamin C in the lemon juice will help your baby's body absorb the iron from the chickpeas and tahini. Celery is packed with anti-inflammatory antioxidants that protect cells, blood vessels, and organs from oxidative damage.

INSTRUCTIONS:

1. Mash the chickpeas in a medium mixing bowl with a fork or potato masher until you reach your desired consistency.

2. Add the remaining ingredients and mix well.

3. Taste it! Does it need anything else? Adjust the seasonings to your child's preference. The optional capers I recommended offer a bold, briny zestiness to this dish. Consider including it for an added depth of flavor.

4. Serve it chilled or at room temperature. Store any leftovers in an airtight container in the refrigerator.

Serving ideas: Smear it onto a few crackers for a light snack or spread onto slices of bread to make a wholesome chickpea "not tuna" sandwich for lunch.

SMASHED AVOCADO CHICKPEA TOAST STICKS

Ages: 6 months+ (makes 3 toasts)

Ingredients:

3 slices of bread

1 (15.5 oz/439 g) can of garbanzo beans (also called chickpeas), drained and rinsed

1 small avocado, peeled and pitted

1 tablespoon lime juice

1 teaspoon ground cumin

salt to taste (omit for infants)

Optional: 1 tablespoon fortified nutritional yeast seasoning

Equipment:

Small mixing bowl

Fork

Toaster

Remember the PB3 Plate on page 73? This snack is a smashing combination of all the food categories you want to tap into for a balanced meal. Not only is it nutrient-dense, but it's also tasty! The lime and cumin add depth to the dish, offering earthy and warm flavors and an edge of tangy citrus.

Health highlights: Reflective of the PB3 Plate, this snack boasts protein-packed chickpeas from the "legumes, nuts, and seeds" category for growth and development, vitamin C–rich avocado from the "fruits and veggies" category for immune support (which also doubles as a rich source of healthy fat for brain health), and wholesome bread from the grains and starches category for healthy digestion. If you add fortified nutritional yeast seasoning to the mix, your baby will benefit from protein and energy-boosting B vitamins.

INSTRUCTIONS:

1. Toast 1 slice of bread.

2. In a small mixing bowl, add the chickpeas and avocado. Mash them together with a fork to a consistency appropriate for your child.

3. Add the remaining ingredients and mix.

4. Spread the mixture onto your toasted bread and slice it into strips wide enough for your little one to grab. Serve it immediately.

5. Store any extra avocado chickpea mixture in a tightly sealed container in the refrigerator for up to 3 days—or use it to make yourself an avocado chickpea sandwich with the other 2 bread slices, so you can eat together! This makes enough spread for at least 3 pieces of toast.

Note: Anytime you cut an avocado, the flesh will begin to brown once exposed to air, thanks to oxidation. It doesn't render the avocado inedible, but the taste may change. That's why I suggest eating these snacks the same day they are made for optimal enjoyment. The lime juice will help slow the browning, but feel free to squeeze a little extra on top if storing in the fridge.

ALMOND BUTTER BANANA BITES

Ages: 6–9 months with modifications, 9 months+ as is (makes 1 serving)

Ingredients:

1 banana, peeled

1–2 tablespoons almond butter (or peanut butter)

¼ teaspoon ground cinnamon (Ceylon if possible), ground nutmeg, or ground cardamom

½ teaspoon shelled hemp seeds

Make it nut-free: Use sunflower seed butter instead of almond butter.

Equipment:

Knife

This is one of the easiest snacks to whip up and it's a guaranteed hit every time with my toddler. If your little one is obsessed with bananas like Beyond is, you'll probably be making this often, so have fun with it! Tweak this recipe each time by switching up the sweet spice you choose to add. This is a convenient way to expose your kiddo to a variety of spices on a snack they love. Some sweet spices I enjoy experimenting with include Ceylon cinnamon, nutmeg, and cardamom.

Health highlights: Hemp seeds and almond butter provide omega-3 ALA for a dose of heart-healthy fats, iron for neurological development, and muscle-building protein. Hemp seeds are a complete protein, which means they have all the essential amino acids your baby needs. Bananas are excellent sources of essential nutrients like vitamin B6, vitamin C, and potassium, which work together to support brain development, iron absorption, and heart health.

INSTRUCTIONS:

1. Cut the banana into round slices.
2. Spread a bit of almond butter (or your preferred nut or seed butter) onto each banana slice.
3. Sprinkle on a sweet spice of your choice, followed by a dash of hemp seeds onto each slice. Since sliced bananas brown quickly, serve this immediately as a fresh, tasty treat. It's also a fantastic lunchbox-friendly snack! Use 2 slices at a time to make little banana sandwich bites to prevent the nut butter from messing up when you pack it.

Infant modification tip: For ages 6–9 months, cut the banana into lengthwise spheres instead of round slices. The nut or seed butter should be applied as a thin layer.

MAPLE ROASTED CHICKPEAS

Ages: 18 months+ (makes about 5 kid-sized snackable servings)

I made these as an airplane snack for Beyond's first vacation. If you want to know the secret to keeping a toddler happy on a plane ride, it's apparently having a boatload of delicious food to munch on. Once he took one bite, it was hard for him to stop. Whether serving these at home, on an airplane, or packing for school, these super snackable Maple Roasted Chickpeas offer a savory-sweet experience that will make your little one's taste buds dance with joy.

Health highlights: The main ingredient, chickpeas, is a nutrient-dense legume rich in protein for growth, fiber for digestion, and carbohydrates for energy. It also provides crucial nutrients such as folate, iron, vitamin B6, choline, and zinc, which collectively support your baby's brain health, metabolism, growth, and taste and smell perception.

Ingredients:

1 (15.5 oz /439 g) can garbanzo beans (also called chickpeas), drained and rinsed

1 tablespoon extra-virgin olive oil

1–2 tablespoons maple syrup

½ teaspoon ground cinnamon, Ceylon if possible

Optional: ¼ teaspoon ground cardamom

pinch of salt

Equipment:

Small mixing bowl

Spoon

Baking sheet

Reusable baking mat (or parchment paper)

INSTRUCTIONS:

1. Preheat the oven to 400°F (200°C) and line a baking sheet with a reusable baking mat or parchment paper.

2. Combine all the ingredients in a small mixing bowl and gently mix them until all the chickpeas are evenly coated. Get your kids involved too! They can help with this step of mixing the ingredients.

3. Spread out the seasoned chickpeas on your prepared baking sheet. Bake for 30 minutes until golden and crispy.

4. Remove it from the oven and allow it to cool completely before serving. Store any leftovers in a tightly sealed container and eat them within a few days.

Tip: These roasted chickpeas will lose their crunchy texture over time, so ideally serve them as a freshly baked tasty snack. They are great on their own or can be used as a hearty addition to a soup or salad.

BLUEBERRY COCONUT BLISS BALLS

Ages: 12 months+ (makes about 14)

Ingredients:

1 cup (180 g) pitted Medjool dates (about 10 dates)

1 cup (90 g) rolled oats

1 cup (80 g) unsweetened shredded coconut (and 2 tablespoons for garnish)

¼ cup (42 g) blueberries

2 tablespoons shelled hemp seeds (alternatives: chia seeds or ground flax seeds)

Optional: 1 teaspoon blue spirulina powder

Equipment:

Small bowl for soaking dates

Food processor

Cookie scoop (optional)

These are especially fun to make with toddlers. It creates a sensory experience for little ones that allows them to get their hands messy. The process is also simple enough for them to follow with the help of an adult. Beyond is fascinated by blue spirulina powder, so I always add it in. He calls it "the blue," and it adds a bright pop of color that even the bluest blueberries could never. The dessert-like dates combined with the bold taste of coconut offer a burst of naturally sweet, nutty flavors. So try this out with your little ones!

Health highlights: Dates are high in disease-fighting antioxidants and contain at least fifteen minerals, including bone-supporting phosphorus, calcium, and magnesium. Oats are loaded with energy-boosting carbohydrates, fiber for digestive health, zinc for immune health, and iron for red blood cell production. Blueberries have one of the highest antioxidant levels of all common fruits and vegetables, which can help protect your baby's cells from damage. Hemp seeds provide omega-3 ALA for a dose of heart-healthy fats.

INSTRUCTIONS:

1. Soak your dates in a bowl of water for 5 to 10 minutes to soften.

2. Place the dates in a food processor and pulse several times until the dates break into small bits.

3. Add the rest of the ingredients and pulse until the mixture has a crumbly texture. Do not go overboard here! You want to avoid it becoming pasty.

4. Use your hands or a cookie scoop to roll the dough into balls of your desired size. To garnish, roll each ball in shredded coconut until lightly covered.

5. Enjoy immediately or store in a tightly sealed container in the refrigerator.

CACAO PEANUT BUTTER PROTEIN BALLS

Ages: 12 months+ (makes about 14)

Cacao? Is that a typo? Surely she meant cocoa. While you can use cocoa powder for this recipe as an alternative, I enjoy raw cacao powder for its nutritional profile, as it contains more minerals and antioxidants. Cacao and cocoa come from the same tree but are processed differently. Cacao has more of an earthy flavor than cocoa and can take time to get accustomed to, so keep that in mind when deciding between them.

Health highlights: Dates and cacao powder are high in disease-fighting antioxidants. Oats are loaded with energy-boosting carbohydrates, fiber for digestive health, zinc for immune health, and iron for red blood cell production. Hemp seeds and peanut butter provide muscle-building protein and brain-supporting healthy fats.

Ingredients:

1 cup (180 g) pitted Medjool dates (about 10 dates)

¼ cup (60 g) peanut butter (or any nut butter of your choice)

½ cup (45 g) rolled oats

1 tablespoon shelled hemp seeds (or chia seeds or ground flax seeds)

3 tablespoons cacao powder (or unsweetened cocoa powder)

Make it peanut-free: Use sunflower seed butter instead of peanut butter

Equipment:

Small bowl for soaking dates

Food processor

Cookie scoop (optional)

INSTRUCTIONS:

1. Soak your dates in a bowl of water for 5 to 10 minutes.
2. Place the dates in a food processor and pulse several times until the dates break into small bits.
3. Add the rest of the ingredients and pulse until the mixture has a crumbly texture. Do not go overboard here! You want to avoid it turning into a paste.
4. Use your hands or a cookie scoop to roll the dough into balls of your desired size. If you want them to be less sticky, you can gently roll them into a little bit of cacao powder. They will slightly resemble powdered donuts.
5. Enjoy immediately or store in a tightly sealed container in the refrigerator.

Tip: If you want to make these extra fun, add chocolate chips!

CHEEZY PIZZA BAGEL BITES

Ages: 18 months+ (makes 6 slices)

Ingredients:

3 vegan mini bagels, sliced

6 tablespoons pizza sauce (or marinara or pasta sauce)

6 tablespoons store-bought vegan mozzarella shreds (or Ooey Gooey Mozzarella Cheeze on page 141)

1½ teaspoons fortified nutritional yeast seasoning

6 fresh basil leaves, chopped

Note: If you can't find mini bagels, use regular-sized ones and adjust the ingredient portions accordingly.

Equipment:

Baking sheet

Reusable baking mat (or parchment paper)

Spoon

The day will come when your little one gets introduced to the concept of pizza. Maybe it's at a kid's birthday party, or perhaps daycare. Best be prepared with a secret vegan pizza weapon you can whip out to get your kiddo to fall in love with mom and dad's version (or grandma, grandpa, auntie, uncle, caregiver, friend, teacher; whoever you are reading this, you wonderful person you). While I enjoy making my own vegan mozzarella cheese, I am presenting you with a simplified and speedy version of my recipe, because let's face it—when there's a pizza party you are rushing to get to, you need a no-fuss vegan pizza treat you can whip up quick, fast, and in a hurry. This is that!

PS: Between these pizza bagel bites and the flatbread recipe on page 204, you have options.

 Health highlights: Fortified nutritional yeast is packed with energy-boosting B vitamins, including vitamin B12. Basil is a source of vitamin K, a nutrient that plays a vital role in blood clotting, as well as beta-carotene that converts to vitamin A, which supports your baby's eye health.

INSTRUCTIONS:

1. Preheat the oven to 400°F (200°C) and line the baking sheet with a reusable baking mat (or parchment paper).

2. Place 6 mini bagel halves on the prepared baking sheet. Top each slice with 1 tablespoon of pizza sauce and 1 tablespoon of vegan mozzarella. Then sprinkle each slice with ¼ teaspoon of nutritional yeast.

3. Bake for 7 minutes or until the bagels are crispy. Remove the pan from the oven and garnish each slice with the chopped basil leaves.

Tip: Check the temperature of the pizza bagel bites before serving them to children, as the sauce and cheese can become hot.

SUN BUTTER JAM STARS

Ages: 9 months+ (makes 4–6 stars)

Saving the world is hard work, so give your super vegan kid a gold star for being the hero we all need. This is a versatile snack that can be adapted into different shapes for different occasions. For example, you could use a heart-shaped cookie cutter and strawberry chia jam to make sunflower butter jam **hearts** for Valentine's Day!

Health highlights: Sunflower seed butter and hemp seeds provide muscle-building protein, omega-3 ALA for a dose of heart-healthy fats, and iron for neurological development. The mango chia jam is an excellent source of vitamin C that will help your baby absorb iron. Bread offers energy-boosting carbohydrates and fiber for digestive health.

Ingredients:

2 slices of bread

2 tablespoons sunflower seed butter (or any nut or seed butter of your choice)

2 tablespoons mango chia jam (page 131)

1 tablespoon shelled hemp seeds

Note: If you don't have time to make mango chia jam, grab any golden-colored jam from the store. Mango, apricot, or peach jam would all work.

Equipment:

Toaster

Star cookie cutter

Knife or spoon

INSTRUCTIONS:

1. Toast your bread slices.
2. Spread the sunflower seed butter on both slices of bread. Spread the mango chia jam on top. Sprinkle them with hemp hearts.
3. Use a star-shaped cookie cutter to cut out star shapes in each slice. How many stars you make will depend on how big your bread slices and star cutters are.

Tip: To prevent food waste, I eat the leftover pieces instead of discarding them.

GRANOLA APPLE DONUT SLICES

Ages: 12 months+ (makes about 6 slices)

Ingredients:

1 red or green apple

peanut butter (or any nut butter of your choice), amount is your preference

granola, amount is your preference

Make it peanut-free: Use sunflower seed butter instead of peanut butter

Note: If you don't have granola, use any crunchy topping concoction of your choice. For example, hemp seeds, nuts, cranberries, and raisins.

Equipment:

Knife

Optional: mini round cookie cutter

Cloth towel or paper towel

These granola apple donut slices are a fun, healthy, and convenient snack option for kids. You can get creative with these because the topping combos are endless. Better yet—get your little ones involved, because they will certainly enjoy finding ingenious ways to experiment with this one. See "alternative topping ideas" at the end of the recipe for some creative ideas!

 Health Highlights: Peanut butter provides muscle-building protein, brain-supporting healthy fats, and iron for neurological development. Apples offer fiber for digestive health and vitamin C to help absorb iron.

INSTRUCTIONS:

1. Cut the apple horizontally into round slices for your child.

2. Cut a hole in the center of each slice to turn it into a donut. Use your knife or a mini round-shaped cookie cutter small enough to do the job, if you have one.

3. Use a cloth towel or paper towel to blot any excess moisture off of the apple slices. This will help the spread go on smoothly.

4. Spread the peanut butter onto each slice and sprinkle them with granola on top. If involving your kids, put a variety of spreads and toppings in small bowls and have them spoon their desired combinations on their apple donuts.

Storage: While these are best served fresh, you can store them in an airtight container in the refrigerator for up to 2 days. They may start browning, but that is okay. They are still edible, and the toppings will hide the browning.

Alternative Topping Ideas:

- ★ Vegan frosting and Coconut Rainbow Super Sprinkles (page 143)
- ★ Hazelnut spread and coconut shreds
- ★ Chocolate sunflower seed butter and blueberries
- ★ Dairy-free vanilla yogurt and vegan chocolate chips
- ★ Vanilla cinnamon sunflower seed butter and raspberries
- ★ Vegan cream cheese and toasted poppy seeds for a savory twist

CARROT FRIES AND LEMON DILL CHIVE DIP

Ages: 9 months+ (makes 2 kid servings)

Ingredients:

Carrot Fries:

3 large carrots, washed and peeled

½ tablespoon extra-virgin olive oil or avocado oil

1 teaspoon fresh parsley, chopped (or dried parsley)

¼ teaspoon garlic powder

pinch of black pepper

salt to taste (omit for infants)

Lemon Dill Chive Dip:

3 tablespoons plain dairy-free yogurt of choice, unsweetened

¼ teaspoon lemon juice

¼ teaspoon fresh or dried chives

¼ teaspoon fresh or dried dill

⅛ teaspoon garlic powder

salt to taste (omit for infants, if desired)

Equipment:

Knife

Medium mixing bowl

Small bowl

Baking sheet

Reusable baking mat (or parchment paper)

Spoon

These carrot fries offer a more nutrient-dense alternative to traditional fast-food fries. The zesty dip complements the fries to enhance the overall flavor. These are great alone as a healthy snack or they can contribute to a larger well-balanced meal, alongside other nutritious foods. I love serving these with Refried Bean Burritos (page 218) and Lentil Sloppy Joes (page 224).

Health highlights: Carrots are loaded with fiber for digestive health, vitamin B6 for immune health, and carotenoids that convert to vitamin A in the body to support your baby's vision. Store-bought dairy-free yogurt is often fortified with probiotics that help your child maintain a healthy gut microbiome.

INSTRUCTIONS:

1. Preheat the oven to 400°F (200°C) and line the baking sheet with a reusable baking mat (or parchment paper).

2. Cut the carrots in half lengthwise, and then cut each piece in half widthwise. Then, cut each into roughly ¼-inch sticks. Place them into a medium mixing bowl. Add the oil, parsley, garlic powder, black pepper, and salt. Toss to combine.

3. Place the seasoned carrot slices on the prepared baking sheet. Bake for 20 minutes, flipping part way through (15 minutes on one side, 5 minutes on the other). Keep an eye on them to prevent burning.

4. Prepare the dip while the carrot fries are baking: Add all the dip ingredients in a small bowl and stir together with a spoon. Refrigerate until ready to use.

5. Remove your fries from the oven and allow them to cool. Serve fresh with the dip! Store these in an airtight container in the refrigerator. Reheat them in an oven or air fryer.

Tip: Use any leftover dip for dunking other snackable foods—like fresh veggies!

SWEET POTATO FRIES

Ages: 9 months+ (makes 2 servings)

Ingredients:

1 medium sweet potato

½ tablespoon extra-virgin olive oil or avocado oil

¼ teaspoon garlic powder

⅛ teaspoon paprika

salt to taste (omit for infants, if desired)

Equipment:

Cutting board

Knife

Medium bowl

Baking sheet (if using an oven)

Optional: air fryer (as an alternative to using an oven)

Okay, what kid **doesn't** love fries? Growing up, it's the thing I looked forward to the most when my parents took me to fast-food restaurants. Then, one sweet day, I grew up and learned I could make healthier, tastier fries from the comfort of my home. These flavorful fries will expand your baby's palate more than overly salted fast-food fries. Strongly consider using an air fryer for better consistency and presentation, as it is easy to burn sweet potato fries in an oven.

Health highlights: Sweet potatoes are a healthy choice for fries. They contain fiber to aid in digestion and high amounts of beta-carotene that convert to vitamin A, which supports your baby's eye and skin health.

INSTRUCTIONS:

Option 1: If using an oven

1. Preheat the oven to 425°F (220°C) and lightly grease your baking sheet with oil or line with parchment paper.
2. Cut the ends off the sweet potatoes.
3. Cut the sweet potato in half horizontally. Stand half up on the cutting board and slice it into several pieces vertically. Then slice those pieces into thin uniform fry shapes. Repeat for the other half and for the other sweet potato.
4. Place the sweet potato slices in a bowl and toss them with oil. Then, add garlic powder, paprika, and salt. Use your hands to mix everything.
5. Place the fries on your baking sheet and space them out. Do not overcrowd them to prevent burning. Bake the fries on the top rack of your oven for 15 minutes. Flip the fries over and bake for another 10 minutes. Monitor

the fries to make sure they don't burn. They can quickly go from "just right" to burnt if you leave them in the oven too long.

6. Remove them from the oven and let them cool. Taste and adjust the seasonings, if needed.

Option 2: If using an air fryer (highly recommended for ease)

1. Follow steps 2–4.
2. Place them in an air fryer and take care not to overcrowd them.
3. Bake them at 400°F (200°C) for about 15 minutes. Check on them halfway through to ensure they are cooking evenly. Move them around if necessary.

Storage: Keep these in an airtight container in your refrigerator. Reheat them in an air fryer or oven for optimal taste and texture.

Tip: Whether you peel the sweet potato skin or leave it on is your personal preference. I leave the skin on to retain more fiber, nutrients, and antioxidants. Most fiber is concentrated in the skin. Just be sure to wash it thoroughly!

CINNAMON ROASTED SWEET POTATO BITES

Ages: 9 months+ (makes 6 kid snackable servings)

Ingredients:

2 medium sweet potatoes

1 tablespoon extra-virgin olive oil

1 tablespoon ground cinnamon, Ceylon if possible

Optional: 1 tablespoon maple syrup, for extra sweetness

Equipment:

Knife

Large mixing bowl

Baking sheet

Beyond went on his first trip a couple of months before his second birthday. One of the best tips I have for keeping a toddler calm and occupied on a plane ride is to arm yourself with plenty of delicious snacks. Is it guaranteed to prevent meltdowns? Of course not! It sure can help though. These cinnamon roasted sweet potato bites were one of many airplane snacks I made at home and brought with us, and he couldn't get enough of them. These are quick and easy to bake and made with simple, healthy ingredients. You just might find yourself sneaking some for yourself.

Health highlights: Sweet potatoes contain fiber for digestive health and high amounts of beta-carotene that convert to vitamin A, which supports your baby's eye and skin health. Small amounts of cinnamon provide disease-fighting antioxidants and manganese, a mineral that helps with bone health.

INSTRUCTIONS:

1. Preheat the oven to 400°F (200°C).

2. Cut the ends off the sweet potatoes. Chop the sweet potatoes into 1-inch cubes.

3. Place the sweet potato cubes in a large mixing bowl and toss with the oil. Add the cinnamon and optional maple syrup. Use your hands to mix everything.

4. Spread the seasoned sweet potatoes out evenly onto a baking sheet and bake them for twenty to twenty-five minutes, giving the pan a good shake halfway through. When they are done, they should be fork-tender and rich in color. Serve fresh and store any extra in an airtight container in the refrigerator.

Tip: Whether you peel the sweet potato skin or leave it on is your personal preference. I leave the skin on to retain more fiber, nutrients, and antioxidants. Most of the fiber is concentrated in the skin. Just be sure to wash it thoroughly!

NO-BAKE CHEWY FRUITY SNACK BARS

Ages: 9 months+ (makes 5 rectangular bars or 10 square bars)

This healthy snack offers a powerhouse of nutrients for your little one. It's soft enough for an infant to sink their gums into and sweet enough for a toddler to jump for joy over. It gets its sweetness from dates, a fruit high in naturally occurring sugar, so be mindful of how much you serve your child at one time.

Health highlights: Dates, dried cranberries, dried apricots, and cocoa powder are high in disease-fighting antioxidants. Chia seeds, pumpkin seeds, almonds, and sunflower seed butter provide muscle-building protein and brain-supporting healthy fats.

INSTRUCTIONS:

1. In a food processor, pulse the dates, cranberries, apricots, nuts, and seeds and process until shredded into pieces.

2. Add the cocoa powder, sunflower seed butter, and coconut oil, and process until well combined.

3. Transfer mixture to an 8x4-inch baking dish. With the back of a spoon, firmly press down until the surface is smooth.

4. Refrigerate for 2 hours or more. They will firm up as they cool. Remove from the refrigerator and slice it into bar shapes before serving. Store these in an airtight container in the fridge.

Ingredients:

1 cup (180 g) pitted Medjool dates (about 10 dates)

¼ cup (32 g) dried cranberries (or another dried fruit of choice)

¼ cup (47 g) dried apricots (or another dried fruit of choice)

¼ cup (32 g) almonds (or another nut of choice), unsalted

¼ cup (30 g) pumpkin seeds

1 tablespoon chia seeds (or shelled hemp seeds)

2 tablespoons cocoa powder (or cacao powder or vegan chocolate chips)

¼ cup (64 g) sunflower seed butter (or another seed or nut butter of choice)

3 tablespoons liquid coconut oil

Make it nut-free: Replace the almonds with granola

Equipment:

Food processor

8x4-inch baking dish

Spoon

Knife

CUMIN LIME AVOCADO

Ages: 6 months+ (makes 1 serving)

Ingredients:

1 avocado, peeled and pitted

juice of ¼ a lime

½ teaspoon ground cumin

Optional: pinch of salt (omit for infants)

Equipment:

Knife

This is the easiest, quickest snack ever and perfect for kids under one to grip. Plus, the tangy lime and aromatic cumin offer infants a chance to expand their palates. As a toddler, this can be a great addition to larger meals. I enjoy serving this alongside soul-warming soups, such as Corn & Potato Chowder (page 248) or Three-Bean Chili (page 244).

 Health highlights: Avocado is a nutritious, concentrated source of brain-supporting healthy fats and offers fiber for digestive health, vitamin K to help with blood clotting, and vitamin E for a healthy immune system. Cumin is a spice that contains iron for neurological development, and the vitamin C in lime will aid the iron's absorption.

INSTRUCTIONS:

1. Slice the avocado flesh vertically into appropriately sized strips for your child's age.
2. Squeeze the lime juice over the avocado slices.
3. Sprinkle it with some cumin (and optionally a pinch of salt for older kids).

CUCUMBER TOMATO TODDLER SALAD

Ages: 12 months+ (makes 1 large family-sized serving)

If your toddler doesn't like this, more for you! This was one of my favorite first-trimester pregnancy snacks, because the tanginess of the vinegar and onions was oh-so-satisfying. Simple, refreshing, and flavorful, this is my go-to whenever I want to make a quick snackable salad, and you can even blend this into a salsa for more versatility.

Health highlights: Cucumbers are 95 percent water, which helps promote hydration. Tomatoes and onions provide disease-fighting antioxidants, vitamin C for immune health, and fiber for digestive support.

INSTRUCTIONS:

1. Mix all the ingredients in a medium mixing bowl with a spoon.

2. Place it in the refrigerator. The flavors intensify when left to marinate in the fridge for a few hours or overnight. Eat it within two or three days for the best taste and freshness.

Ingredients:

1 small cucumber, diced

1 small tomato, diced

½ red onion, finely chopped

2 tablespoons balsamic vinegar, rice vinegar, or apple cider vinegar

salt to taste

Equipment:

Medium mixing bowl

Spoon

09

BREAKFAST OF CHAMPIONS

BANANA CHOCOLATE CHIP BREAKFAST COOKIES

Ages: 12 months+ (makes 10–12, depending on your desired size)

Ingredients:

1 medium ripe banana

1 cup (90 g) rolled oats

1 tablespoon ground flax seeds

¼ cup (64 g) sunflower seed butter (or any nut or seed butter of choice)

¼ cup (40 g) vegan chocolate chips

Optional: 1 tablespoon maple syrup, for extra sweetness

Equipment:

Large baking sheet

Silicone baking mat (or parchment paper)

Medium mixing bowl

Fork

Spoon

Cookie scoop

"More, more, more," my son Beyond has both signed and verbally requested anytime I've given him one of these cookies. One won't be enough for your child, so you'll be glad to make a whole batch to use as a healthy and fun breakfast option!

If limiting sugar, omit the optional maple syrup. The bananas are sweet enough without it. If making for the whole family and some members want that extra sweetness, you can leave out the maple syrup initially when mixing the batter, make several dough balls, and then add in some maple syrup to the remaining batter. That way half of the batch will have it, and the other half won't. There are always creative methods to make these recipes work for everyone in the fam!

Health highlights: Oats are loaded with energy-boosting carbohydrates, fiber for digestive health, zinc for immune health, and iron for red blood cell production. The vitamin C in the banana can help your baby absorb the iron from the oats. Sunflower seed butter and flax seeds supply muscle-building protein and omega-3 ALA for a dose of heart-healthy fats.

INSTRUCTIONS:

1. Preheat the oven to 325°F (165°C) and line a large baking sheet with a silicone baking mat (or parchment paper).

2. Mash the banana with a fork in a medium mixing bowl. Add the rest of the ingredients and mix until a thick, chunky dough is formed.

3. Use your hands or a cookie scoop to form dough balls to your desired size. Place each dough ball on the prepared baking sheet and flatten slightly. They will not spread in the oven, so the shape that goes in is the shape that will come out.

4. Bake for 15 minutes or until the edges are lightly browned. Remove it from the oven and allow these yummy cookies to cool before serving. Store these in an airtight container at room temperature for 2 or 3 days or in the refrigerator for up to a week.

Variation tip: Want to try something else? Replace the chocolate chips with dried fruits, such as raisins or dried cranberries, for a different twist.

HAZELNUT CINNAMON BANANA TOAST

Ages: 6–12 months with modifications, 12 months+ as is (makes 1 slice of toast)

Ingredients:

1 slice of bread, toasted

1 tablespoon vegan hazelnut butter

1 teaspoon shelled hemp seeds

1 small banana

sprinkle of ground cinnamon, Ceylon if possible, to taste

Make it nut-free: Use chocolate sunflower seed butter instead of hazelnut butter.

Equipment:

Toaster

Knife or spoon

There's a reason you keep seeing bananas in this cookbook. Nope, it's not your imagination. Babies and toddlers can go through phases where they aren't in the mood to eat all the wonderful new dishes you whip up. That can be disheartening, especially when **you** know what you made is delicious. If only they'd just take one bite and see!

The humble banana is one of the few constants that has never failed to pique my son's interest. It was the first solid he was introduced to, and he's been in love ever since. Plus the taste of bananas doesn't change, does it? Raspberries might be sweet one day and sour the next. But not a good ol' reliable banana. Bananas never disappoint.

Going through a selective eating phase? Try this combo! Kids love cinnamon. Kids love bananas. Kids love toast. Cinnamon banana toast to the rescue.

Health highlights: Bread offers energy-boosting carbohydrates and fiber for digestive health. Hemp seeds and hazelnut butter provide muscle-building protein, brain-supporting healthy fats, and iron for blood health. The vitamin C in the banana helps the body absorb iron. Small amounts of cinnamon provide disease-fighting antioxidants and manganese, a mineral that helps with bone health.

INSTRUCTIONS:

1. After toasting 1 slice of bread, use a knife or spoon to spread your hazelnut butter onto the toasted bread.
2. Sprinkle on the hemp seeds.
3. Take your banana and make 9 round slices. Layer them on top of the toast, 3 slices in 3 rows.
4. Finish it off by sprinkling on your desired amount of cinnamon. Slice the toast in half and serve!

Infant modification: Slice the toast into appropriately sized strips. In a small bowl, thin out the tablespoon of hazelnut or sunflower seed butter by mixing it with a little bit of human milk, infant formula, or water. Stir in some hemp seeds and a pinch of cinnamon. Then spread the mixture onto the toast strips. Serve the banana on the side, sliced in half.

Variation tip: You can try this with any nut or seed butter spread you like! Instead of hemp seeds, you can try ground flax. Instead of cinnamon, you can experiment with cardamom or nutmeg. Have fun with it.

SILLY ANIMAL FACE TOAST, THREE WAYS

Ages: 12 months+ (makes 1 slice each)

Ingredients:

Kitty Cat Toast

1 slice of 100-percent whole grain bread, toasted

1–2 tablespoons sunflower seed butter (or any nut or seed butter of choice)

1 blueberry, sliced in half (for the eyes)

1 raspberry (for the nose)

1 strawberry sliced in half (for the ears)

1 strawberry, cut into 6 thin strips (for the whiskers)

Teddy Bear Toast

1 slice of 100-percent whole grain bread, toasted

1 tablespoon hazelnut spread or chocolate sunflower butter

2 blueberries, sliced in half (for the eyes and nose)

3 banana slices (for the ears and nose)

Owl Toast

1 slice of 100-percent whole grain bread, toasted

1 tablespoon sunflower seed butter (or any nut or seed butter of choice)

4 banana slices (for the eyes and belly)

1 blueberry sliced in half (for the eyeballs)

1 raspberry, sliced in half (for the beak)

1 strawberry, sliced in half (for the wings)

Equipment:

Toaster

Knife

Spoon

The first time I posted my teddy bear toast on social media, I received multiple comments expressing how even adults would love to be served something as cute as this! Babies and toddlers, whether vegan or not, often have an instinctive affection for animals. They love mimicking the sounds of animals, cuddling with animal stuffies, and reading books with animal characters. These silly animal face toast recipes offer you and your little one a fun, engaging conversational experience. When you present the kitty cat toast, for example, ask them questions like, "What animal does this look like?" and "What sound does the kitty cat make?" These cute breakfast toasts bring both a nourishing mix of protein, grains, and fruits as well as a burst of joy to your little one's morning.

 Health highlights: Bread offers energy-boosting carbohydrates and fiber for digestive health. Nut and seed butters offer muscle-building protein, healthy fats for brain development, and iron for blood health. The vitamin C in fruits helps the body absorb iron.

INSTRUCTIONS:

Kitty Cat: Spread your seed or nut butter on the toast in a circular face shape. Place each half of the strawberry at the top of the face for the ears, 2 blueberry halves below the ears for the eyes, 1 raspberry below that for the nose, and 3 strawberry strips on the left and right side of the nose for the whiskers.

Teddy Bear: Spread hazelnut or chocolate sunflower seed butter on the toast in a circular face shape. Place 2 banana slices at the top of the face for the ears, 2 blueberry halves below the ears for the eyes, 1 banana slice below that for the nose, and 1 blueberry half on top of the banana slice for the nose tip.

Owl: Spread seed or nut butter on the toast in a circular shape for the whole body. Place 2 banana slices at the top of the body for the eyes and 2 blueberry halves on top of the bottom inner corners of the banana slices for the eyeballs. Place 1 raspberry half at an angle below the eyes for the beak. Place each half of the sliced strawberry to the sides of the nose to create the wings. Place the remaining 2 banana slices at the bottom to create the owl's belly.

SPEEDY SCRAMBLED TOFU

Ages: 6 months+ (makes 4 kid servings)

Ingredients:

1 tablespoon extra-virgin olive oil, for cooking

1 block extra firm tofu, drained and pressed

1 teaspoon ground turmeric

½ teaspoon garlic powder

½ teaspoon onion powder

½ teaspoon ground paprika

1 tablespoon fortified nutritional yeast seasoning

pinch of black pepper

salt to taste or pinch of kala namak (**Tip:** omit for infants and salt your portion separately)

1 handful leafy greens of choice, chopped (for example, watercress or kale)

Note: Kala namak is also called black salt—it provides an eggy flavor and is found in Indian stores or online.

Equipment:

Tofu press (optional)

Medium pan

Cooking spoon

This is meant to be a quick, nutritious staple breakfast dish any baby, toddler, or older kid will love to chow down on—and any parent will be happy to throw together when you don't have a lot of time! While I love making scrambled tofu with chopped and sautéed veggies, we're skipping that for this speedy version. This is for the busiest of mornings, so we're replacing the traditional fresh garlic, onion, and bell peppers with simple sprinkles of garlic powder, onion powder, and ground paprika.

The two secret ingredients that will trick your brain into swearing you just cooked the same scrambled eggs from your childhood are turmeric and kala namak. The turmeric will give your scrambled tofu its signature golden glow, and the kala namak, also called black salt, has a distinct egg-like odor and taste, thanks to its sulfur content.

 Health highlights: Tofu is a complete protein that is loaded with heart-healthy omega-3 ALA, as well as iron for neurological development and zinc for immune function. The addition of leafy greens provides vitamin C to help absorb the iron. Fortified nutritional yeast is packed with energy-boosting B vitamins, including vitamin B12, which is essential for brain health.

INSTRUCTIONS:

1. Heat the oil in a medium pan over medium heat. After you drain the water from the package of tofu and press some of the moisture out of the tofu, use your hands to crumble it into the pan. Or put the tofu in the pan first and use your cooking spoon to crumble it.

2. Add the turmeric first and stir it in. The tofu will turn yellow to resemble scrambled eggs. Then, add all the remaining seasonings and stir together. Cook and stir for 2 to 3 minutes.

3. Lastly, add the chopped leafy greens and stir for another minute, or until softened. If your child is turned off by the sight of greens, try making a batch without them. Taste it and adjust the seasonings, if needed. Serve it fresh and store any extra in an airtight container in the fridge.

Fun fact: Did you know paprika is a fancy-sounding name for dried red bell peppers? Yep. That's all it is.

CHIA PUDDING, TWO WAYS

Ages: 6 months+

Need a simple yet satisfying healthy snack or breakfast idea for your little? I got you. You can make chia pudding in two ways. The traditional way—and the "I don't have time for that" way. I love these because there's no baking involved, it's a fantastic grab-and-go snack or breakfast meal prep idea, and you can make them as basic or as fancy as you desire.

Traditional chia pudding only requires three ingredients: a plant-based milk, chia seeds, and a sweetener—plus time to chill in the fridge.

"I don't have time for that" chia pudding also has three ingredients, but there's no need to chill it: a plant-based yogurt, chia seeds, and a topping.

Then to fancify either one, there are tons of fruit combinations, sweet spices, and other pantry staples you can experiment with.

P.S. Nine times out of ten, I'm choosing the "I don't have time for that" recipe and it is my son's hands-down favorite dish. We don't go a day without hearing a request for "yogurt, yogurt, yogurt" and "chia seeds, chia seeds, chia seeds" in his irresistibly adorable toddler voice. I don't even add a sweetener to it. He particularly enjoys the novelty of helping me pour in the chia seeds and his deeply loved toppings like shelled hemp seeds and granola.

Consider this to be one of my ultimate super vegan mom hacks.

Health highlights: The small but mighty chia seeds in both recipes are loaded with heart-healthy omega-3 ALA, antioxidants to protect cells from damage, and fiber for digestive health. Recipe 2 offers a boost in probiotic gut health from the live active cultures found in store-bought fortified vegan yogurts.

Recipe 1: Traditional Chia Pudding
(makes 4 kid servings)

Ingredients:

4 tablespoons chia seeds

1 cup (237 mL) fortified dairy-free milk of choice, unsweetened

1 teaspoon vanilla extract

Optional: 1 teaspoon maple syrup (omit for infants)

Equipment:

Small mixing bowl

Spoon

Serving dish

INSTRUCTIONS:

1. Place all the ingredients in a mixing bowl and use a spoon to mix well.

2. Place the bowl in a fridge for at least 2 hours or overnight to chill. This will allow the ingredients to gel together into a pudding-like texture.

3. Spoon the desired amount into your child's bowl and add any age-appropriate preferred toppings (such as chopped fruit, granola, or shelled hemp seeds, or stir in a pinch of blue spirulina powder for a fun splash of color).

Recipe 2: "I don't have time for that" Chia Pudding
(makes 1 serving)

Ingredients:

dairy-free yogurt of choice (preferred serving amount)

½ tablespoon chia seeds

preferred toppings (we like granola, shelled hemp seeds, and chopped fruit)

Equipment:

Spoon

Serving bowl

INSTRUCTIONS:

1. Spoon your desired amount of dairy-free yogurt into your child's serving bowl and stir in the chia seeds.

2. Add any preferred toppings (such as chopped fruit, granola, or shelled hemp seeds, or stir in a pinch of blue spirulina powder for a fun splash of color).

Storage: Recipe 1 makes enough for multiple servings, so store the extras in an airtight container in the refrigerator for up to 5 days. Recipe 2 is meant to be a one-and-done serving that you can quickly throw together for breakfast or pack in a lunch box. However, if you do want to store it, spoon it into a small airtight jar and refrigerate it for up to 5 days.

Topping ideas: This is where you can get fantastically creative, as there are boundless options for customization! You can add fresh fruits, dried fruits, granola, nuts, seeds, different spices like cinnamon and nutmeg, or cocoa powder to make it chocolatey. Different variations I've made have included mango raspberry chia pudding, chocolate blueberry chia pudding, blackberry kiwi chia pudding, and orange coconut chia pudding.

APPLE PIE PORRIDGE

Ages: 9 months+ (Makes a large family-sized batch)

Ingredients:

1 cup (90 g) rolled oats

2 cups (473 mL) fortified dairy-free milk of choice, unsweetened

2 small red apples, cored and chopped into small cubes

1 tablespoon chia seeds

½ teaspoon ground cinnamon, Ceylon if possible

1 tablespoon maple syrup (omit for infants)

Optional: ¼ teaspoon ground nutmeg or ¼ teaspoon ground cardamom

Equipment:

Medium saucepan

Cooking spoon

I'm all about quick dishes for busy parents that also happen to be wholesome, nourishing, and filling. That's exactly what you'll get from this warm apple pie porridge, with the bonus of satisfying sweetness. Where my UK folks at, by the way? Technically, we call this "oatmeal" here in the US, but I like the way y'all say it. **Porridge.** Sounds kinda fancy, at least to this American mama who has only known it as oatmeal her whole life.

Storytime! When Beyond went through a phase of just wanting plain oatmeal for dinner, I had to find creative ways to gently bring him back around to exploring other dishes. Does this sound familiar? If your baby or toddler has ever gone through a selective eating phase, one technique you can use to pull them out of it is remixing their go-to dishes. In this case, the simple addition of stewed apples was the starting point. Next, I became more adventurous by adding fragrant spices like ginger, nutmeg, and cardamom. This was a simple yet effective way to expose him to more variety and reopen the gateway to eating a diverse range of foods.

 Health highlights: Oats are rich in muscle-building protein and fiber for digestion, apples provide disease-fighting antioxidants, and chia seeds are an excellent source of heart-healthy omega-3 ALA.

INSTRUCTIONS:

1. Place all your ingredients into a medium saucepan over medium heat and bring it to a simmer, stirring constantly until the porridge is thick and creamy. When it's ready, the oats should be soft, and the apples should be fork-tender.

2. Taste the porridge and adjust the seasonings, if needed.

3. Portion any leftovers into airtight baby jars (or one big tightly sealed container) and refrigerate the porridge for up to 7 days. You can also freeze the jars or containers for up to 3 months.

Tip: Involve the kids! Toddlers love being included in the decision-making process. Ask them what toppings they would enjoy in their porridge. Perhaps a dollop of nut or seed butter for extra protein. Maybe some granola, nuts, or seeds for added texture. How about some additional fresh fruit for an extra boost of vitamin C?

COCONUT QUINOA PORRIDGE

Ages: 6 months+ (makes about 4–6 kid servings)

Ingredients:

1 cup (180 g) dry quinoa, rinsed

1 (13.5 oz/400 mL) can of unsweetened coconut milk

¼ cup (59 mL) water

1 tablespoon maple syrup (omit for infants)

½ teaspoon pure vanilla extract

Optional: ¼ teaspoon ground nutmeg, ground cinnamon (Ceylon if possible), or ground cardamom

Equipment:

Medium saucepan

Cooking spoon

A recipe for parents bored and burned out from cooking oats.

During my first trimester of pregnancy with my second child, I took a break from being in the kitchen, as my eyeballs couldn't stand the sight of food at the time. My husband did most of the cooking during this time. He makes excellent meals, but when it came time to feed our toddler in the evening, he developed a habit of giving him oatmeal every night. For him, oatmeal was easy to meal prep large batches of and guaranteed to go down without any power struggles, as it was one of Beyond's favorite meals.

During my second trimester, when I was feeling like myself again, I was ready to change that. Who was this oatmeal-eating machine and what had he done with my little foodie who was excited to try anything? I came up with the idea of easing him out of his comfy oat haven, by swapping it with something similar—quinoa porridge.

So if you're anything like me and ever get tired of oats being your go-to baby comfort food, switch it up with a dish that has a similar texture but a completely different set of nutrients! Just like other breakfast porridges, you can make this as basic or as fancy as you like. Up to you, so have fun experimenting!

 Health highlights: The main ingredients, quinoa and coconut milk, provide a variety of nutritional benefits for your child. Quinoa is a seed (not a grain) that's packed with complete plant-based protein, as well as other nutrients like iron for neurological development, zinc for wound healing, and magnesium for muscle function. Coconut milk adds healthy fats for brain development.

INSTRUCTIONS:

1. Place a medium saucepan on medium heat, and pour in the quinoa, coconut milk, water, maple syrup, and vanilla extract. Stir the ingredients and then place the lid on. Allow it to sit and cook until the porridge is brought to a simmer. Then reduce the heat to low.

2. Cook the porridge on low heat for about 15 to 20 minutes until most of the liquid is absorbed and the porridge is soft and creamy. Then remove the saucepan from the heat.

3. Taste the porridge. If you think your little one would enjoy additional spices like Beyond does, stir in ¼ teaspoon of nutmeg, cinnamon, or cardamom to elevate the flavor profile.

4. Serve with any of the suggested toppings below to add more flavor, sweetness, and depth.

Topping ideas: Try granola, fresh or dried fruit, shredded coconut, nuts, or seeds.

Quinoa alternatives: While quinoa is not a grain, you may enjoy experimenting with different grains to make porridge. Oats, millet, amaranth, teff, and buckwheat are all interesting options for making porridge.

PEACHES 'N' CREAM OVERNIGHT OATS

Ages: 12 months+ (makes 1 serving)

Ingredients:

¼ cup (22 g) rolled oats

¼ cup (59 mL) fortified dairy-free milk of choice, unsweetened

1 tablespoon coconut yogurt

1 teaspoon chia seeds

½ tablespoon maple syrup

¼ teaspoon vanilla extract

¼ teaspoon ground nutmeg or ground cinnamon (Ceylon if possible)

a few peach slices, chopped (frozen or fresh)

Optional topping: a few peach slices (frozen or fresh)

Equipment:

Serving bowl

Spoon

A five-minute "prep and pop in the fridge 'til the next day" kinda recipe. This portion size has about 6 g of protein. Babies ages one to three need approximately 13 g of protein a day, so this is almost half of your baby's protein needs for the day! You really have to either chuckle or sigh deeply whenever someone assumes vegan babies aren't getting enough protein.

Side note, I now have 112's 2001 hit song "Peaches & Cream" stuck in my head. Most of us had no business singing this as kids, but I mean, how many of us actually knew what the lyrics meant back then? The innuendos in '90s and 2000s R&B were so subtle that you'd think these guys genuinely loved dessert.

Health highlights: Oats and chia seeds provide energy-boosting carbohydrates, fiber for digestive health, zinc for immune health, and iron for red blood cell production. The vitamin C in the peaches helps absorb the iron. Coconut yogurt offers brain-supporting healthy fats. Fortified dairy-free milks have muscle-building protein, calcium for bone health, and vitamin D to help absorb the calcium.

INSTRUCTIONS:

1. Mix all the ingredients together in your child's serving bowl (except for the optional peach topping).

2. Top it with the optional extra peach slices and refrigerate overnight.

3. Serve your Peaches 'n' Cream Overnight Oats chilled the following morning or heat it up if your little one prefers it warm.

BANANA OAT PANCAKES

Ages: 6 months+ (makes 8–10 mini pancakes)

Ingredients:

1 cup (90 g) rolled oats

1 ripe banana

1 cup (237 mL) fortified dairy-free milk of choice, unsweetened

½ tablespoon baking powder

½ tablespoon ground cinnamon, Ceylon if possible

¼ teaspoon ground nutmeg

Optional: 1 tablespoon maple syrup (omit for infants)

extra-virgin olive oil, as needed, for cooking

Suggested Toppings:

Fortified dairy-free yogurt, nut or seed butter, shelled hemp seeds, granola, and/or sliced fruit.

Equipment:

Blender

Large mixing bowl

Fork or potato masher

Whisk or spoon

Optional: basting brush, for oiling the skillet

Spatula

Large Skillet

Is it getting cooler outside? The cinnamon and nutmeg flavors combined with the warmth of fresh banana pancakes make this the perfect autumn and winter breakfast for kids. Hot and sunny outside? Great. Nothing changes. It doesn't matter what time of year it is—the time is always right for these golden brown, fluffy vegan banana pancakes! You can make a big batch of baby-sized pancakes with this recipe, which means you can refrigerate the leftovers and serve the following days or freeze for much later. Boom. Less work for you throughout the week.

Health highlights: Oats are packed with energy-boosting carbohydrates, fiber for digestive health, zinc for immune health, and iron for red blood cell production. The vitamin C in the banana helps absorb the iron. Fortified dairy-free milks have muscle-building protein, calcium for bone health, and vitamin D to help absorb the calcium.

INSTRUCTIONS:

1. Blend the rolled oats into a powder. Boom—now you have oat flour!

2. In a large mixing bowl, mash your banana with a fork or potato masher until it's smooth and creamy.

3. Add the oat flour you just made and the remaining ingredients (except the cooking oil) to the bowl with the mashed banana and mix well with a whisk or spoon.

4. Warm a large skillet over medium heat. Once hot, lightly oil the pan. I use a basting brush to coat the pan with a thin layer of oil. Slowly pour 3 tablespoons of batter per pancake into the pan. I usually cook 4 pancakes at a time. Cook until the pancakes slightly puff up, are golden underneath, and the batter is bubbling, about 2 to 3 minutes.

5. Use a spatula to gently test the edges and then flip them over. Cook until the other sides are golden brown. Remove your pancakes from the pan and repeat the process with any remaining batter.

6. Serve these warm with the suggested toppings. Refrigerate any extras in an airtight container.

Freezer tip: Spread the pancakes out on a baking sheet and place them in the freezer until frozen. This step will prevent them from sticking together. Then, place the frozen pancakes in a freezer-safe container or storage bag and store in the freezer for up to 3 months. To reheat them, pop them in a toaster!

CURRY-SPICED TODDLER BREAKFAST BURRITO

Ages: 9–12 months with modifications, 12 months+ as is (makes 6 burritos)

Ingredients:

For the Filling

1 tablespoon extra-virgin olive oil, for cooking

1 bell pepper, any color, diced

1½ cups (150 g) mushrooms, cleaned and chopped (we enjoy baby bella)

1 block extra firm tofu, drained and pressed

1 teaspoon ground turmeric

1 teaspoon garlic powder

1 teaspoon onion powder

1 teaspoon mild curry powder

2 tablespoons fortified nutritional yeast seasoning

pinch of black pepper

salt to taste (**Tip:** omit for infants and salt your portion separately)

Optional: pinch of kala namak (also called black salt, it adds an "eggy" flavor to vegan dishes and can be found in Indian stores or online)

1 handful spinach (about ½ a cup), chopped

For the Wrap

6 medium soft whole wheat tortillas

6 tablespoons mild taco sauce

Optional: 1 teaspoon olive oil, for cooking (if you desire a crispy burrito)

Equipment:

1 medium pan

Spatula

Spoon

The first time I made this for my son was when he was about fifteen months old. Instead of taco sauce, I used tomato chutney, but regardless of the sauce the result is always the same. He positively annihilates it. Parents can sometimes feel hesitant to introduce spices to kids, but it's perfectly safe, and even encouraged by health professionals (see the Q&A with plant-based pediatrician Dr. Shayna Smith on page 108 for more reassurance). That being said, this recipe does involve some seasonings that may overwhelm your little one's taste buds, like curry powder, if not accustomed to these flavors. Adjust the amount of spices, or even remove some, as needed to accommodate your child's preferences. Consider gradually exposing them to these seasonings to expand their palates.

Health highlights: Tofu is a complete protein loaded with heart-healthy omega-3 ALA, as well as iron for neurological development and zinc for immune function. The vitamin C in the bell pepper helps the body absorb iron. Curry powder and turmeric have disease-fighting anti-inflammatory properties and black pepper helps the body absorb the turmeric. Fortified nutritional yeast and mushrooms are packed with energy-boosting B vitamins.

INSTRUCTIONS:

1. Heat the oil in a medium pan over medium heat and sauté the chopped bell peppers and mushrooms for two to three minutes.

2. Use your hands to crumble the tofu into the pan.

3. Add the seasonings and stir together. The tofu will turn yellow to resemble scrambled eggs with the help of the turmeric. Cook for another 3 minutes.

4. Add the chopped spinach and stir until slightly wilted, about 1 minute. Remove the pan from the heat.

5. Take a soft tortilla, spread 1 tablespoon of taco sauce near the bottom center and spoon one-sixth of the scrambled tofu over the sauce. Begin to roll the burrito, tucking in the sides firmly around the filling as you go. Continue to roll the burrito tightly to secure. Repeat for the remaining 5 burritos.

6. Optional additional step for crispy burritos: Wipe the pan clean and return to medium heat with 1 teaspoon of oil. Add 1 burrito seam-side down and cook until golden brown, 1 to 2 minutes per side.

7. Cut the burrito in half and serve.

Recipe Notes:

Storage: Refrigerate the other 5 burritos in an airtight container to grab throughout the week or wrap in parchment paper, place them in a freezer-safe container or bag, and store in the freezer for up to 3 months.

Reheating: When ready to serve them, follow step 6 by reheating them in a pan.

Infant modification: For infants ages 9–12 months, deconstruct the burrito to make it easier for them to eat. You can start by serving the filling with a slice of tortilla on the side. Corn tortillas work well for infants, and you can switch to whole wheat tortillas after 12 months.

Allergens: If your child has a soy allergy, try black beans or chickpeas instead of tofu.

FRENCH TOAST STICKS

Ages: 6 months+ (makes 2 servings)

Ingredients:

½ cup (118 mL) fortified dairy-free milk of choice, unsweetened

2 tablespoons ground flax

1 teaspoon ground cinnamon, Ceylon if possible

¼ teaspoon ground nutmeg

1 teaspoon maple syrup (omit for infants)

2 slices thick bread (such as Texas toast)

½ tablespoon extra-virgin olive oil, for cooking

Equipment:

Small mixing bowl

Spoon

Knife

Medium pan

Spatula

French toast was always one of those sweet breakfast delights I looked forward to on weekends as a kid. Now you can recreate that childhood nostalgia but without the dairy and eggs. These delightfully sweet French Toast Sticks are easy for you to whip up and even easier for your little ones to grasp in their tiny hands.

 Health highlights: Bread offers energy-boosting carbohydrates, muscle-building protein, and fiber for digestive health. Small amounts of cinnamon provide disease-fighting antioxidants and manganese for bone health. Flax seeds offer omega-3 ALA for a dose of heart-healthy fats.

INSTRUCTIONS:

1. Mix the dairy-free milk, flax, cinnamon, nutmeg, and maple syrup in a small mixing bowl and refrigerate for 10 minutes to allow the batter to thicken.

2. While the batter is thickening, prep the bread. Cut the 2 slices of bread into sticks. Ensure the cuts are an appropriate size for your child's age and eating abilities.

3. Remove the batter from the fridge. Heat the oil in a medium pan over medium heat. Quickly dip the bread sticks into the batter on each side and shake off any excess. Avoid soaking the bread sticks in the batter to prevent them from becoming soggy. Place each stick in the pan and cook for about 1 minute on both sides or until they are golden brown.

4. Serve it warm with any desired toppings—fresh berries or bananas work well! Refrigerate any extra in an airtight container.

SAVORY CHICKPEA SCRAMBLE

Ages: 6 months+ (makes 3–4 kid servings)

Ingredients:

1 (15.5 oz/439 g) can garbanzo beans (also called chickpeas), drained and rinsed

1 tablespoon extra-virgin olive oil, for cooking

2 garlic cloves, minced

½ small yellow onion, chopped

½ bell pepper or tomato, chopped

1 tablespoon fortified nutritional yeast seasoning

½ teaspoon turmeric

½ teaspoon cumin

½ teaspoon smoked paprika

¼ cup (59 mL) vegetable stock (page 237 or store-bought)

salt to taste (**Tip:** omit for infants and salt your portion separately)

pinch of black pepper

Equipment:

Small mixing bowl

Fork

Medium pan

Cooking spoon

When my baby boy was thirteen months old, we took him out for a family Valentine's Day vegan brunch. There was one dish on the menu that caught our eyes: chickpea scramble. What was that? Was it like scrambled tofu but made with chickpeas? Did it taste the same? To our delight, it was different from what we imagined. It didn't taste anything like scrambled tofu, nor was it supposed to. It was a unique thing and most importantly, Beyond couldn't get enough of it! In fact, Daddy was moving too slowly for him. He kept grabbing Daddy's arm to feed him faster. After witnessing his feasting session, I was of course obligated to recreate this recipe at home. So voilà, enjoy the savory sensations of this creamy, garlicky, umami-flavored breakfast dish, filled with a medley of flavors and spices to expand your child's palate.

Health highlights: Chickpeas are an excellent source of brain-supporting healthy fats, muscle-building protein, and iron for neurological development. The vitamin C in the bell pepper helps your baby's body absorb iron. Fortified nutritional yeast is packed with energy-boosting B vitamins, including vitamin B12 for brain development. Turmeric has disease-fighting anti-inflammatory properties and black pepper helps absorb the turmeric.

INSTRUCTIONS:

1. Pour the chickpeas into a small mixing bowl and mash with a fork to your desired consistency.

2. Heat the oil in a medium pan over medium heat. Add the garlic, onion, and bell pepper and sauté until the veggies are tender, about 2 to 3 minutes.

3. Stir in the nutritional yeast, turmeric, cumin, and smoked paprika, and sauté for another minute until the spices are fragrant.

4. Pour in the veggie broth and mashed chickpeas and stir it all together. Season it with salt and pepper. Cook for another minute, stirring occasionally, until creamy. Taste it and adjust the seasonings, if needed.

5. Serve warm and store any leftovers in a sealed container in the refrigerator.

Easy chickpeasy!

APPLE LENTIL "SAUSAGE" PATTIES

Ages: 6 months+ (makes 8–10 patties)

Ingredients:

2 tablespoons extra-virgin olive oil, for cooking (half for first step and half for last step)

½ medium red onion, roughly chopped

1 cup (100 g) mushrooms, any kind, cleaned and chopped

1 red apple, roughly diced

½ teaspoon ground thyme

¼ teaspoon ground sage

1 tablespoon maple syrup (**Tip:** omit for infants and add maple syrup to your serving as a topping)

1 cup (90 g) rolled oats

1 (15 oz/425 g) can black lentils, drained and rinsed

1 cup (120 g) raw sunflower seed kernels (also called hulled sunflower seeds)

salt to taste (**Tip:** omit for infants and salt your portion separately)

Equipment:

Large pan

Cooking spoon

Food processor or high-speed blender

Spoon

Spatula

Cutting board

I enjoyed the unique challenge of creating a homemade plant-based breakfast sausage recipe that encapsulates the sweet and savory flavors people know and love, without the high sodium content that typically accompanies it. After all, we want to minimize added salt for our toddlers, and often avoid them for our kids under one. To master that delicate balance, I tapped into the power of two fragrant spices: ground sage and ground thyme. The maple syrup adds a familiar sweet taste to these breakfast patties that make them a traditional morning delight.

Health highlights: Oats, lentils, and sunflower seeds are loaded with muscle-building protein, energy-boosting carbohydrates, fiber for digestive health, zinc for immune health, and iron for red blood cell production. The vitamin C in the apple helps absorb iron. Mushrooms are packed with energy-boosting B vitamins.

INSTRUCTIONS:

1. Heat 1 tablespoon of oil in a large pan over medium heat and add the chopped onions and mushrooms. Sauté for 3 to 4 minutes, until they soften.

2. Add the apples and season with thyme, sage, and maple syrup. Stir and cook for 3 to 4 minutes or until the apples are soft. Remove the pan from heat and set it aside.

3. Add the rolled oats to a food processor or blender and process until it turns into a powder. Now you have oat flour!

4. Add the sautéed ingredients to that same food processor, along with the lentils, sunflower seed kernels, and salt. Pulse until all the ingredients are combined well. The texture will be moist, but that will change when you cook it. Taste the mixture and make sure the seasonings are to your liking before forming your patties.

5. Next you'll create 8–10 patties. Since the mixture is moist, use a table spoon to scoop out each portion and place it on a cutting board. The patties do not need to be perfectly shaped at this point. You can shape them in the pan.

6. Using the same pan from earlier, heat 1 tablespoon of oil on medium heat and transfer the patties to the pan using a spatula. This is when you can start shaping them into round patty shapes, gently rounding the edges and pressing down to flatten them a bit as they firm up in the pan. Cook the patties on both sides until beautifully browned, about 3 minutes per side. Remove the patties from the heat and set them aside. They will firm up even more as they cool.

7. These patties are perfect for serving inside flaky biscuits or with a plate of Speedy Scrambled Tofu (page 176) and fresh fruit. Refrigerate any extras in an airtight container.

ROASTED BREAKFAST POTATOES

Ages: 6–9 months with modifications, 9 months+ as is (1 large family-sized serving)

Ingredients:

2 Yukon Gold potatoes, unpeeled, diced into 1-inch cubes

1 tablespoon extra-virgin olive oil

½ teaspoon garlic powder

½ teaspoon onion powder

½ teaspoon ground paprika

1 teaspoon dried parsley

salt to taste (**Tip:** omit for infants and salt your portion separately)

Equipment:

Large mixing bowl

Baking sheet

It is always a delight to see Beyond grab a fistful of these. Their bite-sized shapes and soft texture make these earthy roasted breakfast potatoes simple for a baby or toddler to grab and sink their mouths into. Plus, don't you love a dish where the oven does most of the work?!

Health highlights: Potatoes have folate for cell function, iron for neurological development, energy-boosting B vitamins, and zinc for wound healing. Extra-virgin olive oil offers a dose of healthy fat for brain health.

INSTRUCTIONS:

1. Preheat your oven to 400°F (200°C) and lightly grease a baking sheet with a bit of oil.

2. In a large mixing bowl, add your diced potatoes. Drizzle them with oil and use your hands or a spoon to evenly distribute the oil throughout. Next, add all the spices and mix well.

3. Spread your seasoned potatoes onto the prepared baking sheet evenly, taking care not to overcrowd the pan. Pop it in the oven for 30 minutes, giving the pan a good shake halfway through. The potatoes are done when they are golden on the outside and light and fluffy on the inside.

4. Serve warm alongside Speedy Scrambled Tofu (page 176) and fresh fruit for a well-balanced breakfast. Refrigerate any extra in an airtight container.

Infant modification: Cut these into large wedges instead of cubes for infants aged 6–9 months.

BREAKFAST BANANA SPLIT

Ages: 9 months+ (makes 1 serving)

This dessert-looking breakfast dish encourages kids to eat fruit and dairy-free yogurt by presenting it in an exciting way! It's giving protein. It's giving healthy fats. It's giving probiotics. It's giving antioxidants. It's giving what it needs to give for little effort, okay? Listen, it takes little effort to put this together. This easy, fun, and healthy breakfast can be thrown together on even the busiest of mornings.

Health highlights: Sunflower seed butter is packed with muscle-building protein, omega-3 ALA for a dose of heart-healthy fats, and iron for neurological development. The vitamin C in the fruits helps your baby's body absorb iron. Store-bought dairy-free yogurt is often fortified with probiotics for a healthy gut microbiome.

Ingredients:

1 banana, peeled

1–2 tablespoons sunflower seed butter (or any nut or seed butter of choice)

3 teaspoons dairy-free vanilla yogurt of choice

2 medium strawberries, chopped

8–10 blueberries, sliced

1–2 tablespoons of granola (or anything crunchy such as chopped nuts, seeds, or oats)

Equipment:

Knife

Plate

Spoon

Small cookie scoop or melon baller, optional

INSTRUCTIONS:

1. Slice a banana in half horizontally and then slice each half vertically to create 4 small slices. Line them up on your child's serving plate.

2. Drizzle sunflower seed butter over all four slices. Use a small cookie scoop or melon baller to add 3 baby scoops of vegan vanilla yogurt (or you can use a teaspoon). Add chopped strawberries and sliced blueberries across the dish. Sprinkle some granola or a crunchy topping of your choice on top.

3. Serve it immediately and enjoy watching your little one light up.

10

MAINS & SIDEKICKS

TODDLER TAQUITOS

Ages: 12 months+ (makes 12 taquitos)

Ingredients:

1 tablespoon extra-virgin olive oil for cooking (½ for first step and ½ for last step)

½ bell pepper, finely diced

1 small onion, finely diced

salt to taste (**Tip:** omit for infants and salt your portion separately)

pinch of black pepper

1 (15 oz/425 g) can beans, any kind, drained and rinsed (we love black or kidney beans)

1 teaspoon ground cumin

1 teaspoon garlic powder

½ teaspoon dried oregano

½ cup (118 mL) water

6 soft medium tortillas

Equipment:

Medium pan

Cooking spoon

Potato masher (optional)

This dish is a win-win for parents and kiddos alike. Babies and toddlers will adore its crunchiness and ease of holding one of these in their little fists. Parents will love these for their protein content and ease of throwing this together in a pinch. You can whip this together for family Taco Tuesday night and pack the extras in your little one's lunch box for daycare or school. Serve with some Baby-Friendly Guacamole (page 134) and Mango Salsa (page 135) on the side, and you'll have a winning meal the entire fam can get down with.

Health highlights: Beans are excellent plant-based sources of muscle-building protein. They also supply iron for neurological development and zinc for immune function, two nutrients that tend to be lacking in infant diets. The bell pepper provides immune-supporting vitamin C that can help your baby's body absorb iron. Onions offer additional disease-fighting antioxidants and extra-virgin olive oil provides healthy fats for brain health.

INSTRUCTIONS:

1. Heat ½ tablespoon of oil in a medium pan over medium heat. Add the bell pepper and onion. Season with salt and pepper and sauté until they soften, about 3 to 4 minutes.

2. Add the beans and season with cumin, garlic, and oregano. Stir for a minute, and then add the water.

3. Turn the heat down to low and let the mixture simmer until some of the water evaporates.

4. Use a spoon or a potato masher to lightly mash the beans until you reach your desired consistency. You can mash the beans until they resemble the consistency of refried beans or lightly mash them to soften them up.

5. Place ¼ cup of the bean mixture on the bottom of a tortilla. Roll it while tucking the bottom in tightly and continue rolling it into a taquito. Repeat with the remaining tortillas.

6. Wipe down the pan you just used and heat ½ tablespoon of oil over medium heat. Place the taquitos in the pan and heat until both sides are golden brown and crispy.

7. Cut each taquito in half to make them a kid-friendly serving size.

8. Serve warm and refrigerate any extras in an airtight container.

F'SH STICKS & TARTAR DIP

Ages: 6 months+ (makes about 10 f'sh sticks)

Ingredients:

F'sh Sticks

1 cup (60 g) Japanese-style Panko breadcrumbs (or any vegan breadcrumbs), divided

1 (14 oz/400 g) can hearts of palm, drained·

½ cup (60 g) all-purpose flour

¼ cup (40 g) cornmeal

½ cup (118 mL) fortified dairy-free milk of choice, unsweetened

1 tablespoon lemon juice

½ teaspoon garlic powder

½ teaspoon onion powder

2 tablespoons seaweed flakes, such as dulse or nori (you can find this online or improvise by crumbling some seaweed snacks into flakes)

1 tablespoon Old Bay seasoning

Tartar Dip

¼ cup (61 g) plain dairy-free yogurt of choice

½ teaspoon mustard

1 tablespoon capers

1 teaspoon lemon juice

½ teaspoon dill weed seasoning

½ teaspoon garlic powder

pinch of celery salt (omit for infants)

Optional: 2 dill pickle slices, finely chopped

Equipment:

Baking sheet

Silicone baking mat (or parchment paper)

Food processor

Small mixing bowl

Spoon

No fish in this dish. You just need a lil' taste of the sea to recreate this childhood fave in a compassionate way. In the opening of Chapter 8, I mentioned that it's not the marine animals you crave but the seasonings. So this recipe is an example of how you can replicate the aromas and flavor profiles of traditional "seafood" dishes without the animal. Crunchy on the outside, tender on the inside, and paired with a creamy, tangy dipping sauce, your kids will have a ball with these tasty vegan f'sh sticks.

Health highlights: Hearts of palm is a vegetable high in muscle-building protein, including all nine essential amino acids your baby needs, which play a role in repairing damaged tissue. Fortified dairy-free milk has calcium for bone health and vitamin D to help absorb the calcium, while dairy-free yogurt is fortified with probiotics for gut health.

INSTRUCTIONS:

1. Preheat the oven to 400°F (200°C) and line a baking sheet with a reusable baking mat or parchment paper.

2. Combine half of the breadcrumbs and the remaining ingredients listed under "F'sh Sticks" in a food processor and pulse a few times until roughly chopped.

3. Pour the other half of the breadcrumbs into a small mixing bowl. Form the batter into stick shapes, dip them into the breadcrumbs, and turn them to coat all sides.

4. Place your coated f'sh sticks on the prepared baking sheet and bake for 12 minutes. Remove them from the oven and flip them over. Bake for another 5 minutes. They should be crispy and slightly browned.

5. Clean the small mixing bowl and use it to make your dip. Combine all the ingredients for the tartar dip and mix well.

6. Serve the f'sh sticks warm with the tartar dip and refrigerate any extras in an airtight container.

MUSHROOM PESTO FLATBREAD PIZZA

Ages: 12 months+ (makes 4 slices)

Ingredients:

1 tablespoon extra-virgin olive oil (½ for sauteing, ½ for baking)

½ a small yellow onion, cleaned and chopped

¼ cup (25 g) mushrooms, any kind, cleaned and chopped

¼ teaspoon garlic powder

salt to taste (**Tip:** omit for infants and salt your portion separately)

¼ cup (65 g) artichoke hearts, roughly chopped (you can find these jarred or canned)

¼ cup (80 g) roasted red peppers, roughly chopped (you can find these jarred)

1 round flatbread

1 tablespoon vegan pesto (page 132 or store-bought)

1 teaspoon fortified nutritional yeast seasoning

pinch of black pepper

3 slices of tomato

Equipment:

Small pan

Cooking spoon

Baking sheet

Reusable baking mat (or parchment paper)

This one is a classic hit for my son. Mushroom pesto flatbread pizza has never failed to excite him—and there's a Buzzfeed video to prove it. You can see him chowing down on this dish by searching "What a 19-Month-Old Vegan Eats in a Day" online. Beyond was featured on Buzzfeed's healthy lifestyle channel, Goodful, and this is one out of three of the magical meals I made for my baby boy in the video. You can whip this up quickly if pizza is on the menu at your child's school or a birthday party. Of course, you don't need any excuse to make this. It's a flavorful entree for any day of the week.

 Health highlights: Mushrooms are packed with energy-boosting B vitamins. Fortified nutritional yeast is a complete protein that contains vitamin B12, which is essential for brain development. Onions, artichokes, roasted red peppers, and tomatoes are loaded with disease-fighting antioxidants and fiber for digestive health.

INSTRUCTIONS:

1. Preheat the oven to 400°F (200°C) and line the baking sheet with a reusable baking mat (or parchment paper).

2. Heat ½ tablespoon of the oil in a small pan over medium heat and add the onion and mushrooms. Season with garlic powder and salt. Sauté until soft, about 5 minutes.

3. Add in your artichokes and roasted red peppers. Sauté for another 3 minutes, and then remove the pan from the heat.

4. Place the round flatbread on your prepared baking sheet and spread on the pesto. Sprinkle the nutritional yeast and black pepper on top. Layer on the sautéed veggies and add your finishing touch with the tomato slices. Bake your flatbread pizza for 5 minutes until crispy.

5. Remove the flatbread from the oven and slice it into 4 parts or even smaller pieces, depending on what works best for your toddler. Serve warm and refrigerate any extra slices for later.

SAUCY CHICKPEA BALLS

Ages: 6 months+ (makes 15 balls)

Ingredients:

For Mixture

2½ tablespoons ground flax + 6 tablespoons water (this will be your "flax egg")

1 (15.5 oz/439 g) can garbanzo beans (also called chickpeas), drained and rinsed

½ cup (30 g) Japanese-style Panko breadcrumbs (or any vegan breadcrumbs)

1 tablespoon Italian seasoning

½ tablespoon garlic powder

½ tablespoon onion powder

1 teaspoon ground cumin

1 tablespoon fortified nutritional yeast seasoning

pinch of black pepper

salt to taste (**Tip:** omit for infants and salt your portion separately)

For Sauce

½ cup marinara sauce

Equipment:

Small bowl

Spoon

Food processor (or high-speed blender)

Air fryer (or oven)

Small mixing bowl

If baking in the oven, you'll need:

A baking sheet

A reusable baking mat (or parchment paper)

Looking for a meatball alternative to offer your little one? Look no further than the humble chickpea ball. Legumes, in general, are great options to experiment with to replace meatballs in vegan cuisines. I've made kidney bean balls, black bean balls, and lentil balls for Beyond, and he loves them all. You can serve this as part of a classic favorite like spaghetti or plate it alongside other foods like Carrot Fries (page 160) and Veggie Couscous (page 228). Putting a vegan twist on traditional meals is a fantastic way to share your treasured childhood memories with your kids.

 Health highlights: Garbanzo beans (chickpeas) are a nutrient-dense legume rich in protein for growth, fiber for digestion, and carbohydrates for energy. It also provides crucial nutrients such as folate, iron, vitamin B6, choline, and zinc, which collectively support your baby's brain health, metabolism, growth, and taste and smell perception. Fortified nutritional yeast provides vitamin B12, which is essential for brain development.

INSTRUCTIONS:

1. If you use an oven to bake these, preheat the oven to 450° F (230°C) and line a baking sheet with a reusable baking mat (or parchment paper). If using an air fryer, skip this step.

2. Make your egg replacement by using a spoon to mix the ground flax and water in a small bowl. Set your "flax egg" mixture aside for 10 minutes, and it will turn into the equivalent of 2 eggs.

3. Add the chickpeas to a food processor or blender and pulse until they are broken down. Do not over-pulse. You just want the chickpeas to break apart.

4. Once the flax "egg" is ready, pour it into the food processor with the broken-down chickpeas and pulse until combined.

5. Add the remaining ingredients listed under "For Mixture" and blend in the food processor until well mixed. If it's too moist or sticky, add more breadcrumbs. If it's too dry, add a little extra-virgin olive oil. Taste the mixture and adjust the seasonings, if needed.

6. Form the mixture into balls. If using an oven, place these on your prepared baking sheet and bake for 20 minutes, turning them halfway through so they cook evenly. If using an air fryer, bake for about 15 minutes at 375°F (190°C), turning halfway through.

7. Once done baking, place the chickpea balls into a small mixing bowl. Pour the marinara sauce over the chickpea balls and gently mix until all the balls are covered in the sauce. Serve warm and refrigerate any extra in an airtight container.

TOFU "EGG" SALAD SANDWICH

Ages: 6–18 months with modifications, 18 months+ as is (1 large family-sized serving)

Ingredients:

½ block firm tofu, drained and pressed

3 tablespoons plain dairy-free yogurt, unsweetened

1 teaspoon mustard

1–2 scallions, chopped

1 teaspoon fortified nutritional yeast seasoning

¼ teaspoon ground turmeric

¼ teaspoon garlic powder

¼ teaspoon onion powder

pinch of black pepper

pinch of kala namak (also called black salt) or regular salt (**Tip:** omit for infants and salt your portion separately)

2 slices of bread

Equipment:

Medium mixing bowl

Spoon

Here's another vegan twist on a classic childhood dish. Growing up, I was quite fond of egg salad; now we can all recreate it for our kids without using any eggs. Instead, use tofu to replicate the texture, turmeric to recreate the vibrancy, and various flavors to bring out the taste. This simple, speedy recipe can be whipped up on those hectic days when you don't have much time. The best part is you can use any leftovers to spread on crackers for a quick snack!

Health highlights: Tofu is a complete protein that is loaded with heart-healthy omega-3 ALA, as well as iron for neurological development, zinc for immune function, and choline for brain health. Scallions have vitamin C to help with iron absorption. Store-bought dairy-free yogurt is often fortified with probiotics for gut health. Turmeric has disease-fighting anti-inflammatory properties and black pepper helps your baby's body absorb the turmeric. Fortified nutritional yeast has vitamin B12, which is essential for brain development.

INSTRUCTIONS:

1. After pressing the tofu for a few minutes to remove any excess moisture, crumble the tofu in a medium mixing bowl and add the remaining ingredients (except for the bread). Mix it all together.

2. Spread as much of the mixture as desired on the bread and make a sandwich. Refrigerate any extra in an airtight container for later use. I like to serve the extras on crackers as a snack or in wraps for a lunchbox meal!

Infant modification: For infants aged 6–12 months and toddlers aged 12–18 months, serve the tofu "egg" salad on its own. You can toast a bread slice and serve an appropriately sized piece of the toasted bread on the side.

ROASTED VEGGIE ANYTHING

Are you an adult who struggles with the idea that vegetables can taste good? Don't let your kids pick up on that disdain toward veggies—it may affect their perceptions and leave them just as uninterested. One way to develop a better relationship with vegetables is to find a cooking method that enhances the flavors of vegetables in a way that excites your taste buds—and for that, I suggest roasting! Roasting the right way will help your whole family, including kids, fall in love with veggies and see them as more than an obligatory healthy side item. Here is a brief guide to roasting vegetables to help you perfect your method and avoid common mistakes.

 Health highlights: Vegetables supply your child with essential vitamins, minerals, and antioxidants to help protect against chronic diseases later in life. They are superb sources of fiber for digestive health.

What You'll Need:

Ingredients: 2 cups (1 pound) of similar vegetables (uniformly chopped), 1 tablespoon of cooking oil, herbs and spices of choice (try: ½ teaspoon garlic powder, ½ teaspoon ground rosemary, and ½ teaspoon dried thyme), and salt to taste

Equipment: Large mixing bowl, rimmed metal baking sheet, and a spatula

Step 1: Group Similar Vegetables

When grocery shopping, look for fresh or frozen vegetables with similar structures. Vegetables with different densities require different lengths of time in the oven, so grouping related vegetables together will ensure even cooking times. Root vegetables and denser vegetables in general, such as sweet potatoes, carrots, parsnips, beets, onions, and rutabagas, roast nicely together. Cruciferous vegetables and softer vegetables in general, like cauliflower, broccoli, green beans, Brussels sprouts, asparagus, and bok choy, are great to roast together.

Step 2: Preheat the Oven to a High Temperature

You'll want to roast your vegetables at a temperature of at least 450°F (230°C). High heat ensures your vegetables experience deep browning, optimal flavor, and a crispy texture. So preheat your oven and then prepare your vegetables for a beautiful roast.

Step 3: Evenly Cut Vegetables

Cut your vegetables uniformly so they cook evenly. Avoid cutting them into random sizes. Smaller pieces will cook faster, while bigger pieces will take longer.

Step 4: Toss with Oil and Seasonings

Transfer your chopped vegetables to a large bowl. Toss them with 1 tablespoon of oil for every pound (2 cups) of vegetables. Use your hands to massage the oil onto the veggies and make them shine. For the seasoning, you can be as simple or complex as you desire. Get creative and experiment with different flavors you and your family will love! Remember, you don't have to shy away from herbs and spices for babies. To start, try a combination of garlic, rosemary, dried thyme, and salt to taste. For a Mediterranean twist, use olive oil, dried oregano, and lemon zest, or for an Asian flair, try sesame oil, garlic, and ginger.

Feel free to omit salt if you are making this for an infant under one year old. However, if making for the whole family, remember that salt is a powerful flavor enhancer, and you don't have to add much. The goal is to use salt to enhance existing flavors, not make the food taste salty. One approach is to separate your baby's portion and salt any portion for yourself or older family members. Or you can cook without salt and sprinkle it onto your individual portion later when serving.

Step 5: Evenly Space Vegetables

Spread out your vegetables on a rimmed metal baking sheet. The metal will conduct the heat better, and a low rim will help the steam escape. Avoid using glass as it doesn't transmit heat the same way. Space the vegetables out and avoid crowding them. If they are piled on top of each other, they will steam instead of roast.

Step 6: Roast Until Tender

Roasting your vegetables can take 15 to 45 minutes, depending on the vegetable family. Remember that the denser the vegetable, the longer the cooking time. Roast soft vegetables for 15 to 20 minutes, cruciferous vegetables for 20 to 25 minutes, and root vegetables for 30 to 45 minutes, depending on how small you cut them. As mentioned in step 3, the smaller the pieces, the faster they cook. Roast your vegetables until tender and toasted.

Step 7: Finish with an Acidic Topping

Roasting releases the internal sugars of vegetables, making them sweeter. To balance the sweetness, add a form of acid like a squeeze of lemon or create a lemony, herby dairy-free yogurt dipping sauce.

Serve your roasted veggie masterpiece warm, alongside hearty, protein-packed dishes like Refried Mixed Beans (page 216) or Saucy Chickpea Balls (page 206) and flavorful grain-based foods like garlic toast or Cauliflower Mac 'n' Geez (page 226). Refrigerate any extras in an airtight container.

> **Note:** For reference, the vegetables I used in the photo are sweet potatoes and beets, which I chopped into small, uniform, cubed pieces and roasted for about thirty minutes.

GREEN PEA PATTIES & LEMONY SAUCE

Ages: 6 months+ (makes 5 baby patties)

Ingredients:

Green Pea Patties

1 cup (144 g) frozen peas

½ tablespoon extra-virgin olive oil for cooking, plus extra for brushing

½ small red or yellow onion, chopped

2 garlic cloves, peeled and minced

½ cup (60 g) whole wheat flour (or any flour you have access to)

½ teaspoon baking powder

1 tablespoon Italian seasoning

1 teaspoon lemon juice

salt to taste (omit for infants)

Lemony Sauce

¼ cup (61 g) plain dairy-free yogurt of choice, unsweetened

½ teaspoon lemon juice

¼ teaspoon garlic powder

½ teaspoon Italian seasoning

salt to taste (**Tip:** omit for infants and salt your portion separately)

Equipment:

Baking sheet

Reusable baking mat (or parchment paper)

Steamer pot (or saucepan)

Small pan

Food processor or blender

Optional: basting brush, for oiling

Small bowl

Spoon

Patties are fantastic for infants and toddlers alike. They are easy to pick up for babies who haven't yet mastered utensil use. These can also be convenient snacks to pack in a lunchbox or part of a toddler's main meal. However you serve it, don't forget the dip! A tangy lemon-flavored sauce is the perfect pairing to elevate the flavor of these little green pea treasures.

Health highlights: Green peas have muscle-building protein, zinc for immune function, and folate for cell growth. Onions and garlic add disease-fighting antioxidants. Extra-virgin olive oil offers healthy fats for brain development.

INSTRUCTIONS:

1. Preheat the oven to 350°F (177°C) and line the baking sheet with a reusable baking mat (or parchment paper).

2. Steam your frozen peas, covered, in a steamer pot until soft, or cook in a saucepan according to the food package instructions.

3. Heat the oil in a small pan over medium heat. Add onion and garlic and sauté until softened, 2 to 3 minutes.

4. Transfer the cooked peas, onions, and garlic to a food processor or blender and pulse until it becomes a paste. Add the flour, baking powder, Italian seasoning, lemon juice, and salt, and pulse again until combined.

5. Use your hands to form the mixture into patties: For each patty, roll 2 tablespoons of the mixture into a ball and place it on the prepared baking sheet. Then gently flatten it into a patty shape. Once you form the patties, use a basting brush or your hands to lightly brush the tops with extra-virgin olive oil. Bake for 15 minutes until golden brown.

6. While the patties are baking, make your sauce! Combine all the lemony sauce ingredients in a small bowl and mix with a spoon.

7. Once the patties are done, pour the sauce on top (or serve the sauce separately in a small bowl so they can dip it themselves). Allow the patties to cool to an appropriate temperature before serving. Refrigerate any extra patties in an airtight container or place in a freezer-safe container or bag and freeze for later.

REFRIED MIXED BEANS

Ages: 6 months+ (1 large family-sized serving)

Ingredients:

3 (15 oz/425 g) cans of beans of choice, such as kidney beans, black beans, and pinto beans (reserve ¾ cup/177 mL of liquid from the cans and drain the rest)

½ tablespoon extra-virgin olive oil

¼ cup (59 mL) vegetable stock (page 237 or store-bought)

3 tablespoons extra-virgin olive oil

1 teaspoon lime juice

1 teaspoon garlic powder

1 teaspoon onion powder

1 teaspoon ground cumin

1 teaspoon ground paprika

½ teaspoon chili powder

salt to taste (**Tip:** omit for infants and salt your portion separately)

Equipment:

Medium pan

Spatula

Potato masher (optional)

Did you know premade canned refried beans often contain lard? Lard is animal fat, typically extracted from the fatty parts of our pig friends (such as their bellies or butts); therefore, it isn't vegan. Thankfully for us and our little ones, anything can be veganized these days. This straightforward recipe utilizes the "healthy fats" portion of the PB3 Plate guidelines (page 73) by relying on extra-virgin olive oil instead of lard. The versatility of this dish will make it a staple in your arsenal of vegan recipes, as it can be used in a variety of ways. It is one of my go-to meal prep foods that I make in batches, store in jars, and freeze for later.

 Health highlights: Beans are loaded with muscle-building protein, iron for neurological support, fiber for digestive health, zinc for immune function, potassium for fluid maintenance in your baby's cells, and magnesium for bone health. The vitamin C in lime zest helps your baby absorb iron.

INSTRUCTIONS:

1. Don't forget to set aside ¾ cup of liquid from your cans of beans after you open them and drain the rest. You'll be using this later in the recipe as a flavorful cooking liquid to complement the veggie stock.

2. Heat the cooking oil in a medium pan over medium heat and pour in the drained canned beans. Cook for about 2 minutes, stirring occasionally.

3. Remove the pan from heat and mash the beans with a potato masher or the spatula you used for stirring.

4. Pour in the vegetable stock and reserved canned bean liquid. Return the pan to medium heat and cook for about 3 minutes, stirring occasionally.

5. Add the extra-virgin olive oil and lime juice. Then, season your beans with the remaining ingredients. Stir together. Taste the beans and adjust the seasonings, if needed, before serving.

6. Serve warm and store any extra in baby jars. You can refrigerate a few jars and freeze the rest for up to three months.

Serving ideas: Serve your refried beans as is or stuffed into bean taquitos, Refried Bean Burritos (page 218), bean sliders, or spread it on toast or soft tortilla slices!

REFRIED BEAN BURRITOS

Ages: 15 months+ (makes 6 burritos)

Ingredients:

½ cup (90 g) dry quinoa

1 cup (237 mL) water

6 medium tortillas

1 ½ cups (390 g) Refried Mixed Beans (page 216)

Serving suggestions: Serve this with Mango Salsa (page 135) or Baby-Friendly Guacamole (page 134).

Equipment:

Fine mesh colander

Small saucepan

Spoon

The flavorful Refried Mixed Beans recipe on page 216 is incredibly versatile, and in this recipe, I'm going to show you one of the many ways you can utilize it! Burritos are brilliant for kids and this one is loaded with health benefits. Between the quinoa and the refried beans, your little vegan super kid will be fueled and ready to take on the world.

 Health highlights: Quinoa is a seed (not a grain) that's packed with complete plant-based protein. Both beans and quinoa provide carbohydrates for energy, iron for neurological development, zinc for wound healing, and magnesium for muscle function.

INSTRUCTIONS:

1. Rinse the quinoa by pouring it into a fine mesh colander and rinse under running water for at least 30 seconds. Drain well.

2. Add the quinoa and water to a small saucepan over high heat and bring it to a boil. Then reduce the heat and simmer for about 15 minutes until all the water is absorbed. Remove the saucepan from the heat and fluff the quinoa with a fork.

3. Warm your tortillas in the microwave, stovetop, or oven.

4. Spoon ¼ cup of Refried Mixed Beans in a line down the center of each tortilla and leave the ends, top, and bottom uncovered, taking care not to overfill the burritos, as it can make it difficult to roll. Top the beans with about 2 tablespoons of quinoa.

5. Roll the tortillas, folding the sides inward and tucking the tortilla over the filling. Continue rolling until the burrito is seam-side down. Serve warm and refrigerate any extras in an airtight container.

VEGGIE-STUFFED ZUCCHINI BOATS

Ages: 12 months+ (makes 4 kid-sized zucchini boats)

Ingredients:

1 large zucchini

¼ tablespoon extra-virgin olive oil

½ small tomato, diced

¼ small yellow onion, minced

1 tablespoon fresh cilantro, chopped

1 tablespoon fresh basil leaves, chopped

½ teaspoon cumin

½ teaspoon garlic powder

pinch of black pepper

salt to taste (omit if avoiding)

2 tablespoons Japanese-style Panko breadcrumbs (or any vegan breadcrumbs)

Equipment:

Baking sheet

Reusable baking mat (or parchment paper)

Melon baller, cookie scoop, or small spoon

Basting brush, for oiling (or you can use your hands)

Small mixing bowl

Cutting board

Looking for a new way to entice your child to try veggies? Switch up the presentation! Make these cute zucchini boats to encourage your little one to give vegetables a chance. Don't hesitate to experiment with this one either! See my variation tip at the end of the recipe for ideas.

 Health Highlights: The zucchini, tomatoes, onions, cilantro, basil, and garlic all make this dish a disease-fighting antioxidant powerhouse.

INSTRUCTIONS:

1. Preheat the oven to 350°F (180°C) and line the baking sheet with a reusable baking mat (or parchment paper).

2. Trim the ends of the zucchini and cut it in half lengthwise. Use a melon baller, cookie scoop, or small spoon to scoop out the middle bits of each zucchini half and place the insides on a cutting board. Roughly chop the insides and put them in a small mixing bowl.

3. Brush the 2 halves of the zucchini boats with the oil and place cut-side down on your prepared baking sheet. Bake it for 10 minutes, until tender.

4. While the zucchini boats are baking, add the tomato, onion, cilantro, basil, cumin, garlic powder, black pepper, and salt to the bowl with the chopped inside bits. Mix until combined well.

5. Once the zucchini boats are done baking, remove them from the oven. Slice each in half horizontally so you have 4 zucchini boats. Spoon the filling into the zucchini boats and sprinkle ½ tablespoon of breadcrumbs on top of each slice. All 4 slices should each have half a tablespoon of breadcrumbs on top.

6. Bake for another 7 to 10 minutes. Remove the zucchini boats from the oven and let them cool down to an appropriate temperature before serving.

Variation tip: Experiment with mixing it up! You can make it heartier with Refried Mixed Beans (page 216) and mushrooms or make it "cheezy" with Ooey Gooey Mozzarella Cheeze (page 141) or store-bought vegan mozzarella shreds.

CREAMY MUSHROOM PENNE PASTA

Ages: 6–12 months with modifications, 12 months+ as is (makes about 8 kid servings)

Ingredients:

8 oz (½ pound/227 g) of penne pasta

¼ cup (59 mL) pasta water (reserved after cooking the pasta)

2 tablespoons extra-virgin olive oil (½ tbsp for drizzling and 1½ tbsp for sauteing)

2 cups (200 g) mushrooms, any kind, cleaned and sliced

Pinch of black pepper

½ large yellow onion, peeled and diced

1 cup (145 g) green peas, frozen or fresh

1 (13.5 oz /400 mL) can full-fat coconut milk, unsweetened

¼ cup (59 mL) vegetable stock

½ teaspoon Italian seasoning

½ teaspoon garlic powder

salt to taste (**Tip:** omit for infants and salt your portion separately)

Equipment:

Large pot

Strainer

Large pan

Cooking spoon

For today's menu, you're whipping up a creamy, hearty meal the whole family will love. Whether you use penne pasta, farfalle pasta, rigatoni pasta, or any other kind—this dish will provide a burst of flavor for your little one's taste buds. Always double-check the ingredients when shopping for pasta. Some fresh pasta you buy from the grocery store contains eggs as an ingredient, so avoid those. Thankfully, most boxed pasta is vegan, made up of only one or two plant-based ingredients such as semolina and enriched wheat flour. Legume-based pastas, like black bean pasta, chickpea pasta, and lentil pasta, are even more nutrient-dense. You have options!

Health highlights: Pasta is packed with muscle-building protein and carbohydrates for energy, mushrooms and peas have high amounts of disease-fighting antioxidants, and coconut milk provides healthy fats for brain health.

INSTRUCTIONS:

1. Bring a large pot of water to a boil and cook the penne pasta according to the package instructions. Reserve about ¼ cup (59 mL) of the pasta cooking water for use in the sauce. Strain the pasta and return it to the pot. Drizzle it with ½ tablespoon of extra-virgin olive oil and stir to coat.

2. Heat 1½ tablespoons of extra-virgin olive oil in a large pan over medium heat. Add the mushrooms to the pan and season it with a pinch of black pepper. Cook until the mushrooms are lightly browned, stirring occasionally, about 3 to 4 minutes.

3. Add the onions and peas and cook for another 3 to 4 minutes, until the onions soften.

4. Add the coconut milk, vegetable stock, and pasta cooking water. Season it with Italian seasoning and

garlic powder. Cook until the sauce has slightly thickened, stirring occasionally, about 5 minutes. Then, reduce the heat to low.

5. Add the cooked pasta to the sauce. Stir it all together until the pasta is well coated with the sauce. Cook it on low for another 5 minutes to allow the pasta to warm through. Add salt and taste it. Adjust the seasonings, if needed, to your family's taste. Remove the pan from the heat.

6. Allow it to cool down to an appropriate temperature before serving. Refrigerate any extra in an airtight container.

Infant modification: Make sure to flatten any peas that are in the portion you serve to a 6–12-month-old.

HEARTY LENTIL SLOPPY JOES

Ages: 6–18 months with modifications, 18 months+ as is (makes 5 sloppy joes)

Ingredients:

1 tablespoon extra-virgin olive oil, for cooking

1 garlic clove, minced

½ medium yellow onion, diced

½ teaspoon mild chili powder

½ teaspoon ground cumin

½ red bell pepper, diced

1 (15 oz /425 g) can of lentils, drained and rinsed

1 cup (237 mL) of water

1 (6 oz /170 g) can of tomato paste

1 teaspoon apple cider vinegar

1 tablespoon maple syrup

Optional: 1 teaspoon low-sodium soy sauce

salt to taste (**Tip:** omit for infants and salt your portion separately)

5 small burger buns

Equipment:

Medium saucepan

Mixing spoon

Toaster

Rich, filling, and made with wholesome ingredients, these Hearty Lentil Sloppy Joes are a fun vegan twist on a classic childhood sandwich. Lentils are an incredible meat substitute because they are packed with protein and do a stellar job of absorbing flavors. The lentils also outstandingly recreate the traditional sloppy joe texture, and the tomato-based sauce gives the dish an overall balanced experience of sweet and savory sensations for your little one's taste buds.

Health highlights: Lentils are an excellent source of iron and zinc, two nutrients that tend to be lacking in infant diets. Iron is essential for neurological development and blood health, while zinc is needed for metabolism and immune function. The vitamin C in the bell pepper and tomato sauce will help your baby's body absorb the iron from the lentils.

INSTRUCTIONS:

1. In a medium saucepan, heat the oil over medium heat. Add the garlic and onion. Season with the chili powder and ground cumin and cook for about a minute, until fragrant.

2. Add the red bell pepper and cook until softened, stirring occasionally, about 5 to 6 minutes.

3. Stir in the lentils, water, tomato paste, apple cider vinegar, maple syrup, optional soy sauce, and salt. Turn the heat up to high and bring it to a boil.

4. Reduce the heat to low and simmer until the mixture thickens, about 15 to 20 minutes.

5. Toast your buns. Allow the sloppy joe mixture to cool and then spoon about ½ cup of the mixture onto a toasted bun for serving. Refrigerate any extra mixture in an airtight container.

RECIPE NOTES:

Freezing: Let the mixture cool completely. Transfer it into a labeled freezer bag. Seal it while removing as much air as possible, date it, and freeze it for up to three months.

Thawing and reheating: Place the mixture in the refrigerator and thaw overnight. Pour bag contents into a pan over medium heat and cook until completely heated through.

Toppings: Serve your sloppy joes with sliced caramelized onions for added flavor!

Infant modification: For infants aged 6–12 months and toddlers aged 12–18 months, serve the sloppy joe filling on its own with an appropriately sized piece of the toasted bun on the side.

CAULIFLOWER MAC 'N' GEEZ!

Ages: 6 months+ (makes 1 large family-sized serving)

Ingredients:

2 cups (300 g) dry elbow macaroni (+1 tablespoon of extra-virgin olive oil for tossing)

2 tablespoons extra-virgin olive oil, for cooking

¼ medium yellow onion, chopped

1 small head (265 g) of cauliflower, chopped

1 large carrot, chopped

1 cup (237 mL) vegetable stock (page 237 or store-bought)

¼ cup (59 mL) fortified dairy-free milk of choice, unsweetened

¼ cup (15 g) fortified nutritional yeast seasoning

½ tablespoon lemon juice

1 tablespoon garlic powder

½ teaspoon vegan Dijon mustard (or yellow mustard)

pinch of black pepper

salt to taste (**Tip:** omit for infants and salt your portion separately)

Equipment:

1 large pot

1 large pan

Cooking spoon

Food processor or high-speed blender

I impressed myself with this one. This creamy, nut-free mac 'n' geez is perfect for little ones. Many vegan cheese recipes have nut-based ingredients, so I created one that is lunchbox-friendly for kids who attend nut-free daycares and schools. My veganized version of the ever-so-popular mac and cheese dish is nutrient-dense, filling, and downright delicious. Serve it with roasted veggies and a protein-packed dish, like Saucy Chickpea Balls (page 206), for a robust lunchbox meal.

Health highlights: Cauliflower is a rich plant-based source of choline, a nutrient needed for memory, mood, muscle control, and other brain and nervous system functions. Carrots supply vitamin A for eye health, fortified dairy-free milk has muscle-building protein and can help toddlers reach their daily calcium requirements, and fortified nutritional yeast is packed with energy-boosting B vitamins, including vitamin B12, which is essential for brain development.

INSTRUCTIONS:

1. Cook the elbow macaroni in a large pot according to the package directions. Drain the water, return the macaroni to the pot, and toss it with 1 tablespoon of extra-virgin olive oil. Set it aside.

2. While the macaroni is cooking, heat 2 tablespoons of oil in a large pan over medium heat. Add in the onion, cauliflower, and carrots. Sauté the veggies for about 5 minutes, until the onions soften, stirring occasionally.

3. Pour in the vegetable stock and give it a good stir. Reduce the heat to medium-low, cover the pot with a lid, and cook until the vegetables are fork-tender, about 15 minutes.

4. Remove the pan from the heat and allow it to cool for a few minutes. Carefully transfer everything from the pot to a food processor or high-speed blender.

5. Add in the dairy-free milk, nutritional yeast, lemon juice, garlic powder, mustard, black pepper, and salt. Process or blend until it turns into a smooth sauce.

6. Add the "cheese" sauce to your pot of drained macaroni and mix well. Serve warm, and refrigerate any extra in an airtight container.

VEGGIE COUSCOUS

Ages: 9 months+ (makes about 4–5 kid servings)

Ingredients:

1 tablespoon extra-virgin olive oil, for cooking

½ small yellow onion, chopped

½ teaspoon garlic powder

¼ teaspoon ground turmeric

pinch of black pepper

1 large carrot, finely chopped

¼ cup (59 mL) water, for veggies

½ large zucchini, finely chopped

1 small tomato, chopped

¼ cup (34 g) peas, frozen

1 teaspoon Italian seasoning

salt to taste (**Tip:** omit for infants and salt your portion separately)

1 ½ cup (355 mL) water, for couscous

1 cup (165 g) dry couscous

Equipment:

Medium pan

Cooking spoon

Medium pot

Growing up, I ate **a lot** of rice. It was the quintessential side item for most of my dinners and served as a blank canvas for an abundance of savory dishes. Much later in life, I learned that rice and rice products tend to contain higher levels of arsenic, a known human carcinogen, than other grains. Thankfully, there are other filling, neutral-tasting, carbohydrate-rich alternatives to this popular pantry staple that can help diversify your family's meals. Couscous is one of those! Couscous is a wheat-based pasta, but its tiny size and fluffy texture make it a worthy rice substitute. This antioxidant-packed veggie couscous recipe is fantastic to serve your kids either on its own or alongside other flavorful dishes.

 Health highlights: Turmeric has disease-fighting anti-inflammatory properties and black pepper helps absorb the turmeric. Carrots, zucchini, and tomatoes supply vitamins A and C for eye and immune health, onions and garlic add extra disease-fighting antioxidants, couscous has muscle-building protein and energy-boosting carbohydrates, and green peas provide choline, a nutrient needed for memory, mood, muscle control, and other brain and nervous system functions.

INSTRUCTIONS:

1. Heat the oil in a medium pan over medium-low heat. Add the onion and sprinkle on the garlic powder, turmeric, and black pepper. Sauté for about a minute, stirring occasionally.

2. Turn the heat up to medium. Add the chopped carrot and ¼ cup of water. Let the veggies simmer for about 5 minutes until the carrots soften a bit, stirring occasionally.

3. Add the zucchini, tomato, and peas to the pan. Season with Italian seasoning and salt. Reduce the heat to medium-low and cook for about 10 minutes, stirring occasionally, until carrots are fork-tender.

4. While the veggies are cooking, get your couscous going. Bring a medium pot of water to a boil on high heat and then add the couscous. Reduce the heat to low, and let it simmer for 10 minutes. Remove the pot from the heat and let the couscous rest for about 5 minutes.

5. When the veggies are done cooking, remove the pan from the heat. Transfer the couscous to the pan with the veggies and mix it all together. Taste it, adjust the seasonings, if needed, and serve warm. Refrigerate any extra in an airtight container.

CILANTRO QUINOA SLIDERS

Ages: 6–18 months with modifications, 18 months+ as is (makes 6–8 sliders)

Ingredients:

1 tablespoon ground flax + 3 tablespoons water (this is your egg replacement)

½ cup (90 g) dry quinoa

1 cup (237 mL) water

1 (15.5 oz/439 g) can of black beans, drained and rinsed

½ cup (30 g) Japanese-style Panko breadcrumbs (or any vegan breadcrumbs)

¼ cup (15 g) fresh cilantro leaves, chopped

2 tablespoons minced red onion

1 teaspoon garlic powder

salt to taste (**Tip:** omit for infants and salt your portion separately)

pinch of black pepper

2 tablespoons extra-virgin olive oil, for cooking

6–8 mini buns

Equipment:

Fine mesh colander

Medium saucepan

Medium mixing bowl

Fork

Large pan

Toaster

Small bowl

When I first went vegan, I thought beans would be my only option for veggie burgers. Oh, how wrong I was. From falafel burgers to mushroom burgers, I've seen it all, and I'm here for all the variety. These sliders are kid-sized miniature burgers made with wholesome and hearty vegan ingredients, including black beans and quinoa, with the unique flavor twist of fresh cilantro. Serve it with your child's favorite burger toppings and pair it with Carrot Fries and Dip (page 160), Sweet Potato Fries (page 162), or Cumin Lime Avocado (page 166).

Health highlights: Protein-packed quinoa and black beans supply iron for blood health and zinc for immune function, two nutrients lacking in infant diets. They are also both sources of choline, a nutrient needed for memory, mood, muscle control, and other brain and nervous system functions. Cilantro provides vitamin A for eye health and vitamin K, a nutrient that plays a vital role in blood clotting.

INSTRUCTIONS:

1. Make your "flax egg," which is your binder for the patties. Mix the ground flax and the water in a small bowl and set it aside for at least 10 minutes.

2. Clean the quinoa by pouring it into a fine mesh colander and rinse under running water for at least 30 seconds. Drain well.

3. Add the quinoa and water to a medium saucepan over high heat and bring it to a boil. Then reduce the heat and simmer for about 15 minutes, or until all the water is absorbed. Remove from the heat and set aside.

4. Place the beans in a medium mixing bowl and mash them with a fork.

5. Add the breadcrumbs, cilantro, onion, garlic powder, salt, black pepper, and the "flax egg" you made. Mix everything together.

6. Shape the mixture into several patties.

7. Heat 2 tablespoons of oil in a large pan over medium heat and add the patties. Cook for 3 to 4 minutes on each side until heated through and browned on both sides.

8. Toast your buns in a toaster and transfer the patties you'll be serving immediately to their slider buns. Top with a yummy sauce of your choice. Refrigerate the rest of the patties in an airtight container or freeze them for later.

Infant modification: For infants aged 6–12 months and toddlers aged 12–18 months, serve the patty on its own with an appropriately sized piece of the toasted bun on the side.

11

ONE-POT WONDER SOUPS & BEYOND

Reducing Food Waste with Kids

When making soups and stews for your family, you may find yourself experimenting with all sorts of herbs and vegetables. What do you do with all the food scraps? As a kid, I would have thought the obvious answer to that question would be to toss it in the trash. However, there are more eco-friendly ways to utilize those unwanted bits and you can teach your kids how!

About 95 percent of discarded food[96] ends up in landfills. Once there, decomposing food waste produces methane, a strong greenhouse gas that contributes to climate change. You can present this as an interactive learning opportunity to show your kids new ways to activate their world-saving superpowers. Here are a few family-friendly food recycling activities you can practice with your vegan super kids.

Regrow Food

One of my favorite ways to involve Beyond in reducing food waste is to help him regrow food from kitchen scraps. Some vegetables can be regrown from their roots, while some herbs can be regrown from their stems. An easy food to start with is a scallion, also called a green onion. The next time a recipe calls for scallions or green onions, don't throw away the root! Do this instead:

1. **Prep it:** Chop your scallion right above the root.
2. **Plant it:** There are two ways to do this. You can either have your child put the root in a small glass of water or plant the root directly in a pot of soil together.
3. **Grow it:** Place your glass or pot in a sunny location. If doing the glass method, place the glass on a sunny windowsill. If going the potted route, put the pot outside or on a table next to a window.

---

96 Harvard T.H. Chan. n.d. "Food Waste." The Nutrition Source. https://www.hsph.harvard.edu/nutritionsource/sustainability/food-waste/.

You can do this project during any season because it works both indoors and outdoors. During spring, I helped Beyond start his vegetable garden outside on our patio—we planted scallions, mint, and cilantro. Every day, he adorably asks to go outside and water his plants.

Compost

Involve your kids in composting, an earth-friendly way to recycle food scraps into valuable nutrients that can enrich soil. Every time I put food scraps in my compost tumbler, I let Beyond help. He's obsessed with bananas, so he's always throwing banana peels in there and trying to turn the tumbler. You can start out by placing a compost bucket in the kitchen your child can easily reach. Give them the role of placing fruit and vegetable scraps in the bucket. If they are old enough, assign them the role of emptying the bucket into your compost bin or pile.

If you don't have the space to compost at home, see if there are any local community-based composting programs that will collect your food scraps or have designated locations where you and your kids can drop them off.

Make Veggie Stock

Did you know you can make vegetable stock from food scraps? Yes! It's a cost-effective way to create a flavorful base for soups and stews without having to buy vegetable stock from the store. When cooking with your kids, give them the assignment of placing vegetable scraps in a large freezer bag or container and storing it in the freezer. The next recipe will show you the magical method of transforming that bag of frozen scraps into deliciously savory veggie stock.

FLAVORFUL VEGGIE STOCK

Ages: 6 months+ (use this as a base for soups and stews you make for your babies and toddlers)

Homemade veggie stock is a sustainable, cost-effective, and flavorful way to make use of vegetable scraps. It enhances the taste of dishes and can be used as a base for soups, stews, and sauces. The result provides a remarkably more flavorsome and nutrient-packed foundation than cooking those dishes in water alone does. We cook **a lot** in our house, so it doesn't take long to accumulate a colorful variety of vegetable tops, peels, herb stems, fruit cores, and other leftover bits that can have a second chance at life. So, don't throw away those scraps! Collect them during your food prep, store them in your freezer, and whip them out when you have at least four cups of scraps saved up. Follow the steps below to transform it into a deliciously savory veggie stock.

 Health highlights: Homemade vegetable stock is filled with all the vitamins, minerals, and antioxidants found in the vegetables, fruits, spices, and herbs you use to make it!

Step 1: Collect Your Scraps

When prepping your dishes, set aside the leftover skins, tops, stems, fruit cores, and bits you would normally toss. Wash them well and remove any stickers. Seal them in a freezer-safe storage bag or container and place it in your freezer. Continue adding to your collection until you have at least four cups worth of vegetable scraps. Below are some examples of what kind of food scraps work well in stock and which ones to toss into your compost bucket instead.

FOOD SCRAPS TO USE	FOOD SCRAPS TO AVOID
Onions, shallots, and leeks: skins and tops	**Cruciferous vegetables (like broccoli and cauliflower):** may cause the stock to be bitter
Garlic and ginger: skins and tops	**Starchy vegetables (like potato skins):** may cause the stock to look cloudy
Tomatoes and bell peppers: skins, flesh, tops	
Mushrooms: any part, but especially the stems	**Beets and artichokes:** may give the stock an overpowering taste
Scallions and celery: anything you don't use	**Rotten or moldy vegetables:** not safe for consumption
Fruit cores: apples, pears, peaches, etc.	
Carrots: skins and tops	
Herbs: stems	

Step 2: Make Your Stock

Ingredients:

4 cups (or enough to fill a large zip-top freezer bag) of vegetable scraps

4 garlic cloves, peeled and chopped

1 bay leaf

1 teaspoon dried thyme leaves

salt to taste (omit for infants, if desired)

pinch of black pepper

water, as needed (enough to cover the vegetables)

Equipment:

Large stock pot

Fine mesh strainer

Storage containers or mason jars

INSTRUCTIONS:

1. Add all the ingredients (except for the water) in a large stock pot over medium heat and let them sweat in the pot for a minute. "Sweating" is a technique that uses heat to gently bring out the flavors of aromatic vegetables.

2. Next, add enough water to cover the vegetables. Turn the heat to high and bring it to a boil. Then, reduce the heat to medium and let it simmer for about 30 to 45 minutes.

3. Once the stock is done simmering, remove the pot from the heat and let it cool to room temperature.

4. Once the stock is cool, pour it through a fine mesh strainer into whatever you want to store it in. You can store this in a sealed mason jar or another airtight container and refrigerate for up to 7 days. You can also freeze it to make it last longer.

Step 3: Compost the Leftovers

Once you finish making your stock, you can still do one more thing with those leftover veggies! Toss the strained veggies into your compost bin or pile, where it will break down into nutrients for your soil. If you don't have space to compost at home, check to see if your local community has any composting programs. This is a fantastic way to divert food waste from landfills.

Freezer tip: If you want your stock to last longer, freeze it. Pour it into a freezer-safe container or storage bag and place it in the freezer. Or pour your stock into ice cube trays and freeze. Once frozen, pop them out and place the cubes in a freezer-safe container or storage bag for up to three months. When you are ready to use your frozen stock, thaw it overnight in the refrigerator.

TOMATO LENTIL SOUP

Ages: 6 months+ (makes about 10 kid-sized servings)

Ingredients:

1 tablespoon extra-virgin olive oil

½ large yellow onion, peeled and chopped

2 garlic cloves, peeled and minced

1 medium carrot, chopped

1 medium celery stalk, chopped

2 cups (473 mL) vegetable stock (page 237 or store-bought)

5 medium tomatoes, chopped

½ cup (95 g) dry red lentils

handful of fresh basil leaves (about 8 leaves)

1 (13.5 oz/400 mL) can full-fat coconut milk

salt to taste (**Tip:** omit for infants and salt your portion separately)

Equipment:

Large pot

Cooking spoon

Immersion blender (or traditional blender)

Let's boost the nutrient profile of the traditional tomato soup with some hearty, protein-packed lentils. This soup is thick and flavorful with simple ingredients that ideally won't overwhelm kids with sensitive taste buds.

Health highlights: Lentils are excellent plant-based sources of muscle-building protein. They are also loaded with iron and zinc, two nutrients lacking in infant diets. Iron is essential for neurological development and blood health, while zinc is needed for metabolism and immune function. Tomatoes supply vitamin C to boost iron absorption and immunity, celery is packed with anti-inflammatory antioxidants that protect cells, carrots provide vitamin A for eye health, and coconut milk offers healthy fats for brain development.

INSTRUCTIONS:

1. Heat the oil in a large pot over medium heat and add the onion, garlic, carrots, and celery. Sauté until the onions become translucent, stirring occasionally, about 3 minutes.

2. Add the vegetable stock, tomatoes, and lentils to the pot. Turn the heat to high and bring to a boil. Then reduce the heat to low and let it simmer for about 20 minutes, or until the lentils are cooked. Stir it occasionally.

3. Remove the pot from the heat and let it cool. Add the basil leaves and then use an immersion blender to puree the soup until it's smooth. If you don't have an immersion blender, transfer the soup to a traditional blender, blend it until it's smooth, and then return it to the pot. Be careful when blending hot soup, as it can lead to splatters or burns if not handled carefully.

4. Turn the heat to low and add in the coconut milk and salt. Reheat the soup, but don't bring it to a boil.

5. Taste your soup and adjust the seasonings as needed. Serve it warm and store any extras in an airtight container in the refrigerator.

Freezer tip: Ladle the soup into a large freezer bag, squeeze out any excess air, seal the bag, date it, and freeze it for up to four months.

CREAMY BROCCOLI SOUP

Ages: 6 months+ (makes about 8 kid servings)

Ingredients:

1 tablespoon extra-virgin olive oil

2 garlic cloves, peeled and minced

½ medium yellow onion, peeled and chopped

1 large celery stalk, chopped

1 large Yukon Gold potato, chopped

3 cups (710 mL) vegetable stock (page 237 or store-bought)

1 small head (225 g) of fresh broccoli, chopped

salt to taste (**Tip:** omit for infants and salt your portion separately)

pinch of black pepper

1 tablespoon fortified nutritional yeast seasoning

1 teaspoon apple cider vinegar

½ tablespoon lemon juice

½ teaspoon vegan Dijon mustard (or plain mustard)

Equipment:

Large pot

Cooking spoon

Immersion blender (or traditional blender)

This creamy broccoli soup is a healthy and flavorful dish that's perfect for any day of the week. It's made with simple ingredients and can be served either hot or chilled, making it versatile for any season.

Health highlights: Broccoli provides vitamin A for eye health and fiber to aid digestion. Celery is packed with anti-inflammatory antioxidants. Fortified nutritional yeast is a complete protein loaded with energy-boosting B vitamins, including vitamin B12, which is essential for brain development.

INSTRUCTIONS:

1. Heat the oil in a large pot over medium heat and add the garlic, onion, celery, and potatoes. Sauté until the veggies soften, stirring occasionally, about 5 minutes.

2. Stir in the vegetable stock, broccoli, salt, and pepper. Turn the heat to high and bring the soup to a boil.

3. Reduce the heat to low and let the soup simmer until the potatoes are tender, about 15 minutes.

4. Remove the pot from the heat and let it cool. Stir in the nutritional yeast, apple cider vinegar, lemon juice, and Dijon mustard.

5. Use an immersion blender to puree the soup until it's smooth. If you don't have an immersion blender, you can simply transfer the soup to whatever blender you have and blend it. Be careful when blending hot soup, as it can lead to splatters or burns if not handled carefully.

6. Taste your soup and adjust the seasonings as needed. Serve it warm or chill it in the fridge and serve it cold. Refrigerate any leftovers in an airtight container.

Freezer tip: Ladle the soup into a large freezer bag, squeeze out any excess air, seal the bag, date it, and freeze it for up to four months.

THREE-BEAN CHILI

Ages: 9 months+ (makes about 14 kid servings)

Ingredients:

1 tablespoon extra-virgin olive oil

½ small yellow onion, peeled and diced

2 garlic cloves, peeled and minced

1 large carrot, chopped

1 teaspoon ground cumin

½ teaspoon dried oregano

¼ teaspoon mild chili powder

pinch of black pepper

salt to taste (**Tip:** omit for infants and salt your portion separately)

1 (6 oz/170 g) can of tomato paste

1 (14.5 oz /411 g) can of diced tomatoes

2 cups (473 mL) vegetable stock (page 237 or store-bought)

3 (15 oz /425 g) cans of beans of your choice, drained and rinsed (we enjoy kidney beans, black beans, and pinto beans)

2 tablespoons lime juice

Equipment:

Large pot

Cooking spoon

Cooking baby meals that work for the whole family is a complete time-saver. It also makes sense. When you eat together, your baby or toddler may be more inclined to try new foods seeing the rest of the family enjoying the same dish, even if it's just you at the table! Chili is a classic family-style stew that everyone can relish. For this filling Three-Bean Chili recipe, you're making an ample amount to feed your entire household, big or small.

 Health highlights: Beans are excellent plant-based sources of muscle-building protein. They also supply iron for neurological development and zinc for immune function, two nutrients lacking in infant diets. The tomatoes and lime juice provide immune-supporting vitamin C that helps your baby's body absorb iron.

INSTRUCTIONS:

1. Heat the oil in a large pot over medium heat and add the onion, garlic, and carrot. Sauté your vegetables for about 5 minutes, stirring occasionally.

2. Add the cumin, oregano, chili powder, black pepper, and salt and stir for another minute. Then, add the tomato paste, diced tomatoes, and vegetable stock. Turn the heat to high and bring it to a boil.

3. Reduce the heat to low and allow it to simmer for 10 minutes. Then, stir in the beans, cover the pot, and allow it to simmer for another 20 minutes, stirring it occasionally.

4. Remove the pot from the heat and stir in the lime juice. Taste the chili and adjust your seasonings, if needed. Serve it warm and refrigerate any extra in an airtight container.

Freezer tip: Ladle the soup into a large freezer bag, squeeze out any excess air, seal the bag, date it, and freeze it for up to four months.

BUTTERNUT SQUASH BISQUE

Ages: 6 months+ (makes about 8 kid servings)

Ingredients:

1 tablespoon extra-virgin olive oil

½ medium yellow onion, peeled and diced

2 garlic cloves, peeled and minced

2 cups (280 g) fresh or frozen butternut squash, chopped

2 red apples, diced

½ teaspoon ground ginger

½ teaspoon ground rosemary

salt to taste (**Tip:** omit for infants and salt your portion separately)

2 cups (473 mL) vegetable stock (page 237 or store-bought)

Equipment:

Medium pot

Cooking spoon

Immersion blender (or regular blender)

One of my favorite soups for its mix of savory and sweet flavors, this Butternut Squash Bisque offers a unique soup experience for your baby. Everything about it feels pleasantly cozy, from the nutty, fragrant butternut squash to the warm ginger and rosemary spices. Treat your child to this light yet satisfying dish and serve it with a hearty helping of cornbread, Veggie Couscous (page 228), or Saucy Chickpea Balls (page 206).

 Health highlights: Butternut squash is a vitamin A powerhouse for healthy vision. It also offers vitamin B6 for immune function and vitamin E for skin health. Apples, onions, and garlic add extra disease-fighting antioxidants.

INSTRUCTIONS:

1. Heat the oil in a medium pot over medium heat and add the onion, garlic, butternut squash, apples, ginger, rosemary, and salt. Sauté for about 5 to 7 minutes, stirring occasionally.

2. Pour in the vegetable stock, turn the heat to high, and bring it to a boil. Reduce the heat to low and let it simmer for about 30 minutes until the squash is cooked through.

3. Remove the pot from the heat and allow it to cool.

4. Use an immersion blender to puree the soup until smooth. If you don't have an immersion blender, you can simply transfer the soup to whatever blender you have and blend it. *Be careful when blending hot soup, as it can lead to splatters or burns if not handled carefully.

5. Taste your bisque and adjust the seasonings, if needed. Serve it warm and refrigerate any extra in an airtight container.

Freezer tip: Ladle the soup into a large freezer bag, squeeze out any excess air, seal the bag, date it, and freeze it for up to four months.

CORN AND POTATO CHOWDER

Ages: 6–12 months with modifications, 12 months+ as is
(makes about 10–12 kid servings)

Ingredients:

2 tablespoons extra-
virgin olive oil

1 large yellow onion, peeled
and chopped

3 garlic cloves, peeled
and minced

2 large carrots, chopped

3 Yukon Gold potatoes, diced

3 tablespoons all-purpose flour

1 teaspoon ground paprika

1 teaspoon dried thyme

2 tablespoons fortified
nutritional yeast seasoning

1 cup (165 g) frozen or fresh
kernel corn

3 cups (710 mL) vegetable
stock (page 237 or
store-bought)

1 (13.5 oz /400 mL) can coconut
cream, unsweetened

salt to taste (**Tip:** omit
for infants and salt your
portion separately)

pinch of pepper

Equipment:

Large pot

Cooking spoon

Immersion blender (or
traditional blender)

Yet another one of our favorite soups, Corn and Potato Chowder is flavorful, easy for little ones to devour, and filling enough to eat on its own. Beyond was thirteen months old the first time I served him a bowl of this creamy, cozy soup. I paired it with simple Cumin Lime Avocado (page 166) slices, and he merrily guzzled both down. It was satisfying to see!

 Health highlights: Potatoes have folate for cell function, iron for neurological development, energy-boosting B vitamins, and zinc for wound healing. Fortified nutritional yeast is a complete protein that contains vitamin B12, which is essential for brain health. Corn is rich in energy-boosting carbohydrates and fiber for digestive health. Coconut milk provides healthy fats for brain development.

INSTRUCTIONS:

1. Heat the oil in a large pot over medium-high heat. Then, add the onion, garlic, carrot, and potatoes. Sauté until the veggies soften, stirring occasionally, about 5 to 6 minutes.

2. Reduce the heat to medium. Add the flour, paprika, thyme, and nutritional yeast and stir to coat the veggies and potatoes well. Continue to cook for about a minute.

3. Add the corn and vegetable stock and stir it to combine. Turn the heat to high and bring it to a boil. Then, reduce the heat to medium-low. Cover the pot with a lid and let it simmer for about 15 minutes or until the potatoes are fork-tender. Remove the pot from the heat and allow it to cool.

4. Use an immersion blender to puree about half of the soup for a creamier texture, while leaving some chunks. If you don't have an immersion blender, simply transfer

half of the soup to whatever blender you have and puree it. Return it to the pot with the chunkier parts of the soup. Be careful when blending hot soup, as it can lead to splatters or burns if not handled carefully.

5. Turn the heat to low and add in ½ of the canned coconut cream, salt, and pepper. Reserve the rest of the coconut cream for another purpose. Stir it and reheat the soup, but don't bring it to a boil.

6. Taste your chowder. Adjust the seasonings, if needed. Let the chowder rest for a few minutes to allow all the flavors to meld together. Serve it warm and store any extras in an airtight container in the refrigerator.

Freezer tip: Ladle the soup into a large freezer bag, squeeze out any excess air, seal the bag, date it, and freeze it for up to four months.

Infant modification: For babies 6–12 months, puree the entire soup, not just half of it.

CURRIED LENTIL SOUP

Ages: 9 months+ (makes about 8–10 kid servings)

Ingredients:

1–2 tablespoons extra-virgin olive oil

½ small yellow onion, peeled and chopped

2 garlic cloves, peeled and minced

1 large carrot, diced

½ teaspoon ground ginger

½ teaspoon ground cumin

½ teaspoon mild curry powder

½ teaspoon ground coriander

pinch of black pepper

4 cups (946 mL) vegetable stock (page 237 or store-bought)

2 cups (380 g) dry green lentils, rinsed

1 (28 oz /794 g) can of diced tomatoes

1 (13.5 oz/400 mL) can full-fat coconut milk, unsweetened

1 tablespoon lemon juice

Salt to taste (**Tip:** omit for infants and salt your portion separately)

Equipment:

Large pot

Cooking spoon

Thick and hearty, this Curried Lentil Soup is a satisfying meal on its own. It's a flavorsome soup that combines nourishing lentils with wholesome vegetables and a medley of aromatic spices to expand your baby's palate. Adding herbs and spices to baby food is a commonly misunderstood practice. Contrary to popular belief, infants do not require their food to be bland. As Dr. Smith mentioned in Chapter 6, flavors are passed through the placenta, so if the parent ate flavorful foods during pregnancy, then the baby will often enjoy those same flavors in their meals! As always, adjust the spices to your child's taste.

Health highlights: Lentils are packed with muscle-building protein. They are also excellent sources of iron and zinc, two nutrients lacking in infant diets. Iron is essential for neurological development and blood health, while zinc is needed for metabolism and immune function. Tomatoes and lemon juice supply vitamin C for iron absorption, carrots provide vitamin A for eye health, coconut milk offers healthy fats for brain development, and onions and garlic add extra disease-fighting antioxidants.

INSTRUCTIONS:

1. Heat the oil in a large pot over medium heat. Then, add the onion, garlic, and carrot. Season the veggies with ground ginger. Sauté until the veggies are tender, about 6 to 7 minutes, stirring occasionally.

2. Add the cumin, curry powder, coriander, and black pepper. Stir to coat the vegetables with your spices and allow them to cook for a minute.

3. Stir in the vegetable stock, lentils, and diced tomatoes. Turn the heat to high and bring it to a boil.

4. Reduce the heat to low, cover the pot, and simmer the soup for about 30 minutes until the lentils are tender.

5. Stir in the coconut milk and lemon juice and heat through. Add salt to your family's taste. Taste your soup and adjust the seasonings, if needed. Refrigerate any extra in an airtight container in the refrigerator.

Freezer tip: Ladle the soup into a large freezer bag, squeeze out any excess air, seal the bag, date it, and freeze it for up to four months.

12

SWEET VICTORIES

WATERMELON POPSICLES

Ages: 12 months+ (makes 6 popsicles, depending on the size of your molds)

Ingredients:

2 cups (300 g) fresh watermelon, roughly diced

vanilla dairy-free yogurt, 1 tablespoon per mold

3 kiwis, peeled and roughly chopped

1 teaspoon maple syrup (omit if avoiding added sugar)

Optional: a pinch of blue spirulina powder (less than ⅛ teaspoon)

Equipment:

Blender

Popsicle molds

Reusable popsicle sticks (if your molds didn't come with them)

Watermelon popsicles are adorably refreshing treats to throw together, especially when temperatures begin to rise outdoors. What makes these so fun is that they are layered to resemble watermelons! You will use kiwi to represent the skin, dairy-free vanilla yogurt to represent the rind, and actual watermelon to represent itself. The aftermath is a delectable frozen watermelon dessert, the quintessential summertime treat.

 Health highlights: Watermelon and kiwi are packed with vitamin C, a crucial nutrient for immune function, skin health, and other physiological functions. If you use store-bought dairy-free yogurt, most are full of probiotics that support gut health by helping to balance the friendly bacteria in your baby's digestive system.

INSTRUCTIONS:

1. **LAYER 1:** Add the watermelon chunks to a blender and blend until smooth. Pour the blended watermelon into the molds, filling each mold about halfway. Pop the molds into the freezer and freeze until just solid enough to add the next layer, about 2 hours.

2. **LAYER 2:** Remove the molds from your freezer. Add 1 tablespoon of vanilla dairy-free yogurt on top of the frozen watermelon layer. Smooth it out. Pop it into the freezer again and freeze until just solid enough to add the next layer, about an hour.

3. **LAYER 3:** Add your kiwi chunks, maple syrup, and optional pinch of blue spirulina powder to a blender and blend until smooth. Kiwi has a sharp taste, so the sweet maple syrup will help balance the sharpness. A dash of blue spirulina powder will help make the kiwi greener by minimizing its yellow undertones. Remove the molds from your freezer and add the kiwi layer. Slide in the reusable popsicle sticks.

4. Put these back into the freezer and freeze your popsicles overnight. Before serving, hold the bottoms of the molds under warm running water for about 10 seconds to help them come out more easily.

RECIPE NOTES:

★ **Storage:** To keep these fresh, store the popsicles in a sealed freezer bag or airtight container in the freezer. Ideally, finish these within a month. The longer they are kept in the freezer, the more they will lose flavor.

★ **Popsicle molds:** They come in different sizes. The popsicle molds I use are reusable silicone molds that hold 3.3 ounces per mold and make up to 6 popsicles.

★ **No popsicle molds?** No problem! You can get creative and use what you have. Small disposable paper cups or small reusable silicone cups could work, offering a unique shape to present.

★ **Ingredient substitutions:** For yogurt, you can use any vegan yogurt you desire. I usually use vanilla coconut yogurt. Alternatively, you could try coconut cream.

★ **Additional flavor ideas:** You can make popsicles for any taste and occasion! You can turn smoothies into popsicles or experiment with using any of your favorite fruits, such as strawberries, mangoes, peaches, pineapples, raspberries, and blueberries.

FUDGY AVOCADO BROWNIES

Ages: 12 months+ (makes 9 brownies)

Ingredients:

1 cup (90 g) rolled oats

¼ cup (30 g) unsweetened cocoa powder

3 tablespoons coconut sugar

2 teaspoons baking powder

1 teaspoon ground cinnamon, Ceylon if possible

1 medium ripe avocado, peeled, pitted, and mashed

3 tablespoons sunflower seed butter

¾ cup (177 mL) fortified dairy-free milk of choice, unsweetened

¼ cup (59 mL) maple syrup

1 tablespoon vanilla extract

Equipment:

8x8-inch baking dish

Food processor or high-speed blender

Spatula

You may have paused when you read the title of this recipe. **Avocado**? In **brownies**? Hear me out. I had the same reaction the first time I saw avocado brownies served at an event. To my surprise, it was rich, chocolaty, and flavorful! I began to wonder what other unconventional ingredients could be used in brownies. In addition to avocado, I've learned how to make brownies with black beans, sweet potatoes, and pumpkin! These ooey gooey avocado brownies are moist, fudgy, and made with simple ingredients. Pick the right avocado and the taste will be neither bitter nor overly sweet—it will be perfectly balanced for your little one.

Health highlights: Avocado and sunflower seed butter are loaded with healthy fats for brain health. Oats provide protein for growth and fiber for digestion and bowel movement regulation. Cocoa powder packs a powerful antioxidant punch to help protect against inflammation.

INSTRUCTIONS:

1. Preheat the oven to 350°F (180°C) and lightly grease your baking pan with oil.

2. Add all of your ingredients to a food processor or high-speed blender and blend until creamy.

3. Taste the batter! This kid-friendly recipe has less sugar than typical brownie recipes. If you find it needs more sweetness, add a little more maple syrup or coconut sugar, 1 teaspoon at a time, until it reaches your desired sweetness level.

4. Transfer the batter to your prepared baking pan and smooth the top with a spatula. Place it in the oven for 35 to 40 minutes.

5. Remove the brownies from the oven and do the toothpick test to check for readiness—insert a toothpick in the center, and if the toothpick comes out with a few moist crumbs on it, they are done.

6. Allow the brownies to cool before slicing and serving.

★ **Avocado selection:** Using a ripe avocado is the key to ensuring your brownie batter isn't bitter. The avocado shouldn't be too young or too ripe. To know if it is ripe enough, press it with your finger. It should be soft, which means it's not too young. When you peel it, the flesh should be green, which means it's not too ripe.

★ **Sweetness level:** How sweet this is will depend on your goals for your kids. If you are limiting added sugar and training their taste buds to appreciate mildly sweet desserts as opposed to overly sweet ones, then no tweaks are needed! If you know your child likes traditionally sweet desserts and you don't mind adding extra coconut sugar or maple syrup, then adjust to their taste.

★ **Storage:** Store these brownies in an airtight container in the refrigerator. You can also freeze them in an airtight freezer-safe storage container or freezer bag for up to three months.

STRAWBERRY LEMON SORBET

Ages: 6 months+ (makes 1 family-sized batch)

Ingredients:

2 cups (298 g)
  frozen strawberries

1 tablespoon lemon juice

1 tablespoon maple syrup,
  or more if desired (omit
  for infants)

¼ cup (59 mL) warm
  water, as needed

Equipment:

High-speed blender or
  food processor

Mini spatula

Freezer-safe container

Homemade sorbet is a simple frozen treat with a smooth and luscious texture that any kid or adult can enjoy! You can use any of your favorite frozen fruits; however, I have a particular fondness for strawberry lemon. The tartness of the lemon combined with the sweetness of the strawberries creates a divine flavor contrast that will tickle your little one's taste buds. If your child is going through a selective eating phase where they are rejecting fruit, try serving it a different way in the form of a sorbet! This is an exciting, chilled delicacy the entire family can enjoy, especially on a warm, sunny day.

 Health highlights: Strawberries and lemons are packed with vitamin C, which promotes immunity and wound healing. Strawberries are also rich in antioxidants, and lemons are known for their detoxifying properties.

INSTRUCTIONS:

1. Place the strawberries and lemon juice in the blender or food processor and pulse it until the strawberries break up and look crumbly.

2. Add the maple syrup. Then, pour in some of the warm water to help the sorbet loosen, and blend it until smooth. You may need to stop and use a mini spatula to push the mixture down. Blend it for several seconds until it resembles a soft-serve texture. Add more warm water, if needed, to get it there.

3. Taste it. If you want more tartness, add another ½ teaspoon of lemon juice. If you want more sweetness, add a little more maple syrup and blend it again.

4. You can serve this immediately if you like the soft texture. Or you can transfer the sorbet into a freezer-safe container and allow it to solidify more in the freezer for 1 to 2 hours. Allow it to soften on your counter before serving.

★ **Freezer storage:** If you don't plan to eat this immediately, you can store the sorbet in your freezer in an airtight container for up to a month.

★ **Sweeteners:** If you want to avoid added sugar for your baby, leave the maple syrup out. However, if you want to make these sweeter, you can add your preferred sweeteners in your desired amount after you have finished blending and tasted it to see if it needs additional sweetening. Vegan sweetener ideas include maple syrup, date syrup, coconut sugar, and raw sugar.

★ **Switch up the flavor:** Experiment using any of your favorite frozen fruits instead of strawberries. You can follow this recipe with other fruits like mango, pineapple, blueberry, raspberry, watermelon, and more—go wild! Adjust the maple syrup amount, according to how sweet or tart your chosen fruit is.

★ **Fresh fruit:** If all you have is fresh fruit, you must freeze it first. Slice it up, place the fruit on a parchment-lined baking sheet without the slices touching each other, and freeze overnight before using them in this recipe.

KIDDIE PANCAKE DONUTS

Ages: 12 months+ (Makes 6 pancake donuts)

Ingredients:

Dry Ingredients

½ cup (60 g) all-purpose flour

½ teaspoon baking powder

¼ cup (48 g) coconut sugar

¼ teaspoon ground cinnamon, Ceylon if possible

Wet Ingredients

⅓ cup (79 mL) fortified dairy-free milk of choice, unsweetened

½ tablespoon applesauce

½ teaspoon vanilla extract

½ tablespoon liquid coconut oil

Optional Glaze for Adults who want their portions to be sweeter

¼ cup (28 g) organic powdered cane sugar

1 teaspoon water

Equipment:

Donut pan

2 medium mixing bowls

Piping bag or medium plastic food storage bag

1 small bowl (for glaze)

I never thought to bake my toddler homemade donuts until seeing a "Donuts with Dad" event on his school calendar. I didn't even own a donut pan at the time, but I sure do now! This recipe puts a fun twist on traditionally thick donuts and instead creates thin ones. The result is a unique cross between pancakes and donuts! I make half with a powdered sugar glaze for my husband and his sweet tooth and half without for our little one.

Health highlights: These low-sugar donuts have fortified dairy-free milk for muscle-building protein and strength-building calcium, as well as applesauce for vitamin C, which helps kids form and repair red blood cells, bones, and tissues. Small amounts of cinnamon also provide disease-fighting antioxidants and manganese, a mineral that helps with bone health.

INSTRUCTIONS:

1. Preheat the oven to 350°F (180°C) and grease your donut pan with cooking oil or cooking spray.

2. In a mixing bowl, stir together the dry ingredients. In another mixing bowl, stir together the wet ingredients.

3. Pour the wet mixture into the dry mixture and stir to combine into a thick batter.

4. Pour the batter into a piping bag. No piping bag? No problem. Pour it into a medium plastic food storage bag instead and cut a corner of the bag to squeeze the batter out. Use your piping bag or storage bag to smoothly pipe the batter into the donut pan.

5. Bake your donuts for about 8 minutes. Then, remove them from the oven and allow them to cool before serving.

Optional glaze: Mix all the glaze ingredients in a small bowl and dip three donuts in the glaze. This will be for the adults, and the other three for your little one.

Storage: These are best eaten on the day they are made but can be stored in an airtight container in the fridge for up to three days.

CREAMY CHOCOLATE PUDDING

Ages: 12 months+ (Makes 2–3 servings)

Ingredients:

3 pitted Medjool dates

Water, for soaking the dates

1 cup (237 mL) fortified dairy-free milk of choice, unsweetened

½ banana

½ teaspoon vanilla extract

1 tablespoon ground flax

2 tablespoons cacao or cocoa powder, unsweetened

Equipment:

Small bowl

Food processor or high-speed blender

If you grew up on chocolate pudding cups like me, this will feel nostalgic for you. They were easy to grab from the store's refrigerated section and pack in my lunchbox. Now you can make your own for your kiddos without the cow's milk and artificial flavors we were addicted to. This indulgent chocolate pudding brings all the delightful memories of childhood, without the unnecessary additives. Enjoy this easy-to-make, velvety vegan version of a classic childhood favorite dessert.

 Health highlights: Dates are high in disease-fighting antioxidants and contain at least fifteen minerals, including bone-supporting phosphorus, calcium, and magnesium. Fortified dairy-free milk can help toddlers reach their daily calcium requirements. Ground flax is packed with omega-3 ALA for a dose of heart-healthy fats. Bananas and cocoa powder are high in disease-fighting antioxidants.

INSTRUCTIONS:

1. Place the dates in a small bowl and pour enough water to cover them. Soak the dates for about 15 minutes to soften, and then pour out the water.

2. Combine the remaining ingredients, including your soaked dates, in a food processor or high-speed blender and blend until creamy. This can be served immediately or chilled. To store, refrigerate the pudding in an airtight container.

BAKED FRUIT CRUMBLE

Ages: 12 months+ (Makes 8 kid servings)

As with many of the baked goods I learned to make for my little one, I figured this one out after seeing "fruit crumble" on his school menu one day. I try my best to replicate the school menu and make veganized versions to send him off with. This baked fruit crumble can be made using any combination of your little one's favorite fruits. Opt for produce that is in season for the freshest flavors. The result is a simple, sweet, fruit-filled fest that is sure to satisfy your toddler's tastebuds year-round.

 Health highlights: Oats are loaded with energy-boosting carbohydrates, muscle-building protein, fiber for digestive health, zinc for immune health, and iron for red blood cell production. Fruit is an excellent source of vitamin C that helps kids absorb iron and form and repair red blood cells, bones, and tissues.

Ingredients:

Fruit Base

2½ cups (295 g) chopped fresh fruit of choice (I love using 1 red and 1 green apple)

½ cup (65 g) dried cranberries (or another dried fruit of your choice)

½ teaspoon ground cinnamon, Ceylon if possible

Crumble Topping

¾ cup (67 g) rolled oats

¼ cup (30 g) whole wheat flour

2 tablespoons liquid coconut oil

3 tablespoons maple syrup

2 tablespoons liquid coconut oil

½ teaspoon ground cinnamon, Ceylon if possible

Equipment:

8x8-inch square baking pan

Spoon

1 small mixing bowl

INSTRUCTIONS:

1. Preheat the oven to 350°F (180°C).
2. Pour the fruit base ingredients into the square pan and mix well.
3. In a small mixing bowl, stir all the crumble topping ingredients together.
4. Sprinkle the crumble topping evenly over the fruit base in the pan. Bake it for about 20 to 25 minutes until the topping is golden. Remove it from the oven and allow it to cool before serving. Store the fruit crumble in an airtight container in the refrigerator.

CINNAMON CHOCO CHIP BANANA BREAD

Ages: 12 months+ (makes about 8 slices)

Ingredients:

¼ cup (59 mL) fortified dairy-free milk of choice, unsweetened

1 teaspoon apple cider vinegar

3 medium overripe bananas

1 tablespoon maple syrup (omit if avoiding added sugar)

¼ cup (59 mL) liquid coconut oil

1 teaspoon vanilla extract

2 cups (240 g) whole wheat pastry flour or all-purpose flour

1 teaspoon baking soda

1 teaspoon ground cinnamon, Ceylon if possible

½ cup (80 g) vegan chocolate chips (alternative idea: raisins)

Equipment:

9x5-inch loaf pan

Optional: parchment paper

1 small bowl

1 large mixing bowl

Fork or potato masher

One day, I saw banana bread on my toddler's school menu. Naturally, I had to figure out how to make it! I was **beyond** pleased with how it came out; more importantly, he was too. If you have bananas starting to overripe, don't throw them out! Make this cinnamon banana bread instead. It's sweet, moist, and quick to prepare (though it takes a long time to bake), with the bonus delectable surprise of chocolate chips.

Health highlights: Fortified dairy-free milk has muscle-building protein and can help toddlers reach their daily calcium requirements. Bananas are excellent sources of essential nutrients like vitamin B6, vitamin C, and potassium, which work together to support brain development, iron absorption, and heart health. Small amounts of cinnamon provide disease-fighting antioxidants and manganese, a mineral that helps with bone health.

INSTRUCTIONS:

1. Preheat the oven to 350°F (180°C). Lightly grease your loaf pan with a bit of oil. Optionally line it with parchment paper, if desired.

2. Pour the dairy-free milk and apple cider vinegar into a small bowl, stir, and set it aside.

3. Mash the bananas in a large mixing bowl with a potato masher or fork. Stir in the maple syrup, coconut oil, vanilla, and your milk/apple cider vinegar mixture. Mix well.

4. Add the flour, baking soda, and cinnamon, and mix everything together. Gently fold in the chocolate chips, taking care not to over-mix.

5. Pour your batter into the prepared loaf pan and smooth over the top. Bake for 1 hour and 15 minutes. Then, remove it from the oven and check if the bread is done

by inserting a toothpick or fork into the center. If it comes out clean or with a few crumbs clinging to it, the bread is done.

6. Allow it to cool before slicing and serving. Store the bread slices in an airtight container in the refrigerator. You could also place it in a freezer bag or tightly wrap it in plastic freezer wrap and store it in the freezer for up to 3 months.

COCONUT-STUFFED DATES

Ages: 18 months+ (makes 6 stuffed dates)

Ingredients:

6 pitted Medjool dates

6 teaspoons of almond butter, peanut butter, or sunflower seed butter

1 tablespoon (or more) of coconut shreds, unsweetened

Equipment:

Knife

Spoon

This snack-sized dessert is a sublime mix of savory and sweet. Coconut-stuffed dates are easy to prepare and versatile. They can be enjoyed as an on-the-go snack, a party appetizer, or a quick dessert. Don't serve the dates all at once, though! Dates, while packed with nutrients, are high in naturally occurring sugar. This fruit can be used in deliciously sweet snacks and desserts, but in moderation.

 Health highlights: Dates are high in fiber, which supports digestive health; they also contain several types of antioxidants, which may help reduce the risk of developing certain chronic illnesses. The nut or seed butter you add will provide a healthy source of fats for brain health.

INSTRUCTIONS:

1. Use a knife to slice open each date lengthwise halfway, creating an opening. Remove the pits if they aren't pitted already.

2. Add 1 teaspoon of nut or seed butter inside the opening of each date.

3. Sprinkle a pinch of coconut shreds on top of each stuffed date and serve. These can be stored at room temperature in an airtight container for a few days.

APPLE PUMPKIN MUFFINS

Ages: 6 months+ (makes about 9 muffins)

Ingredients:

1 tablespoon chia seeds + 3 tablespoons water (this is your egg replacement)

1 ripe banana

¼ cup (60 g) almond butter or sunflower seed butter

3 tablespoons canned pure pumpkin

¼ cup (60 mL) fortified dairy-free milk of choice, unsweetened

½ tablespoon apple cider vinegar

½ cup (125g) applesauce

¾ cup (90 g) whole wheat pastry flour or all-purpose flour

¾ teaspoon baking powder

½ teaspoon baking soda

½ teaspoon cinnamon, Ceylon if possible

Equipment:

1 small bowl

Spoon

1 small mixing bowl

Fork

Reusable silicone cupcake liners (or disposable liners if you don't have any)

Standard muffin pan

I first made these for my fur baby before I even had my son. Since it is advisable never to give a dog any food with added sugar, my muffin recipe has none, making it a great treat for infants! The bananas and apples help make it naturally sweet for babies. Serve one of these warm muffins for breakfast or offer it as a satisfying anytime-of-day snack.

Note: These even passed the hubby test! However, if you are making these for adults too, remember you may want to separate half of the batter and add your favorite vegan sweetener—like a couple of tablespoons of maple syrup, coconut sugar, or raw cane sugar. Half the muffins can be baby-friendly, and the other half can be adult-friendly!

 Health highlights: Pumpkin is loaded with vitamin A, which can help strengthen a baby's eyesight. Apples are a great source of vitamin C, which supports immunity. The nut or seed butter you use also adds a healthy serving of fats into the mix for brain health.

INSTRUCTIONS:

1. Preheat the oven to 350°F (180°C) and line your muffin pan with the cupcake liners.

2. Make an egg replacement: Mix the chia seeds and water in a small bowl to make a "chia egg." Set aside the mixture for 10 minutes. This will act as your binder.

3. In a small mixing bowl, mash your banana with a fork. Add your "chia egg" mixture, nut or seed butter, pumpkin, dairy-free milk, apple cider vinegar, and applesauce. Mix your ingredients.

4. Next, add the flour, baking powder, baking soda, and cinnamon. Mix well.

5. Spoon the mixture into the cupcake liners and bake for 15 minutes. Then, remove the pan from the oven and allow your muffins to cool before serving. Store these muffins in an airtight container in the refrigerator.

CHOCOLATE DONUT SMASH CAKE

Ages: 12 months+ (makes 1 baby-sized Bundt cake)

Ingredients:

For the Binder

2 tablespoons ground flax + 6 tablespoons water (this will be your "flax egg")

For the Dry Mixture

1¾ cup (210 g) all-purpose flour

¾ cup (90 g) unsweetened cocoa powder

1½ teaspoons baking powder

1½ teaspoons baking soda

½ cup (96 g) coconut sugar (omit if you are not ready to introduce added sugar to your child)

For the Wet Mixture

1 ripe banana, mashed

½ cup (118 mL) liquid coconut oil

1 cup (237 mL) fortified dairy-free milk of choice, unsweetened

2½ teaspoons vanilla extract

Additional Ingredient

1 cup (237 mL) boiling water

For the Optional Ganache Frosting

1 cup (180 g) vegan chocolate chips

½ cup (118 mL) canned full-fat coconut milk, unsweetened

Note: This cake is very moist on its own, so the ganache frosting is optional!

Equipment:

Bundt pan

Small bowl

2 large mixing bowls

Whisk

Small saucepan

If you feel anxious about serving the perfect cake for your baby's first birthday—I encourage you to release that pressure. Not in the mood to bake a cake? Buy one (I did). Want to bake but stressed about added sugar? Leave it out. Not a fan of the smash cake tradition? Skip it! You don't need a cake to celebrate your baby's exciting entrance to toddlerhood.

That said, if you choose to bake and want an unconventional smash cake, make a baby Bundt cake! Bundt cakes have always been my favorite type of cake to make. The batters are easy to whip up and look stunning right out of the pan, even with minimal decorating. Smash cakes tend to be pretty large, so I decided to create something toddler-sized. Rich, moist, and extra chocolatey, this decadent birthday treat kinda looks like a giant chocolate donut, which offers a fun and different alternative to the traditional smash cake.

Health highlights: This low-sugar smash cake relies on bananas for sweetness, with the option of adding coconut sugar for those comfortable with it.

INSTRUCTIONS:

1. Preheat the oven to 350°F (180°C) and grease your Bundt pan with cooking oil or spray.

2. Make your binder ("flax egg"): Combine the ground flax and water in a small bowl. Stir it and set it aside for 10 minutes to thicken. This will be your magical egg replacement.

3. Add the ingredients for the dry mixture to a large mixing bowl. Whisk it and set it aside.

4. In a separate large mixing bowl, combine the ingredients for the wet mixture and whisk it. Then add the "flax egg" you made and mix it well.

5. Slowly add the dry mixture to the bowl with the wet mixture, pouring in a little at a time while mixing it together. Then, add the boiling water and mix it again.

6. Pour your cake batter into your prepared Bundt pan and drop it on the counter a few times to release air bubbles. Bake it for 35 minutes.

7. Make the optional ganache (frosting): While the cake is baking, warm a small saucepan on medium heat. Pour in the chocolate chips and coconut milk and stir them together as the chocolate melts. Remove it from the heat as soon as it melts.

8. Once the cake is finished baking, remove it from the oven. Let it cool for 10 to 20 minutes. Then, flip your Bundt cake over onto a serving dish and let gravity do its job. Loosen it with a mini spatula around the edges of the cake if it seems stuck. Pour the ganache on top and add any desired toppings (see recipe notes)!

RECIPE NOTES:

How to tell if the cake is done: When you remove the cake from the oven, use a toothpick or fork to make sure it's done—gently stick it in the cake and pull it out. If the toothpick or fork is mostly clean, then the cake is ready.

Storage: Store the smash cake in an airtight container in the refrigerator for up to a week. Let it sit on your countertop until it reaches room temperature before serving.

Freezing: Slice the cake and wrap each slice in plastic wrap or foil. Place each wrapped piece in a freezer-safe container or bag.

Thawing: Allow the cake to thaw at room temperature or in the fridge.

Topping ideas: Sliced strawberries or bananas, store-bought vegan sprinkles, or homemade Rainbow Coconut Super Sprinkles (page 143). Add festive cake toppers for a fun, party-like presentation.

Don't want a gooey mess? Skip the ganache and let them grab fistfuls of the moist, fluffy cake without the chocolate coconut sauce. Though, the mess is part of the fun!

13

POWER-UP SMOOTHIES

BUTTERNUT DREAMZICLE

Ages: 12 months+ (makes 2 kid servings)

Ingredients:

1 cup (237 mL) fortified dairy-free milk of choice, unsweetened

¼ cup (28 g) frozen butternut squash cubes

½ cup (35 g) frozen banana

½ mandarin, peeled

¼ cup (61 g) plain dairy-free yogurt of choice, unsweetened

Optional superfood add-in: 1 teaspoon ground flax

Equipment:

High-speed blender

Get ready for some orangey, butternutty goodness! This satisfying smoothie is one of my all-time favorites. It's smooth and creamy with a hint of citrus and tastes like dessert. Even kids who don't like the taste of butternut squash can appreciate this special treat. The sweet and tangy flavors of the bananas and oranges are powerful enough to shine through. Packed with vitamins A and C, this smoothie is an antioxidant-rich drink that offers your little one a nutritional boost with a splash of sweetness.

Health highlights: Butternut squash is a vitamin A powerhouse for eyesight. It also offers vitamin B6 for immune function and vitamin E for skin health. Oranges and bananas add extra disease-fighting antioxidants. Fortified dairy-free milk supplies muscle-building protein, vitamin B12 for brain support, calcium for bone health, and vitamin D to help your baby's body absorb calcium. Store-bought dairy-free yogurt is often fortified with probiotics that help your child maintain a healthy gut microbiome. The addition of ground flax provides a superfood boost of brain-supporting omega-3 ALA.

INSTRUCTIONS:

1. Blend all the ingredients in a blender for a few seconds until you reach a thick and creamy consistency.

2. Taste it! Does the banana overpower the other flavors? Consider adding more butternut squash cubes or orange slices to steer the flavor more in the direction you want.

3. Serve it fresh and store any leftovers in the refrigerator for later.

Tips:

★ **Storage:** Store it in sealed mason jars, silicone refillable baby pouches, or an airtight container and refrigerate for up to twenty-four hours.

★ **Ingredient substitutions:** If you can't find frozen butternut squash, experiment with similar vitamin A–rich ingredients like mango, pure pumpkin puree, or sweet potato puree.

CARROT APPLE DELIGHT

Ages: 12 months+ (makes 2 kid servings)

Ingredients:

1 cup (237 mL) fortified dairy-free milk of choice, unsweetened

½ cup (59 g) red apples, chopped

½ frozen banana

¼ cup (31 g) raw carrots, chopped

¼ teaspoon ground cinnamon, Ceylon if possible

1 pitted date

Optional superfood add-in: 1 teaspoon shelled hemp seeds

Equipment:

High-speed blender

I've always enjoyed the combination of apples and carrots—it's a nourishing, tasty way to get your fruits and veggies all in one go! What gives this deliciously thick smoothie a unique twist is the addition of cinnamon. Sweet, subtly spiced, and everything nice, this carrot apple delight is a delectable treat anyone can appreciate.

Health highlights: This smoothie has dairy-free milk for muscle-building protein, apples for digestion-supporting fiber, carrots for eyesight-developing vitamin A, and bananas for blood pressure-lowering potassium. Dates are high in disease-fighting antioxidants and contain at least fifteen minerals, including bone-supporting phosphorus, calcium, and magnesium. The addition of shelled hemp seeds provides a superfood boost of brain-supporting omega-3 ALA.

INSTRUCTIONS:

1. Blend all the ingredients in a blender until smooth.
2. Taste it! Adjust it as needed and serve it fresh. Store any leftovers in the refrigerator for later.

Tips:

★ **Storage:** Store it in sealed mason jars, silicone refillable baby pouches, or an airtight container and refrigerate for up to twenty-four hours.

★ **Ingredient substitutions:** Want to try a different spice? Cardamom and nutmeg offer pleasantly similar flavor profiles.

STRAWBERRY LEMONADE SMOOTHIE

Ages: 12 months+ (makes about 1 kid serving)

One of my favorite combos, strawberries and lemon go together as naturally as peas and carrots. This refreshing, tangy recipe is a captivating balance of mildly sweet and tart, offering your little one's taste buds a spunky mingling of flavors.

Ingredients:

¾ cup (177 mL) fortified dairy-free milk of choice, unsweetened

½ cup (74 g) frozen strawberries

juice of ¼ lemon

zest of ¼ lemon

Optional superfood add-in: 1 teaspoon chia seeds

Equipment:

High-speed blender

Health highlights: This smoothie has dairy-free milk for muscle-building protein, while strawberries and lemon are excellent sources of vitamin C, which helps kids absorb iron and repair red blood cells, bones, and tissues. The addition of chia seeds provides a superfood boost of omega-3 ALA for heart-healthy fats, antioxidants to help protect against cellular damage, iron for neurological development, and fiber to aid in digestion.

INSTRUCTIONS:

1. Blend all the ingredients in a blender until smooth.
2. Taste it! Too tart? Consider adding a tablespoon of maple syrup or a date.
3. Serve it fresh or store it in the refrigerator for later.

Tips:

★ **Storage:** Store it in a sealed mason jar, silicone refillable baby pouch, or an airtight container and refrigerate for up to twenty-four hours.

★ **Ingredient substitutions:** You can make any kind of berry lemonade smoothie you like! Raspberries, blueberries, or blackberries—use what you have.

BLUEBERRY SPINACH SMOOTHIE

Ages: 12 months+ (makes about 2 kid servings)

Ingredients:

¾ cup (177 mL) fortified dairy-free milk of choice, unsweetened

1 cup (140 g) frozen blueberries

½ cup (15 g) fresh spinach

½ ripe banana

¼ cup (61 g) dairy-free vanilla yogurt, unsweetened

1 pitted date

Optional superfood add-in: 1 teaspoon ground flax seeds

Equipment:

High-speed blender

Spinach where? This recipe may call for spinach, but your kiddo certainly won't taste it or see it. This sweet plum-colored smoothie is a kid-approved way to get all the glorious benefits of their veggies, while enjoying the splendid flavors of their fruits.

Health highlights: Blueberries have one of the highest antioxidant levels of all common fruits and vegetables, which can help protect your baby's cells from damage. This smoothie also has dairy-free milk with muscle-building protein, dairy-free yogurt with probiotics for gut health, bananas with blood pressure-lowering potassium, and spinach with vitamin K, which plays a vital role in blood clotting. The addition of ground flax provides a superfood boost of brain-supporting omega-3 ALA.

INSTRUCTIONS:

1. Blend all the ingredients in a blender until smooth.

2. Taste it! Adjust as needed. Serve it fresh or store it in the refrigerator for later.

Tips:

★ **Storage:** Store it in sealed mason jars, silicone refillable baby pouches, or an airtight container and refrigerate for up to twenty-four hours.

★ **Ingredient substitutions:** While spinach seems to be a popular choice for leafy greens, I encourage you to explore others. Swiss chard, kale, arugula, watercress, and more—you can experiment with all kinds of nutrient-packed, leafy greens.

PB&J SMOOTHIE

Ages: 12 months+ (makes 2 kid servings)

PB&J (peanut butter and jelly) is a beloved classic flavor combo amongst many kids—at least in the US where I grew up. If your little one has a peanut allergy, you can easily use another nut butter in its place, transforming it into a nut butter and jelly smoothie. Of course, you can also opt to use a seed butter instead as well. Rather than using actual jelly, you will utilize strawberries. This smoothie is a savory-sweet duo of flavors swirling in a sea of vibrant pink goodness. It's so thick, creamy, and dessert-like, your kids will think they ordered a milkshake!

Ingredients:

½ cup (75 g) frozen strawberries

½ frozen banana

1 tablespoon peanut butter

1 cup (237 mL) fortified dairy-free milk of choice, unsweetened

Optional superfood add-in: 1 teaspoon shelled hemp seeds

Make it peanut-free: Use sunflower seed butter instead of peanut butter.

Equipment:

High-speed blender

 Health highlights: Strawberries are packed with vitamin C, which powers your baby's immune system and aids the absorption of iron. Bananas supply potassium that helps lower blood pressure, peanut butter offers healthy fats for brain development, and dairy-free milk provides muscle-building protein. The addition of shelled hemp seeds provides a superfood boost of heart-healthy omega-3 ALA.

INSTRUCTIONS:

1. Blend all the ingredients in a blender until smooth.
2. Taste it and adjust as needed. Serve it fresh or store it in the refrigerator for later.

Tips:

★ **Storage:** Store it in sealed mason jars, silicone refillable baby pouches, or an airtight container and refrigerate for up to twenty-four hours.

★ **Ingredient substitutions:** You can experiment with other frozen fruits to recreate different "jelly" flavors like raspberries or cherries.

PEACHES 'N' GREENS DRINK

Ages: 12 months+ (makes about 3 kid servings)

Ingredients:

1 fresh peach, chopped

1 cup (30 g) fresh leafy greens of choice (for example, spinach, arugula, or watercress)

1 clementine, peeled

½ teaspoon vanilla extract

1 cup (237 mL) fortified dairy-free milk of choice, unsweetened

Optional superfood add-in: 1 teaspoon ground flax seeds

Equipment:

High-speed blender

I know this doesn't sound as enticing as peaches 'n' cream, but it sure does make drinking your greens feel a little more inviting. Kids aren't always excited by green foods and drinks, but this just might be the exception. The sweet and tangy peaches balance the earthy greens, the clementine gives it a bright, citrusy note, and the vanilla extract adds a hint of floral flavor. It's a cross between a green juice and a fruity smoothie—behold, the Peaches 'n' Greens Drink.

Health highlights: Peaches and mandarins provide fiber for digestive health and vitamin C to strengthen your child's immune system. Leafy green vegetables are loaded with vitamin K, a nutrient that plays a vital role in blood clotting. Dairy-free milk supplies muscle-building protein. The addition of ground flax provides a superfood boost of brain-supporting omega-3 ALA.

INSTRUCTIONS:

1. Blend all the ingredients in a blender until smooth.

2. Taste it! Adjust as needed. Serve it fresh with a colorful eco-friendly straw to make it fun or store it in the refrigerator for later.

Tips:

★ **Storage:** Store it in sealed mason jars and refrigerate for up to twenty-four hours. Give it a good stir before serving.

★ **Ingredient substitutions:** Can't find clementines? Try a tangerine or any variety of mandarin!

RED VELVET SMOOTHIE

Ages: 12 months+ (makes 1 kid serving)

Red velvet cake is a decadent US Southern delight, which at its core is basically chocolate cake with red coloring added to it. To make a red velvet smoothie, you will be building on that idea with cocoa powder for the chocolate flavor and beets for the crimson hue. The addition of sweet bananas, dates, and flavorful vanilla go on to balance the mildly earthy taste of the beets. The aftermath is a rich and creamy dessert-like smoothie that will tickle your little one's taste buds.

Health highlights: Beets and bananas are high in fiber for digestion support, dates and cocoa powder supply disease-fighting antioxidants, and dairy-free milk offers muscle-building protein. The addition of chia seeds provides a superfood boost of omega-3 ALA for heart-healthy fats.

Ingredients:

¼ cup (34 g) raw beets, peeled and cubed

1 frozen banana

1 teaspoon cocoa powder, unsweetened

1 pitted date

½ teaspoon vanilla extract

½ cup (118 mL) fortified dairy-free milk of choice, unsweetened

Optional superfood add-in: 1 teaspoon chia seeds

Equipment:

High-speed blender

INSTRUCTIONS:

1. Blend all the ingredients in a blender until smooth.
2. Taste it! Adjust as needed. Serve it fresh or store it in the refrigerator for later.

Tips:

★ **Storage:** Store it in a sealed mason jar, silicone refillable baby pouch, or an airtight container and refrigerate for up to twenty-four hours.

★ **Ingredient substitution:** Not into dates? Replace it with another sweetener of choice, such as a tablespoon of maple syrup.

★ **Garnish idea:** Serve the smoothie with a dollop of dairy-free whipped cream to make it more reminiscent of red velvet cake!

PINEAPPLE COCONUT SMOOTHIE

Ages: 12 months+ (makes 1 kid serving)

Ingredients:

1 cup (140 g) frozen pineapple chunks

¼ cup (59 mL) full-fat coconut milk, unsweetened

½ cup (118 mL) fortified dairy-free milk of choice, unsweetened

Optional superfood add-in: 1 teaspoon ground flax seeds

Equipment:

High-speed blender

Tropical fruits are embedded in our roots. My husband's family is Nigerian, my mother is South Indian, and my grandmother on my father's side is Jamaican. So naturally, pineapples and coconuts are our jam! This refreshing pineapple coconut smoothie is packed with vitamins, minerals, and sunshiny flavors that can brighten even the cloudiest of days. The sweet and tangy taste of pineapple perfectly complements the rich, nutty flavors of the coconut, resulting in a creamy, ice-cold taste of the tropics. My toddler loves it and I hope your little one will too!

Health highlights: Pineapples are loaded with vitamin C for iron absorption, folate for cell function, and fiber for digestion support. Coconut milk offers healthy fats for brain development, while dairy-free milk provides a great source of muscle-building protein. The addition of ground flax provides a superfood boost of brain-supporting omega-3 ALA.

INSTRUCTIONS:

1. Blend all the ingredients in a blender until smooth.
2. Taste it! Adjust as needed. Serve it fresh or store it in the refrigerator for later.

Tips:

★ **Storage:** Store it in a sealed mason jar, silicone refillable baby pouch, or an airtight container and refrigerate for up to twenty-four hours.

★ **Ingredient substitutions:** Want to try other tropical flavors? Try frozen mango, papaya, or passion fruit!

DRAGON MANGO BOWL

Ages: 12 months+ (makes 1 smoothie bowl)

Have you ever served a smoothie in a bowl? Well, today you will! A smoothie bowl offers a fun twist on the traditional sip-and-slurp smoothie. It gives you more wiggle room for creativity, as you can present it with a wide variety of tantalizing toppings for your little one to try. You can even use the toppings to make funny faces in the bowl, similar to the ones in my silly animal face toast recipes I shared with you on page 174 in this cookbook. Have some fun with this one!

Ingredients:

½ cup (88 g) frozen mango chunks

½ cup (70 g) frozen pink dragon fruit

½ cup (118 mL) fortified dairy-free milk, unsweetened

Optional superfood add-in: 1 teaspoon chia seeds

Equipment:

High-speed blender

 Health highlights: The dragon fruit and mango are excellent sources of vitamin C for immune support and iron absorption, as well as beta-carotene, which your baby converts to vitamin A for healthy eyes. The dairy-free milk offers muscle-building protein, and the addition of chia seeds provides a superfood boost of omega-3 ALA for heart-healthy fats and iron for neurological development.

INSTRUCTIONS:

1. Blend all the ingredients in a blender until the mixture is thick like soft-serve ice cream.

2. Spoon it into a bowl and add your little one's favorite toppings if desired (see recipe notes). Serve it immediately after preparation to avoid melting.

Tips:

★ **Topping ideas:** Coconut shreds, an array of colorful sliced fruits, nuts, seeds, and/or granola all make excellent toppings. For older toddlers, you can involve them by letting them choose and arrange their toppings.

★ **Ingredient substitutions:** Can't find frozen pink dragon fruit? Try frozen strawberries instead.

Overcoming Challenges: How Jazz Duke Inspired This Next Recipe (and Me)

I chose this next recipe to be the final recipe of my book, because of the talented person who inspired it. Jazz Duke is a vegan lifestyle content creator and influencer known for her refreshingly honest yet comical and relatable brand "Diary of a Mad Black Vegan." Her naturally sunny disposition and entertaining storytelling abilities help motivate, engage, and educate people from all walks of their vegan journey, including myself. In doing so, she probably doesn't know just how much of a role she played in making this book happen.

You see, unbeknownst to Jazz, she is the first person who ever planted the seed in my soul to write this book. As a fellow social media content creator myself, I share vegan lifestyle inspiration that became more family focused after I became a mother. I began posting healthy plant-based recipe ideas for kids and started a series called "What My Vegan Baby Eats in a Day" that unexpectedly went viral. While it was applauded and well-received by many, it was painfully vilified by others who didn't understand veganism or plant-based nutrition. During a time when I was coping with extreme online harassment for raising my child vegan, Jazz left an unforgettable comment on one of my early vegan baby recipe videos that instantly impacted me:

> **"This is the BEST content in these vegan streets!!!! Pleaseeee keep showing us what baby Beyond eats! So many people are so clueless about raising vegan children and you Sis are really doing the work to educate us!!!!!!! THANK YOUUUUUUU!!!! Waiting on the vegan baby guide from you!"**

Before seeing her message, I was debating whether or not to continue posting videos. I had received an incredibly hateful, gut-wrenching comment about my child that nearly discouraged me from persisting with sharing vegan parenting content. But something transformational happened when I read her words. Suddenly, I felt uplifted, empowered, and needed. Just like that, the power was stripped away from any cruel remarks I received going forward.

I stopped taking the negative comments personally and began to recognize them as fear-based reactions resulting from a limited exposure to vegan lifestyles. Education, however, is a powerful way to intercept ignorance. The only way I can fight misconceptions, stereotypes, and misinformation about vegan parenting is through education. So, I decided to keep going—and now have a whole book dedicated to educating and empowering all of you reading this to confidently navigate any challenges and criticisms that may arise during your journeys.

Jazz often posts tantalizing smoothie recipes on her Instagram page, and one caught my eye. She called it the "Chocolate Covered Cherry Smoothie," and the mere sound of it had me drooling. There's nothing **not** to love about chocolate and cherries, and I knew my son Beyond would feel the same way. Something about that ingredient combination radiates love. With food being one of the many vehicles I use to express my love for my son, I thought it would be a blissfully delectable treat to offer him. He delightfully guzzled it down as I hoped, and I immediately messaged Jazz to ask her if I could create a baby-sized version of it for this book!

I encourage you to try making the recipe, continue your exploration of vegan parenting, and always remember to engage with the vegan community in a supportive, positive way. You simply never know who you might impact, just as Jazz impacted me. With that said, I'm sending a big thank you to Jazz for inspiring the final recipe of **The Vegan Baby Cookbook and Guide**—and for inspiring me to make it this far.

JAZZY CHOCOLATE CHERRY SMOOTHIE

Ages: 12 months+ (makes 2 kid servings)

Ingredients:

1 cup (237 mL) fortified dairy-free milk of choice, unsweetened

⅓ cup (51 g) frozen cherries

1 pitted date

1 tablespoon cocoa powder, unsweetened

Optional superfood add-in: 1 teaspoon shelled hemp hearts

Equipment:

High-speed blender

Inspired by Jazz Duke of "Diary of a Mad Black Vegan," I've created this mini version of her decadent chocolate-covered cherry smoothie recipe with the optional addition of nutrient-boosting hemp hearts. The rich, chocolatey flavor is complemented by the sweetness and tartness of the cherries. It reminds me of a luscious chocolate milkshake. Thank you, Jazz, for the delicious inspiration!

Health highlights: Cherries offer fiber to aid in digestion. Fortified dairy-free milk supplies muscle-building protein, vitamin B12 for brain support, calcium for bone health, and vitamin D to help your baby's body absorb calcium. Dates and cocoa powder are high in disease-fighting antioxidants. The addition of shelled hemp seeds provides a superfood boost of brain-supporting omega-3 ALA.

INSTRUCTIONS:

1. Blend all the ingredients in a blender until smooth.
2. Taste it and adjust as needed. Serve this divine Jazzy Chocolate Cherry Smoothie to your little one for a tasty treat that's also packed with nutrients. I hope they enjoy it as much as mine does!

Tips:

★ **Storage:** If not serving immediately, store it in sealed mason jars, silicone refillable baby pouches, or an airtight container and refrigerate for up to twenty-four hours.

★ **Ingredient substitution:** Not into cherries? Try frozen strawberries instead! "Jazzy Chocolate Strawberry Smoothie" does have a nice ring to it.

AFTERWORD

It is my greatest hope that this book brought you joy, insight, inspiration, and confidence. If it touched you positively in any way, I would love to know. Writers often desire to connect with and hear from their readers, so I encourage you to reach out! I welcome all reader feedback (be kind though, please—I know I talk a lot about being a superhero, but superheroes have feelings, too).

If **The Vegan Baby Cookbook and Guide** brought value to your life, share what you learned with your family and friends, post about it online, tag me (@heyashleyrenne) on social media, and write a review on Amazon. If, for some reason, you **didn't** like it, then don't forget what Mama or whoever once taught you: "If you can't say something nice…" Well, you know the rest.

I appreciate you dearly for sticking with me to the end of this thing. Thanks for coming along for this wild vegan parenting ride!

ADDITIONAL RESOURCES

The Vegan Baby Cookbook and Guide

Locate a Plant-Based Health Provider

Plantrician Providers (plantrician.org): An online directory designed to connect patients with healthcare professionals, including pediatricians, who are committed to using whole-food, plant-based nutrition as a cornerstone in practice.

Online Resources

Plant-Based Juniors (plantbasedjuniors.com): Blog and social media platform providing evidence-based guidance delivered by nutrition experts on plant-forward and plant-exclusive diets from pregnancy all the way through the teen years.

Plant Based News (plantbasednews.org): Mission-led impact media platform that will keep you up to date on all the latest vegan news.

The Physicians Committee for Responsible Medicine (pcrm.org): Nonprofit platform featuring information from physicians, dietitians, and scientists who are working with policymakers, industry, the medical community, the media, and the public to create a better future for people and animals—they have a Pregnancy section and Nutrition for Kids section on their website.

NutritionFacts.org: Science-based nonprofit platform that provides free updates on the latest in nutrition research via bite-sized videos, blogs, podcasts, and infographics.

Vegan Health (veganhealth.org): Website providing reviews of the scientific literature related to the health benefits of a vegan diet, discussions about concerns related to vegan nutrition, and recommendations for nutrients that can be low in the diets of some vegans. They have a Life Cycle section that focuses on pregnancy, infants, and children.

Veggie Fit Kids (veggiefitkids.com): Website by board-certified pediatrician Dr. Yami Cazorla-Lancaster offering families tools to help them on their journey to a healthier life for their kids—she also has a podcast called Veggie Doctor Radio.

Vegan Baby-Led Weaning: Facebook group where community members share first foods, food ideas, recipes, stories, photos, and support for anyone on their vegan baby-led weaning journey.

Books

The Plant-Based Baby & Toddler Book by Alexandra Caspero MA, RDN, and Whitney English MS, RDN

Plant-Powered Families by Dreena Burton

The Vegucated Family Table by Marisa Miller Wolfson and Laura Delhauer

A Parent's Guide to Intuitive Eating: How to Raise Kids Who Love to Eat Healthy by Dr. Yami Cazorla-Lancaster

Documentaries

The Game Changers: Documentary about athletes who follow plant-based diets.

Eating Our Way to Extinction: Cinematic documentary that exposes the cost of eating animals by revealing the impact animal agriculture has on the planet.

Forks Over Knives: Documentary sharing the research and connections between nutrition and health.

Cowspiracy: The Sustainability Secret: Documentary focusing on the unsustainable environmental impact of animal agriculture and investigates why the world's leading environmental organizations are too afraid to talk about it.

What the Health: Investigative documentary from the producers of Cowspiracy that explores the influence of government and corporations on our health.

Organizations and Movements

Mothers Against Dairy (mothersagainstdairy.org): A worldwide movement of mothers speaking out against dairy.

Youth Climate Save Movement (genesisforanimals.org/youth-climate-save): Youth-led environmental organization launched by Genesis Butler that focuses on animal agriculture's impact on climate change and works with schools, governments, and hospitals in international communities to help create campaigns, events, and legislation that can help the environment and animals.

Coalition for Healthy School Foods (healthyschoolfood.org): Nonprofit that introduces plant-based foods and nutrition education in schools to educate the whole school community about the health, environmental, and social justice issues of our food choices.

Additional Resources

Tab Time: YouTube Originals series hosted by Tabitha Brown that teaches children how to live fulfilled lives, and in every episode, she shows kids how to make a fun, healthy vegan snack.

Peta Kids (petakids.com): Website and social media platform with educational resources, games, activities, and quizzes that teach kids about animal rights and ways to take action for animals.

Happy Animals: Friends Not Food by Liora Raphael, Glenn Saks, Susan Szecsi (Illustrator): My toddler's favorite book, which takes kids on an entertaining journey through an animal farm sanctuary and introduces the compassion behind the choice to live a vegan lifestyle.

That's Not My Momma's Milk! by Julia Barcalow: A vegan children's board book that helps families teach young children that a momma's milk is meant for her baby.

Charlie Goes Vegan by Charles Leigh Jr.: A book for kids who want to learn about the vegan lifestyle that also serves as a conversation starter for parents who want to teach their children about the benefits of eating their fruits and vegetables.

ACKNOWLEDGMENTS

Thank you, Beyond, my Chief Taste Tester, for instilling within me a joy for cooking that never existed until you came along. Preparing food felt like a chore in the past—now it's one of many vehicles I use to express my love for you. Anytime I felt like giving up on finishing this book, I thought about you and found the strength to keep going. My sweet boy, you are my ultimate inspiration and the reason this book exists. I hope you are proud of what we created together. Mommy loves you.

Thank you, Wonder, for showing me that if I can write a book while pregnant, I can do **anything**. You have been here with me every step of the way on this book-writing journey, reminding me with a good ol' kick to my belly that I'm not on this path alone. As fate would have it, I went into labor minutes after finalizing this book manuscript. Eight hours later, you entered the world, and I had the honor of meeting my writing buddy. Mommy is thrilled you're finally here.

Thank you, Karl, my loving husband and soulmate, for recognizing that fatherhood is not about being an assistant to your wife, but rather an active, present, and equal partner. You hold it down in the kitchen, nurture our family, and take care of our household just as passionately as I do. The mental, emotional, and physical support you provide is next level. I love and appreciate you dearly for that.

Thank you, Mommy, my personal superhero, for being both my son's and dog's best friend in the eleventh hour when I needed help the most with getting this book done. Without you flying all the way from India to the United States to stay with us and help take care of Beyond and our fur baby Kayden, I would have never finished this thing, especially with a newborn due to enter the world in a matter of days! You are the most kind, compassionate, and patient human I know. Your love and warmth are the lights that guide our whole family. We love you, ammachi.

Thank you to the intelligent, insightful, and fierce ladies who helped take this book to the next level! You three superheroes were kind enough to lend your time, expertise, and wisdom to my project when you had a zillion other things going on in your lives and careers:

★ Dr. Shayna Smith: You took the time to answer my questions about introducing solids to infants, enriching parents with the knowledge they need to begin their journeys.

★ Dr. Yami Cazorla-Lancaster: You reviewed and fact-checked my nutrition chapter for accuracy, helping parents gain the confidence they need to succeed on their journeys.

★ Genesis Butler: You shared your soul-stirring journey in the foreword, ultimately giving parents a beautiful example of how a vegan super kid truly can help change the world.

Thank you to my photographer, Alex Questo, who brought my book cover to life and to the Mango Publishing team who brought my entire book vision to life. I appreciate you taking a chance on me as a new author tackling a topic that isn't discussed nearly enough. With your help, this book will change that, providing a much-needed resource for parents all around the globe.

Finally, I want to acknowledge myself. Writing and photographing my first book while pregnant and taking care of my toddler was a uniquely challenging first-time experience, but I did it and I'm **beyond** proud of myself for pushing through! Now, the **Vegan Baby Cookbook & Guide** is out in the world, and I couldn't be more overjoyed—I hope my children are too.

ABOUT THE AUTHOR

Ashley Nsonwu is a Black American and South Asian environmental, health, and animal rights advocate, author, and mom dedicated to helping the next generation of sustainable, vegan families.

After spending over a decade working in the video and media departments of large corporations, she left the corporate world to build her personal brand around her passions. She started out as a travel blogger, until a 2015 trip to Bali, where witnessing the horrific effects of environmental pollution inspired her to change her lifestyle, and eventually, the direction of her brand. Fueled by her love for animals, she adopted a vegan lifestyle in 2016, and then in 2017, she learned of the blatant connections between animal agriculture, climate change, and health disparities. As a result, her platform naturally shifted over time to focus on educating others on how we can all help safeguard animals, the earth, and our health through a sustainable, vegan lifestyle. In 2019, she officially rebranded from a travel blogger to her self-titled brand **Hey Ashley Renne**.

After becoming a mom in 2021, she began using her social media platforms in 2022 to share family-focused vegan lifestyle inspiration, healthy plant-based menu ideas for kids, sustainable parenting tips, and animal rights education. After her online video series "What My Vegan Baby Eats in a Day" featuring her baby Beyond reached millions of viewers, she was inspired to author her first cookbook and guide, uniquely created for vegan and vegan-curious families all around the world, which she wrote in 2023 while pregnant with her second child, Wonder.

Ashley has been interviewed on television networks and shows, including CNN and **Good Morning America**, her work has been highlighted in numerous magazines and online publications, and she was invited by the White House multiple times to speak with the president and vice president in 2022 and 2023. Through her work, she aims to motivate her community to bridge individual action with systemic change to help end animal exploitation, protect the environment, and make plant-based nutrition education accessible for parents and children in schools—especially in communities of color disproportionately impacted by climate change and health problems.

She would love for you to join her community, follow her on social media, and subscribe to her newsletter. Keep up with Ashley and her family's adventures, initiatives, projects, recipes, and tips:

Website: www.ashleyrenne.com
Social Media: @heyashleyrenne

Index

Mango Publishing, established in 2014, publishes an eclectic list of books by diverse authors—both new and established voices—on topics ranging from business, personal growth, women's empowerment, LGBTQ studies, health, and spirituality to history, popular culture, time management, decluttering, lifestyle, mental wellness, aging, and sustainable living. We were named 2019 **and** 2020's #1 fastest growing independent publisher by **Publishers Weekly.** Our success is driven by our main goal, which is to publish high-quality books that will entertain readers as well as make a positive difference in their lives.

Our readers are our most important resource; we value your input, suggestions, and ideas. We'd love to hear from you—after all, we are publishing books for you!

Please stay in touch with us and follow us at:

Facebook: Mango Publishing
Twitter: @MangoPublishing
Instagram: @MangoPublishing
LinkedIn: Mango Publishing
Pinterest: Mango Publishing
Newsletter: mangopublishinggroup.com/newsletter

Join us on Mango's journey to reinvent publishing, one book at a time.